The dynamics of military revolution, 1300–2050

The Dynamics of Military Revolution, 1300–2050 aims to bridge a major gap in the emerging literature on revolutions in military affairs. It suggests that two very different phenomena have been at work over the past centuries: "military revolutions," which are driven by vast social and political changes, and "revolutions in military affairs," which military institutions have directed, although usually with great difficulty and ambiguous results. The work provides a conceptual framework and historical context for understanding the patterns of change, innovation, and adaptation that have marked war in the Western world since the fourteenth century – beginning with Edward III's revolution in medieval warfare, through the development of modern military institutions in seventeenth-century France, to the military impact of mass politics in the French Revolution, the cataclysmic military–industrial struggle of 1914–1918, and the German Blitzkrieg victories of 1940. The work's case studies and conceptual overview offer an indispensable introduction to revolutionary military change – which is as inevitable as it is difficult to predict – in the twenty-first century.

MacGregor Knox served in Vietnam as a rifle platoon leader with the 173rd Airborne Brigade, and is now Stevenson Professor of International History at the London School of Economics and Political Science. His other works include *Mussolini Unleashed, 1939–1941; Common Destiny: Dictatorship, Foreign Policy, and War in Fascist Italy and Nazi Germany*; and *Hitler's Italian Allies*.

Williamson Murray served with the United States Air Force in Southeast Asia. He has taught at Yale University, the Ohio State University, the Naval War College, the Army War College and Marine Corps University. His extensive work on twentieth-century military history includes co-authorship of the acclaimed history *A War to be Won: Fighting the Second World War*.

The dynamics of military revolution, 1300–2050

The dynamics of military revolution
1300–2050

Edited by

MACGREGOR KNOX
*The London School of Economics
and Political Science*

WILLIAMSON MURRAY
Institute for Defense Analyses

CAMBRIDGE
UNIVERSITY PRESS

PUBLISHED BY THE PRESS SYNDICATE OF THE UNIVERSITY OF CAMBRIDGE
The Pitt Building, Trumpington Street, Cambridge, United Kingdom

CAMBRIDGE UNIVERSITY PRESS
The Edinburgh Building, Cambridge CB2 2RU, UK
40 West 20th Street, New York, NY 10011-4211, USA
10 Stamford Road, Oakleigh, VIC 3166, Australia
Ruiz de Alarcón 13, 28014 Madrid, Spain
Dock House, The Waterfront, Cape Town 8001, South Africa

http://www.cambridge.org

First published 2001

Printed in the United States of America

Typeface Sabon 10/12pt.   *System* 3B2

A catalog record for this book is available from the British Library.

Library of Congress Cataloging in Publication Data
The Dynamics of military revolution, 1300–2050 / [edited by] MacGregor Knox,
Williamson Murray.
p. cm.
Includes bibliographical references and index.
ISBN 0-521-80079-X
1. Strategy – History. 2. Military art and science – History.
3. Revolutions – Europe – History. 4. Military history, Modern.
5. Europe – History, Military.
6. United States – History – Civil War, 1861–1865.
I. Knox, MacGregor.
II. Murray, Williamson
D25 D96 2001
355.02–dc21   00-066704

ISBN 0 521 80079 X hardback

To those members of the armed forces of the United States and of its allies who believe that "the maximum use of force is in no way incompatible with the simultaneous use of the intellect" (*On War*, Book I.1.3).

Contents

Contributors

Brigadier Jonathan B. A. Bailey
  MBE, ADC
Director Royal Artillery
British Army

Mark Grimsley
Professor of History
The Ohio State University

Holger H. Herwig
Professor of Strategy
The University of Calgary

MacGregor Knox
Stevenson Professor of International
  History
The London School of Economics
  and Political Science

John A. Lynn
Professor of History
The University of Illinois at
  Urbana-Champaign

Williamson Murray
Senior Fellow
Institute for Defense Analyses

Clifford J. Rogers
Professor of History
The United States Military
  Academy

Dennis E. Showalter
Professor of History
Colorado College

Acknowledgments

This book has been long in gestation, but the issues it addresses are not likely to disappear soon. We owe thanks above all to our contributors for their skill and patience. We remain abidingly grateful to The Marine Corps University and The Marine Corps University Foundation, Quantico, Virginia, for the generous support and hospitality they offered to the April 1996 conference on "Historical Parameters of Revolutions in Military Affairs" from which this book evolved. Finally, we wish to express our lasting appreciation to Andrew W. Marshall, always a light in the darkness, for his contributions over many years to the understanding of military effectiveness, and to the security of the United States and of its allies. All have added in one way or another to the book's strengths; its remaining weaknesses are above all our responsibility.

MacGregor Knox   Williamson Murray
London   Alexandria, Virginia

Figures and tables

1

Thinking about revolutions in warfare

WILLIAMSON MURRAY AND MACGREGOR KNOX

The term "revolution in military affairs" (RMA) became decidedly fashionable in the course of the 1990s. It lies at the heart of debates within the Pentagon over future strategy and has gained increasing prominence in Washington's byzantine budgetary and procurement struggles. Yet few works throw light on the concept's past, help situate it or the phenomena it claims to describe within a sophisticated historical framework, or offer much guidance in understanding the potential magnitude and direction of future changes in warfare. This book is an effort to answer those needs.

CONCEPTUAL ROOTS

Current notions of revolutions in military affairs derive from two principal sources: early modern historians and Soviet military theorists. The closely related concept of "military revolution" emerged in 1955 in an inaugural lecture by the British historian Michael Roberts.[1] Roberts argued that in the early seventeenth century, under the leadership of the warrior-king

---

1 Michael Roberts, *The Military Revolution, 1560–1660* (Belfast, 1956), reprinted in Michael Roberts, *Essays in Swedish History* (London, 1967), and in Clifford J. Rogers, ed., *The Military Revolution Debate, Readings on the Military Transformation of Early Modern Europe* (Boulder, CO, 1995). For a different view see Geoffrey Parker, "The 'Military Revolution,' 1560–1660 – A Myth?" and "In Defense of 'The Military Revolution,'" in Rogers, *The Military Revolution Debate*. See also Geoffrey Parker, *The Military Revolution: Military Innovation and the Rise of the West, 1500–1800* (Cambridge, 1988). It is significant that the Rogers book, published in 1995, used the singular of "Revolution" in its title. The extent of scholarly interest is suggested by the following list of articles: Gunther E. Rothenberg, "Maurice of Nassau, Gustavus Adolphus, Raimondo Montecuccoli, and the 'Military Revolution' of the Seventeenth Century," in Peter Paret, Gordon A. Craig, and Felix Gilbert, eds., *Makers of Modern*
(continued)

Gustavus Adolphus, Sweden had embarked on a military revolution that had swept away traditional approaches to military organization and tactics throughout the West.[2] That claim provoked several decades of furious debate over the extent and nature of the changes in sixteenth- and seventeenth-century warfare.[3] In the end, most specialists came to agree that Roberts had been correct in suggesting that European warfare in this period had undergone fundamental systemic changes. But until the 1990s, military historians focused on other periods of Western history had largely ignored the concepts developed in the debate that Roberts had opened.[4]

The second major influence on the development of the notion of revolutions in military affairs was the writings of Soviet military theorists from the 1960s onward. Marxist–Leninist indoctrination made the Red Army, from its beginnings, receptive to notions of major revolutionary change. Soviet theorists had pioneered in analyzing the overall impact of the First World War on military technique in the 1920s and early 1930s.[5] Stalin's attempts to ensure the "security of the rear" and his own uncontested domination by massacring his military elite checked the Red Army's development of modern operational theories from 1937 onward. But the catastrophes of

(continued)

Strategy (Oxford, 1986); K. J. V. Jespersen, "Social Change and Military Revolution in Early Modern Europe: Some Danish Evidence," *The Historical Journal* XXVI (1983); Bert S. Hall and Kelly R. Devries, "Review Essay – the 'Military Revolution' Revisited," *Technology and Culture* (1990); George Raudzens, "War-Winning Weapons: The Measurement of Technological Determinism in Military History," *Journal of Military History* (1990); David A. Parrott, "Strategy and Tactics in the Thirty Years' War: the 'Military Revolution,'" *Militärgeschichtliche Mitteilungen* (1985) (reprinted in Rogers, *The Military Revolution Debate*); Edward M. Furgol, "Scotland Turned Sweden: The Scottish Covenanters and the Military Revolution, 1638–1651," in J. Morrill, ed., *The Scottish National Covenant in Its British Context* (Edinburgh, 1990); and Mahinder S. Kingra, "The *trace italienne* and the Military Revolution during the Eighty Years' War, 1567–1648," *Journal of Military History* (1993). One of the best surveys of the period remains Hans Delbrück, *History of the Art of War*, vol. 4, *The Dawn of Modern Warfare* (Lincoln, NB, 1990).

2   For the context of Roberts's claims for a Swedish military revolution, see his *Gustavus Adolphus: A History of Sweden, 1611–1632*, II (London, 1958).

3   See particularly Clifford J. Rogers, "The Military Revolution in History and Historiography," in *The Military Revolution Debate*; see also Parker, "In Defense of 'The Military Revolution,'" ibid.

4   The best introduction to the literature is Rogers, *The Military Revolution Debate*, but see also William H. McNeill, *The Pursuit of Power, Technology, Armed Force, and Society Since A.D. 1000* (Chicago, 1982), for a wide-ranging discussion of the major issues and trends; Jeremy Black, *European Warfare, 1660–1815* (London, 1994) is also worth consulting. On the specific processes on building the modern state through military power see John A. Lynn, *Giant of the Grand Siècle: The French Army, 1610–1715* (Cambridge, 1997) and Bruce D. Porter, *War and the Rise of the Modern State* (New York, 1993).

5   See especially the 1929 work of V. K. Triandafillov, *The Nature of Operations of Modern Armies* (London, 1994).

1941 – in which the German Blitzkrieg came close to destroying the Soviet Union – offered an unforgettable demonstration of the possibility of revolutionary change in war.[6] Soviet operational art belatedly recovered, and by 1945 had surpassed even the achievements of the Germans. From the late 1940s Soviet development of missile and nuclear systems likewise came to rival that of the West.

Yet the appearance in the 1970s of striking new technologies within the American armed forces – precision-guided munitions (PGMs), cruise missiles, and stealth – suggested to Soviet thinkers that a further technological revolution was taking place that had potentially decisive implications for the Soviet Union. Given their close attention – grounded in ideology – to material factors, the Soviets focused on the technological aspects of what they perceived as an emerging "military–technical revolution." Marshal Nikolai V. Ogarkov, chief of the Soviet general staff from 1977 to 1984, commented that these advances "ma[de] it possible to sharply increase (by at least an order of magnitude) the destructive potential of conventional weapons, bringing them closer, so to speak, to weapons of mass destruction in terms of effectiveness."[7]

From the Soviet perspective this was a particularly frightening prospect. The new "smart" high-technology weapons that the American armed forces were developing and deploying threatened the very bases of Soviet operational art and of Soviet strategy: the immense armored masses, deployed in depth and aimed at swiftly submerging NATO's outnumbered defenders.[8] Analysis of the highly effective use the U.S. Air Force had made of laser-guided bombs in the 1972 LINEBACKER air campaigns undoubtedly heightened Soviet unease.[9] That discomfiture

---

6 See among others V. G. Reznichenko, *Taktika* (Moscow, 1978), p. 9 of the Foreign Broadcast Information Service translation in *Joint Publications Research Service Report*, "Soviet Union, Military Affairs," JPRS-UMA-88-008-L-1, 29 June 1988; and S. Davydov and V. Chervonobab, "Conventional, but No Less Dangerous," *Energiya: Ekonomika, technika, ekologiya*, no. 7, 1987.

7 Interview with Marshal of the Soviet Union N. V. Ogarkov, "The Defense of Socialism: Experience of History and the Present Day," *Krasnaya zvezda*, 1st ed., 9 May 1984.

8 Soviet and East German planners envisaged reaching the French–Spanish border by D+30–35; see especially Mark Kramer, trans., "Warsaw Pact Military Planning in Central Europe: Revelations from the East German Archives," *Cold War International History Project Bulletin*, Issue 2 (1992), pp. 1, 13–19.

9 In the Gulf War of 1991, USAF aircraft used approximately 9,270 precision-guided munitions (PGM) out of 227,100 expended. In the LINEBACKER campaigns, air force aircraft had expended over 29,000 PGMs. The tactical emphasis of the LINEBACKER campaigns had prevented American analysts from seeing anything revolutionary in the greater accuracy of laser-guided bombs. The Soviets, who had access to the North Vietnamese lessons-learned studies as well as the direct results of the Arab–Israeli clashes, concluded otherwise. See Barry D. Watts, "American Air Power," in Williamson Murray, ed., *The Emerging Strategic Environment: Challenges of the Twenty-first Century* (Westport, CT, 1999).

could only have grown as Soviet planners absorbed the implications of the wide use of air defense suppression weapons and PGM by the Israeli Air Force in the Yom Kippur War and in subsequent air battles against the Soviet Union's Arab proxies.[10] At the same time the Soviets were watching U.S. developments such as the "Assault Breaker" program, which aimed at developing short-range ballistic missiles armed with clouds of precision sub-munitions targeted – to the full depth of the theater of war – against the follow-on echelons of any Red Army drive toward the Channel and the Pyrenees. The ability to threaten and – if opportunity arose – to conquer western Europe on the ground after 1944–45 had been the basis, even more than the nuclear arsenal acquired from 1949 onward, of Soviet Russia's world position. By the 1970s that position was in mortal peril.

Andrew W. Marshall and his Office of Net Assessment within the Pentagon were the first to register the significance of Soviet writings on "military–technical revolution." From the mid-1980s through the early 1990s, the commentaries on Soviet doctrine and on the concept of "revolutions in military affairs" emerging from Net Assessment proved increasingly influential within the U.S. defense community.[11] Marshall and his office emphasized above all the conceptual and doctrinal, rather than the purely technological aspects of RMAs.[12] Net Assessment's explicit use of the term "revolution in military affairs" instead of the Soviet "military–technical revolution" indeed aimed at focusing the attention of the American armed forces on issues far broader than technological change. Marshall also argued repeatedly that the U.S. armed forces had not yet realized a revolution in military affairs, but were in reality no further along than were the British in the mid-1920s when they first began experimenting with armored and mechanized warfare.[13]

---

10 See Barry D. Watts and Thomas A. Keany, *Effects and Effectiveness*, Report II, vol. 2, *The Gulf War Air Power Survey* (Washington, DC, 1993), pp. 67–71.

11 Marshall testified to Congress in 1995 that "available and foreseen technological capabilities in areas such as PGMs, computing power, and surveillance systems could transform war to the extent that occurred during the interwar period with armored warfare, strategic bombing, and carrier aviation" (Andrew W. Marshall, "Revolutions in Military Affairs," Statement for the Subcommittee on Acquisition and Technology, Senate Armed Services Committee, 5 May 1995, p. 1).

12 The fact that the Office of Net Assessment was willing to support a number of historically-based studies on military innovation during this period underlines this point.

13 Andrew W. Marshall, "Some Thoughts on Military Revolutions," Office of Net Assessment memorandum, 27 July 1993. In testimony before the Senate Armed Services Committee Marshall made explicit that the creation of a revolution in military affairs is inevitably a long process: "The term 'revolution' is not meant to insist that change will be rapid – indeed past revolutions have unfolded over a period of decades – but only

(continued)

America's crushing victory in the Second Gulf War raised interest throughout the U.S. armed forces in the revolutionary prospects of current and foreseeable technologies to an almost uncontrollable pitch. But it also had three decidedly negative consequences. First, the mastery seemingly demonstrated in the Gulf revived the very worst feature of U.S. defense culture: the recurring delusion that war can be understood and controlled in the mechanized top-down fashion of Robert Strange McNamara and his entourage in the 1960s.[14] Second, victory provided the services with yet another argument in favor of procurement of new and enormously costly platforms such as the F-22, while unleashing claims from specialized pressure groups such as the "info-war" community.[15] Finally, victory through technology appeared to promise the strategic freedom in the age of the masses seemingly lost in the paddies and jungles of Vietnam. "Virtual war" with minimal bloodshed could render unnecessary the presidential leadership, military statesmanship, and popular commitment to the fight that was seemingly in such short supply.

Advocates of U.S. leadership of a revolution in military affairs outside the Office of Net Assessment made little effort to place this putative future in some sort of historical perspective. Attempts to examine the nature and limits of such revolutions in the past might – to the common-sense mind – appear to offer a means of gauging both the possibilities and the pitfalls inherent in radical changes in war. The writings of the enthusiasts have nevertheless displayed an astounding lack of historical consciousness.[16]

(*continued*)
that the change will be profound, that the new methods of warfare will be far more powerful than the old. Innovations in technology make a military revolution possible, but the revolution itself takes place only when new concepts of operations develop and, in many cases, new military organizations are created. Making these organizational and doctrinal changes is a long process" (Marshall, "Revolutions in Military Affairs," 5 May 1995). For an outsider's review of the development of thinking within the Pentagon see Thomas E. Ricks, "Warning Shot: How Wars Are Fought Will Change Radically, Pentagon Planners Say," *The Wall Street Journal*, 15 July 1994, p. A1.

14 See Williamson Murray, "Clausewitz Out, Computers In, Military Culture and Technological Hubris," *The National Interest*, Summer 1997. For a vivid snapshot of the McNamara approach by two of his systems analysts, see Alain C. Enthoven and K. Wayne Smith, *How Much is Enough? Shaping the Defense Program, 1961–1969* (New York, 1971).

15 On "platform fever," see Williamson Murray, "Hard Choices: Fighter Procurement in the Next Century," The CATO Institute, *Policy Analysis*, paper no. 334 (Washington, DC, 1999).

16 One of the foremost proponents of the claim that history is irrelevant is James Blacker; see in particular his "Understanding the Revolution in Military Affairs: A Guide to America's 21st Century Defense," *Defense Working Paper No. 3*, Progressive Policy Institute (Washington, DC, 1997), and "Crashing Through the Barricades," *Joint Forces Quarterly*, Summer 1997.

PATTERNS AND CONCEPTS: MILITARY REVOLUTIONS

While Pentagon debates swirled around issues of immediate interest to the
services – such as which multibillion-dollar weapons platform might best
support the coming "revolution in military affairs" – historians had nevertheless begun to look beyond the seventeenth century for examples of revolutionary military change. A paper delivered at the spring 1991 meeting of
the Society of Military History suggested that the history of Western military institutions since the fourteenth century had involved periods of violent
change followed by periods of relative calm in which armies had adapted to
major changes in their environment, a pattern which evolutionary biolo-
gists have called punctuated equilibrium.[17] Such an approach offers one –
admittedly metaphorical – way of understanding revolutionary change in
warfare.

The difficulties inherent in understanding the pattern of past revolutions
arise from the enormous complexities, ambiguities, and uncertainties in the
historical record. The two distinct concepts already sketched out best
describe radical military innovation.[18] The first and most far-reaching in
consequences is the military revolution. Its defining feature is that it fundamentally changes the framework of war. Five military revolutions have had
that effect in Western history:

- the creation in the seventeenth century of the modern nation-state,
  which rested on the large-scale organization of disciplined military
  power;
- the French Revolution of the late eighteenth century, which merged
  mass politics and warfare;
- the Industrial Revolution of the late eighteenth century and after,
  which made it possible to arm, clothe, feed, pay, and move swiftly to
  battle the resulting masses;
- the First World War, which combined the legacies of the French and
  Industrial Revolutions and set the pattern for twentieth-century war;
- the advent of nuclear weapons, which contrary to all precedent kept
  the Cold War *cold* in the decisive European and northeast Asian
  theaters.

These five upheavals are best understood through a geological metaphor:
they were earthquakes. They brought systemic changes in politics and

---

[17] The paper eventually received the Moncado Prize from the Society of Military History
for the best article in the *Journal of Military History* in 1994. For its most recent
iteration see Rogers, "The Military Revolutions of the Hundred Years' War," in
Rogers, *The Military Revolution Debate*.
[18] The remarks that follow draw particularly on discussions at the conference at Quantico
in 1996 mentioned in the acknowledgments, and on the work of Cliff Rogers.

society. They were uncontrollable, unpredictable, and unforeseeable. And their impact continues. The leaders of North Vietnam in their wars against French and Americans drew inspiration from the French Revolution (and its Bolshevik and Maoist progeny) as well as from Vietnamese nationalism.[19] Those who expect the "information revolution" – if it is indeed a revolution – to bring radical military change will consequently find the direction, consequences, and implications of any change that may result to be largely unpredictable.

Military revolutions recast society and the state as well as military organizations. They alter the capacity of states to create and project military power. And their effects are additive. States that have missed the early military revolutions cannot easily leap-frog to success in war by adopting the trappings of Western technology. Oil bought Saddam Hussein fabulous quantities of Soviet, French, and American hardware. But hardware alone could not confer battlefield effectiveness on forces conscripted from a society that possessed neither a modern state, nor the solidarity and resilience generated through mass politics, nor the breadth and depth of technological skill common throughout societies that had passed through the Industrial Revolution. Whereas the Vietnamese Communist movement, which combined the revolutionary fervor of the French Revolution (derived equally from its French colonial masters and its Muscovite and Chinese patrons) with a bureaucratically organized and profoundly xenophobic traditional culture, defeated one Western great power and one superpower.

The first of the five great military revolutions introduced a degree of order and predictability into an activity – war – that since the collapse of Rome had largely been the province of anarchic improvisation. Governments – insofar as the personal entourages of kings and princes merited that name – had with few exceptions exercised only the loosest control over armies and fleets. Employers frequently failed to pay their troops; subsistence through pillage was the usual result. In 1576, the unpaid soldiers of the Spanish monarchy mutinied and sacked the great city of Antwerp – an action that wrecked Spanish policy in the Netherlands and advanced the cause of the rebellious Dutch. The mutiny reflected both the inherent indiscipline of the soldiery and the inability of the financially decrepit Spanish state to compensate them for their sacrifices. Similar episodes recurred throughout the Thirty Years' War that devastated Germany and central Europe from 1618 onward.

But other powers tamed disorder. The Swedish Articles of War of the early seventeenth century made clear that soldiers would dig when they

[19] General William Westmoreland was as little acquainted with the history of the French Revolution as with that of East Asia; it is therefore unsurprising that he botched the conduct of the war in South Vietnam.

were told to dig – an uncommon notion up to that point. Impersonal military discipline focused upon the state made European military organizations of the mid- to late seventeenth century infinitely more effective on the battlefield than the feudal levies, mercenary companies, and haphazardly organized hostilities-only forces that they replaced. And the new disciplined military instruments were self-reinforcing: they backed with force the state's collection of the taxes needed to pay the troops regularly. In return for pay, the state could and did demand that its soldiers maintain a disciplined obedience in garrison as well as on the battlefield; Western societies could thenceforth take for granted the order and responsiveness of their military institutions. That was indeed a revolution, as the consequences of its absence in Latin America and much of the Third World during the nineteenth and twentieth centuries make clear.

The French Revolution further widened and deepened the state's grip upon the wealth and manpower of its citizens. The secular ideology of equality and its correlative, nationalism, injected into war a ferocity that far outstripped the religious fanaticism of the preceding century. Two immense world conflicts resulted: the French War of 1792–1815 and the German War of 1914–1945. Faced with a foreign invasion that they had themselves provoked through nationalist lunacy, the leaders of France in 1793 declared a *levée en masse* that placed the French people and their possessions at the state's disposal for the duration of the war:

> From this moment, until our enemies have been driven from the territory of the Republic, the entire French nation is permanently called to the colors. The young men will go into battle; married men will forge weapons and transport supplies; women will make tents and uniforms, and serve in the hospitals; children will make old cloth into bandages; old men will have themselves carried into public squares to rouse the courage of the warriors, and preach hatred of kings and the unity of the Republic.[20]

The French thus tripled their army in less than a year, and although the new troops long remained less effective than their opponents on a unit-by-unit basis, they could accept casualties and fight on a scale that no other eighteenth-century army could match. The Prussian philosopher of war, Carl von Clausewitz, saw the new French armies at first hand, and later wrote that

> Suddenly war again became the business of the people – a people of thirty millions, all of whom considered themselves to be citizens . . . The people became a participant in war; instead of governments and armies as heretofore, the full weight of the nation was thrown into the balance. The resources and

---

[20] *Archives parlementaires de 1789 à 1860*, première série (Paris, 1867–1980), vol. 72, p. 674.

efforts now available for use surpassed all conventional limits; nothing now inhibited the vigor with which war could be waged, and consequently the opponents of France faced the utmost peril.[21]

French conquest and tyranny ultimately forced upon the other peoples of Europe a willingness – in the unintentionally ironic words of a twentieth-century American president – to bear any burden, pay any price. France's adversaries brought France to heel through the same measures – the national mobilization of resources and manpower – that had given France its battlefield edge. And the revolutionary example influenced others across time as well as space. The combatants of the American Civil War and of the two world wars replicated with even greater ruthlessness and effectiveness the social and political mobilization that the French revolutionaries had pioneered.[22]

Concurrently with the French Revolution, the first stages of the Industrial Revolution were already under way in Britain. That upheaval changed radically the economic underpinnings of British society and placed hitherto unimagined resources in the hands of the nation's leaders. Yet industrial technology offered the armed forces no major battlefield innovations until the mid-nineteenth century; the British Army under Wellington fought in thoroughly traditional fashion. Yet behind the scenes, the Industrial Revolution nevertheless provided the British government with the enormous wealth needed to cobble together and sustain the great coalitions that eventually defeated Napoleon. The alliance of 1813 that brought together Britain, Austria, Russia, and Prussia at last mobilized the continent's resources sufficiently to overwhelm Napoleon's tactical–operational genius. Britain's financial power was the decisive force behind that mobilization.

The Industrial Revolution first influenced the battlefield in the Crimean War: rifled muskets, telegraphy, and steamships combined to let Britain and France project forces as far afield as southern Russia, where they ultimately defeated numerically superior Russian forces. But no party to that conflict was willing to mobilize the national passions, manpower, and resources required to fight the war to a finish. It was left to the opposing sides in the American Civil War, South as well as North, to begin the process of combining the ostensible benefits of technology (railroads, steamboats, telegraphs, rifled muskets, breech-loading rifles, and improved artillery) with

---

21 Carl von Clausewitz, *On War*, eds. and trans. Michael Howard and Peter Paret (Princeton, NJ, 1976), p. 592.
22 As did Ho Chi Minh's Party, which combined the precepts of the French Revolution with a xenophobic ferocity all its own. Vo Nguyen Giap's many filmed and videotaped encounters with French interviewers inadvertently convey the immensity of Vietnamese Communism's debt to Robespierre and Saint-Just.

the French Revolution's mobilization of belief. Between 1861 and 1918 Americans and Europeans then married the two great revolutions at the end of the eighteenth century – the French and Industrial Revolutions – into an even more terrifying new military revolution.

For those who fought the American Civil War, the result was a frighteningly lethal conflict that lasted four years and in the end destroyed the antebellum South as a society. The grim "bummers" of Sherman's army who turned the towns of Georgia and South Carolina into "Chimneyvilles" were the precursors of Bomber Command's "dehousing" of Hitler's followers.[23] Almost concurrently with the U.S. Civil War, the Europeans fought three major wars in 1859, 1866, and 1870–71 that also pointed the way toward the future, if less conclusively than the conflict across the Atlantic. The last of the three, the Franco-Prussian War, might have turned into a war as all-devouring as the U.S. Civil War. But Napoleon III and his high command displayed such extraordinary ineptitude during the war's opening phases that they destroyed the entire French professional army at Metz and Sedan.[24] Those disasters prevented the French from repeating the *levée en masse* successfully; the new Third Republic that succeeded Napoleon III lacked the experienced cadres needed to create effective armies from the recruits it called to arms.

It was thus not until 1914 that the Europeans experienced in full the ferocity of a war that combined industrial firepower and logistics with the fighting power and staying power that nationalism could generate. The First World War had the most profound impact of all Western military revolutions to date. Politically, the consequences of 1914–18 convulsed Europe until the final collapse in 1991 of the Communist empire created in 1917–23. Militarily, the Great War was equally revolutionary. The armies that fought it developed the wholly new and three-dimensional forms of combined-arms tactics and operations described in Chapter 8 as the "modern style of warfare"; the navies likewise explored war in three dimensions and three elements, pioneering submarine warfare, carrier operations, and – despite dramatic failure at Gallipoli – amphibious warfare; and strategic bombing made its first grim appearance. The as yet rudimentary development of the internal combustion engine – a defect remedied in the Great War's even more lethal continuation in 1939–45 – still limited the development of these and other military techniques. But the

---

[23] In fairness to Sherman, Union forces allowed Southern civilians to escape before "dehousing" them, while Bomber Command, facing a barbaric enemy and prisoner of an inflexible technology, flattened and incinerated both Hitler's cities and their inhabitants. For the war on civilians in 1861–65, see Mark Grimsley, *The Hard Hand of War: Union Military Policy Toward Southern Civilians, 1861–1865* (Cambridge, 1995).

[24] Michael Howard, *The Franco-Prussian War, 1870–1871* (London, 1961) remains by far the best book in English on the war.

extent of the revolution is clear enough. A British or German battalion commander from summer 1918 could have understood the underlying concepts governing warfare in 1940, 1944, or even 1991. But a 1914 battalion commander magically transported to the Western Front battlefields of summer 1918 would have had great difficulty in understanding what he saw.[25]

The development and use of nuclear weapons in 1941–45 constituted the most recent military revolution. In the ensuing Cold War the United States and the Soviet Union deployed massive arsenals incorporating two leading-edge technologies – the American nuclear bomb and the German ballistic missile – that threatened destruction of their opponents and of the rest of humanity many times over. Yet that very destructive power inhibited the two contenders from seeking through the use of force to "compel [the] enemy to do [their] will." That two heavily armed powers, whose hostility was thrice overdetermined – by ideology, geopolitics, and, on the Soviet side above all, by the requirements of totalitarian domestic stability – failed to fight the long-anticipated Third World War was historically wholly without precedent. Only the existence of nuclear weapons – and the historical accident that the power that enjoyed a brief but unique monopoly over them was democratic rather than totalitarian – explains Europe's post-1945 "long peace."[26] The Cold War is over but nuclear weapons remain; their future pacific influence in the hands of rulers less responsible than those of the Cold War era should be a perennial subject of anxious speculation.

REVOLUTIONS IN MILITARY AFFAIRS

The great military revolutions that have rocked the West and much of the rest of the world since the seventeenth century offer small comfort to the military professional. Those who passed through the fires of the great wars that rent Europe from the seventeenth century to the mid-twentieth, or faced the rigors and anxieties of the nuclear era, came to recognize the grim face of revolutionary change; they could rarely aspire to do more than hang on and adapt. If an information revolution that may parallel in magnitude the advent of the modern state, the mobilization of whole peoples through secular ideology, the mechanization of killing through science and technology, and the ultimate terror of thermonuclear annihilation is indeed in the process of enveloping the world, then the resulting uncontrollable onrush of events will sweep nations and military organizations before it.

---

25 See Chapter 7 of this work.
26 For brave but unpersuasive efforts to argue otherwise, see John E. Mueller, "The Essential Irrelevance of Nuclear Weapons: Stability in the Postwar World," *International Security* 13:2 (1988), pp. 55–79, and *Retreat from Doomsday: The Obsolescence of Major War* (New York, 1989).

The record of the past nevertheless suggests the existence – alongside and within the great military revolutions – of clusters of less all-embracing changes. These lesser transformations are best conceptualized as the "revolutions in military affairs" already described. They do appear susceptible to human direction, and in fostering them, military institutions that are intellectually alert can gain significant advantage.

Military organizations embark upon an RMA by devising new ways of destroying their opponents. To do so, they must come to grips with fundamental changes in the social, political, and military landscapes; in some cases they must anticipate those changes. Revolutions in military affairs require the assembly of a complex mix of tactical, organizational, doctrinal, and technological innovations in order to implement a new conceptual approach to warfare or to a specialized sub-branch of warfare. The most effective mix is rarely apparent in advance; innovation and adaptation are messy, and even historians – with all the benefits of documentation and hindsight – find it difficult to reconstruct past events with precision. Yet in the end, battlefield outcomes usually make pitilessly clear which military organization has innovated most effectively.

The linkages between past RMAs and the great military revolutions are best sketched in outline form (Table 1.1). RMAs have a number of salient characteristics. First, even in war – the most powerful accelerating force conceivable – most take considerable time to develop. Twentieth-century peacetime RMAs have sometimes required decades, and delays of that magnitude have inevitably led to argument over the appropriateness of the term *revolutionary*. Perspective also matters. To French and British officers in northern France in May 1940, the German breakthrough from the Meuse to the Channel appeared *revolutionary*. To the Germans, the doctrine and forces that destroyed the Allied armies in the battle of France were an evolutionary development with a history that stretched back at least to 1917 and in some respects to 1807.[27] Moreover, some German officers engaged in the fighting believed that *Wehrmacht* success was due as much to political indoctrination and racist fanaticism as to tactical skill.[28] Given that some German infantry companies attacking across the Meuse suffered upward of 70 percent casualties and kept fighting, it would be foolish to dismiss that view.

[27] For the development of German combined-arms concepts see Williamson Murray, "Armored Warfare," in Murray and Allan R. Millett, eds., *Military Innovation in the Interwar Period* (Cambridge, 1996); for the contribution of pre-1917 traditions, MacGregor Knox, "The 'Prussian Idea of Freedom' and the Career Open to Talent: Battlefield Initiative and Social Ascent from Prussian Reform to Nazi Revolution, 1807–1944," pp. 186–226 in Knox, *Common Destiny: Dictatorship, Foreign Policy, and War in Fascist Italy and Nazi Germany* (Cambridge, 2000).
[28] See Chapter 9 of this work.

Table 1.1. *Revolutions in military affairs and military revolutions*

Anticipatory RMAs of the Middle Ages and early modern era – longbow, offensive–defensive strategy, gunpowder, new fortress architecture. **Military revolution 1:** *the seventeenth-century creation of the modern state and of modern military institutions* Associated and resultant RMAs: – Dutch and Swedish tactical reforms, French tactical and organizational reforms, naval revolution, Britain's financial revolution; – French military reforms following the Seven Years' War. **Military revolutions 2 and 3:** *the French and Industrial Revolutions* Associated and resultant RMAs: – national political and economic mobilization, Napoleonic warfare (battlefield annihilation of the enemy's armed forces); – financial and economic power based on industrialization (Britain); – technological revolution in land warfare and transport (telegraph, railroads, steamships, quick-firing smokeless-powder small-arms and artillery; automatic weapons); – the Fisher revolution in naval warfare: the all-big-gun battleship and battlefleet (1905–14). **Military revolution 4:** *the First World War irrevocably combines its three predecessors* Associated and resultant RMAs: – combined-arms tactics and operations, Blitzkrieg operations, strategic bombing, carrier warfare, submarine warfare, amphibious warfare, radar, signals intelligence. **Military revolution 5:** *nuclear weapons and ballistic missile delivery systems* Associated and resultant RMAs: – precision reconnaissance and strike; stealth; computerization and computer networking of command and control; massively increased lethality of "conventional" munitions.

Creating a revolution in military affairs in wartime is difficult enough, even when battle produces clear lessons paid for in blood. The combined-arms RMA that emerged in the course of the First World War consisted, at its core, in the development of accurate indirect artillery fire in combination with decentralized infantry tactics that emphasized fire, maneuver, and exploitation. But this revolution emerged only in late 1917, after three years of inept slaughter. And the RMA's essence and lessons were far from clear even by 1918, as the dogged refusal of the British and French armies to come to grips with it in the ensuing two decades showed.[29] Their

29 See Murray, "Armored Warfare."

failure, and the fact that adequate analysis of the 1914–18 battlefield – with exceptions such as G. C. Wynne's brilliant *If Germany Attacks* – was not available until the 1980s, emphasizes the extent to which the fear, uncertainty, and confusion of war had created or exacerbated the intractable systemic problems facing Europe's armies in 1914–18.[30]

If adapting to wartime conditions is desperately difficult, those involved in peacetime innovation confront almost insoluble problems: it is here that the leaders of military institutions earn their pay. The twentieth-century record suggests that many have not. As a retired senior U.S. Army officer has noted, in summarizing the lessons of a series of case studies on the effectiveness of military institutions in the first half of the century:

> [I]n the spheres of operations and tactics, where military competence would seem to be a nation's rightful due, the twenty-one [case studies] suggest for the most part less than general professional military competence and sometimes abysmal incompetence. One can doubt whether any other profession in these seven nations during the same periods would have received such poor ratings by similarly competent outside observers.[31]

Yet military organizations do confront immense obstacles to peacetime innovation. Michael Howard has compared their problems to those facing surgeons who must prepare to operate without the benefit of experience on live patients.[32] Armies, navies, and air forces must be prepared to function at short notice in extraordinarily trying circumstances that by definition cannot be replicated except by killing large numbers of people. Moreover, they frequently lack the lavish financial support and staunch political backing needed for peacetime experimentation and realistic training. Yet the record – the German campaign against western Europe in 1940 once again suggests the possibilities – shows that some have done far better than others. Discerning how and why some organizations have succeeded and charting the nature and implications for the future of the military revolutions and RMAs of the past is the principal purpose of the case studies that follow.

30 G. C. Wynne, *If Germany Attacks. The Battle in Depth in the West* (London, 1940); Timothy T. Lupfer, "The Dynamics of Doctrine: The Changes in German Tactical Doctrine During the First World War," *Leavenworth Papers* 4 (1981); Timothy Travers, *The Killing Ground: The British Army and the Emergence of Modern Warfare, 1900–1918* (London, 1987) and *How the War Was Won: Command and Technology in the British Army on the Western Front 1917–1918* (London, 1992); Martin Samuels, *Command or Control? Command, Training and Tactics in the British and German Armies, 1888–1918* (London, 1995).
31 Lieutenant General John H. Cushman, "Challenge and Response at the Operational and Tactical Levels, 1914–1945," in Allan R. Millett and Williamson Murray, eds., *Military Effectiveness*, vol. 3, *World War II* (London, 1988), p. 322.
32 Michael Howard, "The Uses and Abuses of Military History," *Journal of the Royal United Services Institution*, vol. 107, no. 165 (February 1962), pp. 4–10.

2

"As if a new sun had arisen": England's fourteenth-century RMA

CLIFFORD J. ROGERS

During the reign of Edward III (1327–77), England underwent a genuine and dramatic revolution in military affairs. The country's abrupt transformation from a third-rate military power into the strongest and most admired martial nation in Europe was obvious even to contemporaries. The great humanist Francesco Petrarca observed in 1360 that

> In my youth the Britons . . . were taken to be the meekest of the [non-Italians]. Today they are a fiercely bellicose nation. They have overturned the ancient military glory of the French by victories so numerous that they, who were once inferior to the wretched Scots, have reduced the entire kingdom of France by fire and sword.[1]

At about the same time, the Liégeois knight–cleric–chronicler Jean le Bel, who had served on Edward III's first campaign against the Scots in 1327 and had followed the English monarch's later military career with great interest, remarked that

> When the noble king Edward [III] first reconquered England in his youth [in 1326], the English were generally not held in high regard, and no one spoke of their prowess or their boldness . . . [but] they have learned skill-at-arms so well in the time of this noble King Edward . . . that they are [now] . . . the best fighters known.[2]

---

[1] Quoted in R. Boutruche, "The Devastation of Rural Areas During the Hundred Years' War and the Agricultural Recovery of France," in P. S. Lewis, ed., *The Recovery of France in the Fifteenth Century* (New York, 1972), p. 26.

[2] Jean le Bel, *Chronique de Jean le Bel*, eds. Jules Viard and Eugène Déprez (Paris, 1904), vol. 1, pp. 165–6: "quant ce noble Roy Edowart premierement reconquist Angleterre en sa joeunesse, on ne tenoit riens des Anglès communement, et ne parloit on point de leur proesse ne de leur hardiesse. . . . Or ont ilz sy apris les armes au temps de ce noble roy Edowart, qui souvent les a mis en oeuvre, que ce sont plus nobles et les plus frisques combastans qu'on sache." "Frisques" is difficult to translate adequately with one word: it carries connotations of boldness, vigor, and gallantry.

The chronicler Henry Knighton commented that in the reign of Edward's father "two Englishmen were hardly a match for one feeble Scot"; a generation later, by contrast, "a hundred Frenchmen hardly either wished or dared to meet twenty Englishmen in the field, or to give them battle."[3]

The battlefield verdicts of Edward's reign support these views. Dupplin Moor, Halidon Hill, Sluys, Crécy, Neville's Cross, Poitiers, and Nájera constitute a roll of honor equaled by no other English monarch in history. Indeed, no other European nation achieved a comparable string of battlefield successes between the fall of Rome and the French Revolution and Empire. Edward's list compares well even with the victories of Napoleon, for English[4] forces overcame heavy numerical odds in all of their fights – conservative estimates are 10:1 (yes, *ten to one*) at Dupplin Moor, 2:1 at Halidon Hill, 2:1 at Crécy, 1.9:1 at Neville's Cross, 2.3:1 at Poitiers, and 1.5:1 at Nájera.[5] The figures are all the more remarkable when we consider that Clausewitz, writing in the mid-nineteenth century, was able to find only two examples in all modern history of a defeat of a larger European army by one half its size.[6]

These battles, moreover, were not merely defeats for Edward's enemies: they were all *crushing* defeats. At Dupplin Moor, 1,500 Englishmen defeated 15,000 Scots, killed the regent of Scotland and four of the five Scottish earls present, captured the fifth, and killed about 3,000 Scots. Cases in which an army has killed twice its own numbers in enemies against a technologically comparable opponent on an open battlefield are rare indeed. Subsequently, at Halidon Hill, the English killed the new regent

---

[3] Henrici Knighton, *Chronicon*, ed. J. R. Lumby (London, 1895), vol. 1, p. 451: "duo Angli vix valebant debilem Scotum"; *Anonimalle Chronicle 1333–1381*, ed. V. H. Galbraith (Manchester, 1927), p. 43: "apayn c Fraunceis ne voidreount ne oseount vint Engleis en chaumpe encountrere ne a eux bataille doner." See Andrew of Wyntoun, *Orygynale Cronykil of Scotland*, ed. David Lang (Edinburgh, 1872), vol. 2, p. 489: "Yit think me and I ware to ta / Ane Ingliss man worthe Franche twa," and Blaise de Monluc's observation that "we had heard our predecessors say, that one Englishman would always beat two Frenchmen," cited in Michael Harbinson, "The Longbow as a Close Quarter Weapon in the Fifteenth Century," *Hobilar: The Journal of the Lance and Longbow Society*, No. 15 (January 1995), p. 2. The English of Edward III's day also thought of themselves as unbeatable: see M. McKisack, *The Fourteenth Century* (Oxford, 1959), pp. 150–1, 151 note.

[4] Here and elsewhere I use the term "English" loosely to include other subjects or allies of Edward III – Gascons, Scots, Welshmen, Spaniards, etc.

[5] These ratios are calculated based on figures taken from the "best guess" estimates in Clifford J. Rogers, *War Cruel and Sharp: English Strategy under Edward III, 1327–1360* (Woodbridge, 2000), with two exceptions. The Nájera ratio is based on C. W. Oman, *A History of the Art of War in the Middle Ages* (London, 1924), vol. 2, p. 187. For Neville's Cross, see Clifford J. Rogers, "The Scottish Invasion of 1346," *Northern History* XXXIV (1998), pp. 57–60.

[6] Rossbach and Leuthen: *Vom Kriege*, ed. Werner Hahlweg (Bonn, 1952), p. 273 (Book 3, Chapter 8); *On War*, eds. and trans. Michael Howard and Peter Paret (Princeton, NJ, 1976), p. 195.

of Scotland, another four earls, and more thousands of Scots. At Sluys, more Frenchmen perished than at Agincourt (or Waterloo, or Dienbienphu); Edward's outnumbered fleet won the largest naval battle of his century even more decisively than Napoleon's fleet lost Trafalgar. According to the king himself, the English captured 166 of the 190 French ships, whereas Nelson's fleet at Trafalgar captured only eighteen of the thirty-three French and Spanish ships, while eleven escaped to Cádiz. At Crécy, England thoroughly smashed the French royal army. The king of Bohemia, 1,500 other nobles, and numberless infantrymen lay dead on the field; among those who fled were the king of France (wounded by multiple arrows), the king of Majorca, and a future Holy Roman Emperor. At Neville's Cross, the English captured the King of Scots; at Poitiers King John II of France suffered the same fate at the hands of the Black Prince, Edward's eldest son.[7] And Edward never "met his Waterloo" – nor Leipzig nor Borodino. England won all its major land battles during his fifty-year reign.

These tactical triumphs led to political settlements that were highly impressive, if far from enduring. Scotland twice fell under English domination, in 1333 and 1335, and would have stayed there – as even the Scots admitted – had not the struggle with a greater foe, France, distracted Edward.[8] In that great contest, English arms won a remarkable triumph with the 1360 Treaty of Brétigny by which the Valois agreed to surrender a full third of France to English sovereign rule.[9] Further south, the Black Prince's intervention in Iberia temporarily restored the English-sponsored Pedro "the Cruel" to the throne of Castile. And Edward III's martial successes so impressed European opinion that the English king was offered the crown of the Holy Roman Empire, as "the most worthy, most vigorous, most powerful knight of Christendom."[10] Things had

---

7 For all these fourteenth-century battles, see Rogers, *War Cruel and Sharp*.
8 See John of Fordun, *Chronica Gentis Scotorum* [Historians of Scotland, vol. I] ed. W. F. Skene (Edinburgh, 1871), p. 363, note 5, and the related text in the *Liber Pluscardensis*, ed. F. J. H. Skene [Historians of Scotland, vol. VII] (Edinburgh, 1877), p. 286: "The mortal war between Edward III and the king of France revived, fortunately for the realm of Scotland; for if the King of England had continued the war he had begun [against the Scots], without doubt he would have subjugated all the realm of Scotland to his commands." It is also worth noting that in the 1350s, Edward persuaded the childless David Bruce (who had been captured at the battle of Neville's Cross) to settle the inheritance of the Scottish crown on Edward or one of his sons, and in the meantime to become the Plantagenet's vassal, though David was unable to secure enough political support in Scotland for this settlement to enact it (see E. W. M. Balfour-Melville, *Edward III and David II* [London, 1954], pp. 15–16).
9 Though the final transfer of sovereignty never actually took place, the French did agree to it.
10 Knighton, *Chronicon*, vol. 2, p. 55; Thomas Gray, *Scalacronica*, ed. Joseph Stevenson (Edinburgh, 1836), p. 301; H. S. Offler, "England and Germany at the beginning of the Hundred Years' War," *English Historical Review* LIV (1939).

clearly changed since the days of Edward II, "always lily-livered and luckless in war."[11] Indeed, wrote the chronicler Thomas Walsingham, "it seemed to the English almost as if a new sun had arisen, because of . . . the glory of their victories."[12]

Medieval historians have recently begun to examine this remarkable transformation in war-making ability from the perspective of the early modern "military revolution" thesis – either within a purely British context, as part of an "Edwardian military revolution," or, along with the accomplishments of Flemings, Swiss, Scots, and others as part of the "infantry revolution" of the early fourteenth century.[13] This essay will take it as given that England *did* undergo a fourteenth-century revolution in military affairs, and will reexamine Edward's wars to see what they can tell us about the relationships linking technology, organization, tactics, strategy, and individual leadership within an RMA.

TECHNOLOGY

Commentators often view RMAs as driven above all by technology – but with the proviso that the development from innovation to revolution requires organizational and doctrinal adaptation before the tactical and strategic potential of new weapon systems can be realized. The formulation of Andrew Krepinevich is typical. Military revolutions comprise four elements: technological change, systems development, operational innovation, and organizational adaptation. Each of these elements is in itself a neces-

---

11 *Chronicon de Lanercost*, ed. Joseph Stevenson (Edinburgh, 1839), pp. 247–8: "qui semper fuerat cordis pavidi et infortunatus in bellis."

12 Thomas Walsingham, *Historia Anglicana*, ed. H. T. Riley (London, 1863), vol. 1, p. 272, on the aftermath of Crécy and Calais: "videbatur Anglicis quasi novus sol oriri, propter pacis abundantiam, rerum copiam, et victoriarum gloriam."

13 Edwardian: Michael Prestwich, *The Three Edwards: War and the State in England 1272–1377* (London, 1980), p. 62; much more fully developed in his *Armies and Warfare in the Middle Ages. The English Experience* (New Haven, CT, 1996), and in Andrew Ayton, *Knights and Warhorses: Military Service and the English Aristocracy under Edward III* (Woodbridge, 1994), Chapter 1, "The Military Revolution in Edwardian England"; see also idem, "English Armies in the Fourteenth Century," in Anne Curry and Michael Hughes, eds., *Arms, Armies and Fortifications in the Hundred Years' War* (Woodbridge, 1994). Infantry Revolution: Clifford J. Rogers, "Military Revolutions of the Hundred Years' War," in *Journal of Military History* (1993), reprinted with revisions in idem, ed., *The Military Revolution Debate* (Boulder, CO, 1995), pp. 55–93 [citations below are to the latter version], and John F. Guilmartin, Jr., "The Military Revolution: Origins and First Tests Abroad," also in *The Military Revolution Debate*, p. 304. See also Kelly R. DeVries, *Infantry Warfare in the Early Fourteenth Century* (Woodbridge, 1996).

sary, but not a sufficient, condition for realizing the large gains in military effectiveness that characterize military revolutions.[14]

The obvious technological component of the English fourteenth-century RMA is the famous yew longbow – a weapon basically similar to the wooden selfbows in use since the Neolithic age, but longer, with a heavier draw weight (and so more power) than earlier weapons. Although one historian has recently challenged the traditional view of the weapon's killing power, a careful examination of the contemporary sources reaffirms the conclusion that the fourteenth-century longbow was lethal even against armored troops.[15] In the hands of a strong and skilled archer, it could fire at least three times as fast as a contemporary composite-bowed crossbow, could shoot farther and (beyond point-blank distance) with much greater accuracy, and could strike with enough impact to penetrate armor and inflict serious or even lethal wounds on men or horses. Many contemporary sources attest its importance for Edward III's victories.[16] Take for example his first battle, at Halidon Hill in 1333: the chroniclers describe the English archers as having "inflicted a tremendous massacre on the Scots," and as "striking them down by the thousands."[17]

Yet by 1333 the longbow was scarcely a new technology; it had been a principal weapon of the English monarchy's armed forces for half a century. Of the English force that Robert the Bruce's Scots crushed at Bannockburn in 1314, the longbowmen probably formed the majority.[18] For all their fine qualities, Edward II's archers failed to prevent one of the

---

14 Andrew F. Krepinevich, "Cavalry to Computer: The Pattern of Military Revolutions," *The National Interest* 37 (1994), pp. 30–42. For a proposed differentiation between military revolutions and RMAs, see Rogers, " 'Military Revolutions' and 'Revolutions in Military Affairs': A Historian's Perspective," in Thierry Gongora and Harald von Riekhoff, eds., *Toward a Revolution in Military Affairs? Defense and Security at the Dawn of the 21st Century* (Westport, CT, 2000).

15 See Rogers, "The Efficacy of the English Longbow: A Reply to Kelly DeVries," *War in History* 5 (1998), pp. 233–42.

16 Giovanni Villani, *Cronica*, in Roberto Palmarocchi, *Cronisti del Trecento* (Milan, 1935), p. 397; Jean Froissart, *Oeuvres*, ed. Kervyn de Lettenhove (Bruxelles, 1870), vol. 5, pp. 37–78; Rogers, "The Efficacy of the English Longbow."

17 Thomas Burton, *Chronica Monasterii de Melsa*, ed. E. A. Bond (London, 1866–68), vol. 2, p. 106 ("Anglici sagittarii maximam stragem perfecerunt"); British Library, London, Cottonian MS Cleopatra D III (a *Brut* manuscript), fo. 101v ("ils lour mistrent avale par plusours millers").

18 It was usual in the later wars of Edward I for the majority of the infantry to be archers, and this was probably the case in 1314 as well. The writs of array for the Bannockburn campaign mostly do not specify the armament of the infantry (*Rotuli Scotiae*, ed. David Macpherson [London: Record Commission, 1814], vol. 1, pp. 120, 124, 126, 129), but in the few cases where arms are specified, bows are always emphasized (ibid., p. 114 [1,500 archers with bows from Durham], p. 120 [40 crossbowmen and 60 archers from Bristol], p. 122 [4,000 infantry, archers and others, from Ireland]). Furthermore, in the canceled writs of 9 March for the array of the counties, archers were specified: J. E. Morris, *Bannockburn* (Cambridge, 1914), p. 40. The change may indicate that Edward
(continued)

worst humiliations inflicted upon an English army between Hastings and the fall of Singapore, even though the army in question was perhaps the largest and best-equipped expeditionary force an English monarch had assembled up to that point, and far outnumbered its Scottish opponents.[19] Edward II, for all his longbowmen, clearly did not benefit from an RMA, and so, equally clearly, the adoption of the longbow had not produced one.

Finding a technological cause for the radical transformation of English military effectiveness under Edward III requires a search for changes in the Plantagenet army's military equipment which developed specifically in the years between Scottish victory at Bannockburn (1314) and Scottish defeat at Dupplin Moor (1332). Two such changes stand out: the introduction of gunpowder weapons and the dramatic improvement in the armor and war-horses of the English men-at-arms.

Edward III's first campaign, in 1327, was the first in Europe in which gunpowder weapons are recorded as having been used,[20] and the king remained on the cutting edge of artillery technology for most of his career. The cannon his troops fired at Crécy may have been the first ever used in a field battle, and his provision of ten guns (including two "*grossa*") for the siege of Calais in 1346-47 was impressive for its day.[21] Equally striking to contemporaries was the dramatic improvement in English men-at-arms' armor and equipment. At the time of Bannockburn, most English knights relied on mail armor and pot helms for protection. Documents describing

---

(continued)

II was willing to accept having a portion of his army armed otherwise than with bows, but it seems most likely that the majority continued to be archers. Finally, the chroniclers make repeated mention of "the English archers" at Bannockburn, but none of "the English spearmen." E.g. *Chronicon de Lanercost*, p. 225; John Barbour, *The Bruce*, ed. W. W. Skeat (London, 1889), pp. 307-09. The conclusion of J. E. Morris (*Bannockburn*, p. 39) that "The reign of Edward II is the bad period in this history of the evolution of the English archer" is not persuasive. It is hard to imagine how Edward III could have found so many trained archers in 1333 had there not been a regular call for them during his father's reign. Infantry was by far the largest element of the Bannockburn host; the army probably consisted of 2,500 cavalry and 15,000 foot (ibid., p. 41).

[19] *Vita Edwardi Secundi*, ed. N. Denholm-Young (London, 1957), p. 50.
[20] Barbour, *The Bruce*, ed. A. A. M. Duncan (Edinburgh, 1997), 402; A. E. Prince, "The Importance of the Campaign of 1327," *English Historical Review* L (1935), pp. 301–02; illumination of 1326 in Richard Humble, *Medieval Warfare* (Wigston, 1989), p. 147.
[21] Crécy: see Burne, "Cannons at Crécy," *English Historical Review* LXXVII (1962), pp. 335–42, but note that Burne does not give the full text (or very good translations) of the references to the cannon in Villani and the *Storie Pistoresi* (*Storie Pistoresi*, ed. Muratori [Rome: Rerum Italicarum Scriptores, ser. XI, vol. 5], p. 223; G. Villani, *Cronica*, pp. 397–8). The version of the *Grandes Chroniques* (better translated in Burne) is probably more accurate than the Italian chroniclers'. For Calais, see Paris, Bibliothèque Nationale, MS Fr. 693, fo. 267; T. F. Tout, "Firearms in England in the Fourteenth Century," *English Historical Review* XXVI (1911), pp. 689–91. Materials for over 5,000 pounds of gunpowder were also supplied.

equipment forfeited after the battle of Boroughbridge in 1322 show that by then a well-equipped knight might well have had some plate protection, but the testimony of Jean le Bel indicates that as late as 1327 most English men-at-arms still wore neither plate armor nor bascinets, but only mail hauberks and old-fashioned great helms.

The example of the Hainaulter knights who came to England to serve Edward in 1326 and 1327, and the demands of his frequent campaigns (reinforced by the king's own example of extravagant spending on war-horses and military equipment) quickly brought England's chivalry up to continental standards. Indeed for the next century English cavaliers were among the best-armed in Europe.[22] Comparison between the funeral brass of the English knight Sir Robert de Bures (c. 1331) and the illumination of a knight in the Walter de Milemete manuscript of 1326 on the one hand and the brass of Sir John d'Abernon (c. 1340) on the other illustrates the difference. The first two show men clad in mail armor with little or no plate reinforcement; d'Abernon, by contrast, has almost his entire body protected by plate as well as mail (including torso and groin, which are covered by a coat-of-plates, the external rivets of which are visible beneath the front of his surcoat).[23]

During this period, English knights and esquires also appear to have improved substantially the quality of their battle-horses, as indicated by the greatly increased average and maximum prices found in the *restor* rolls, the records kept so that the government could fairly compensate men-at-arms for horses killed in service.[24] Andrew Ayton, the leading expert on the subject, has described this development as an "Edwardian horse-breeding revolution."[25]

22 Jean le Bel, *Chronique*, vol. 1, p. 156 (1327); Michael Prestwich, "*Miles in Armis Strenuus*: The Knight at War," *Transactions of the Royal Historical Society* (1996), p. 208; idem, *Armies and Warfare*, p. 22; Nigel Saul, *Knights and Esquires* (Oxford, 1981), p. 24.
23 David Edge and John Miles Paddock, *The Arms and Armour of the Medieval Knight* (New York, 1988), pp. 84, 78; Humble, *Medieval Warfare*, p. 147. The illumination of c. 1338 in BL MS Egerton 3028, fo. 18, shows a level of armor comparable to that of d'Abernon's.
24 Horses: The average value of the knights' and men-at-arms' horses evaluated for the 1324–25 Gascon campaign (at the end of Edward II's reign) was £11.6; for the 1311–15 Scotland campaign it was £11.9 (the highest before 1338). For Edward's 1338–39 expedition to France, however, the average value had risen to a remarkable peak of £16.4. For the 1342–43 Brittany expedition it was an almost equally remarkable £14.3. That state of affairs did not outlast the English triumphs in the first stage of the Hundred Years' War: from 1359 onward the mean horse value was much lower, around £8–9 (Ayton, *Knights and Warhorses*, p. 195). Edward himself set an example of extravagance in horse buying, spending the truly phenomenal sum of £168 on a single destrier in 1337, the equivalent of over eighty years' income for a well-off peasant family! (Prestwich, *Armies*, p. 34). Rising prices presumably reflected increases in quality – at least in part – rather than simply rising demand.
25 *Knights and Warhorses*, p. 212.

From the standpoint of a study of revolutions in military affairs, however, the most interesting thing about these impressive improvements in
arms and equipment is that they made little difference on the battlefield – an important warning against the assumption that correlation
equates to causation. Doubtless their improved armor benefited English
men-at-arms as they withstood the shock of a French charge (the idea
that dismounted heavy cavalry were helpless lobsters is a myth),[26] but it
was far from decisive. Swiss halberdiers and pikemen of the same era,
although lightly armored, proved equally effective at the same task.
Although the improvements in English men-at-arms' equipment after
1327 did keep them from being at a major disadvantage when fighting
French knights and esquires at Crécy and Poitiers, they did not make any
positive contribution to the English victories there – for the French had also
adopted plate armor. Conversely, Edward II's men-at-arms had already
possessed a significant advantage in armor over the even-worse-equipped
Scots – but this had not helped at Bannockburn. A £15 charger might have
a radically greater impact on an equestrian's aesthetic sense than a £10
warhorse, but the battlefield effect was less significant – especially since
English men-at-arms almost without exception mounted only for pursuit,
after winning the battle. As for the cannon, the chronicler who records their
first use in 1327 describes them as "novelties" that apparently made an
impression mainly because of the noise they produced (he calls them "cra-
kys" of war). His account gives no indication they were of military importance.[27] English cannon may have frightened off a few Italians at Crécy,
and were useful adjuncts to springalds and trebuchets at sieges, but they did
not have a revolutionary impact on siege warfare until the 1420s, and not
until even later did they play an important battlefield role.[28]

Changes in the material culture of war during Edward III's "revolution in
military affairs" were thus far from decisive, and the most important technological development – the longbow – had been in use far earlier, but
without effecting an RMA. It is therefore safe to say that the stunning
improvement in British military effectiveness from the 1330s to the 1350s
was not technologically driven, though technological development was a
significant contributing factor.

---

26   E.g. A. H. Burne, *The Agincourt War* (London, 1956; reprint, Greenhill, 1991), p. 38:
      "Being less encumbered with armor than the men-at-arms, the archers were more
      nimble and *therefore more effective in the hand-to-hand fighting*" (emphasis added).
      Armor was expensive, and it is most difficult to believe that medieval soldiers would
      have accepted heavy cash outlays in order to acquire something that would lower their
      combat effectiveness. Cf. the opinion of John Barbour: "agane armyt men to ficth/May
      nakit men haff litill mycht" [i.e. "unarmored men have little ability to fight with
      armored men"] (Barbour, *The Bruce*, p. 309).
27   *The Bruce*, ed. Duncan, p. 402.
28   Revolutionary effect in 1420s–30s: Rogers, "Military Revolutions of the Hundred
      Years' War," pp. 64–5. Crécy: Burne, "Cannons at Crécy."

ORGANIZATION

The English army underwent important organizational, structural, and administrative changes in the decades between Bannockburn and the opening of the Hundred Years' War. The armies of the first half of Edward II's reign still retained a partially feudal character: the magnates who brought their large retinues of men-at-arms into Scotland in 1314 did so in order to fulfill their obligations as vassals of the crown, and appear to have served at their own expense.[29] The infantry of the English army at Bannockburn, however, had been recruited almost entirely through commissions of array. Each pair of counties, typically, had two officials (usually the sheriff and a clerk) appointed to muster the adult freemen of the shire, to examine their arms and equipment, and to select the most suitable, up to the number specified in the king's writ, for service in the coming campaign. Their community then provided these men with any necessary equipment they did not already own, and sent them off to the gathering point of the royal host. After their arrival there, they received royal pay.[30]

That system changed rapidly in the decades after Bannockburn. All magnates who served in the campaign of 1322 received royal wages.[31] Edward III's first campaign, in 1327 (the last before the "Shameful Peace" of 1328 acknowledged Robert Bruce's victory in the first Scottish War of Independence), was also the last of his reign in which he issued a formal feudal summons. It seems unlikely, furthermore, that any of the men who answered the summons performed the traditional forty days of unpaid service; the one head of retinue for whom the pay records still exist received wages for his men starting on the day of their assembly at York.[32] As A. E. Prince has observed, "if it was the voice of feudalism which uttered the call

---

[29] Morris, *Bannockburn*, p. 24, writes of the 1314 campaign that "we have no Marshal's Register because it was not a strictly feudal campaign." This is somewhat misleading: Morris is referring to the fact that Parliament did not agree to the summons for the campaign, but that makes the summons all the more a "strictly feudal" one, i.e. one based on the military obligation that a vassal owed for his fief (see *Vita Edwardi Secundi*, p. 50 ["Rex igitur debita seruitia ab omnibus exegit"] and *Parliamentary Writs*, vol. II/2, pp. 421–2 ["toto servicio nobis debito . . . in fide et homagio quibus nobis tenemini"], p. 423 ["summoneri fac' . . . qui de nobis tenent per servicium militare vel per serjancia . . ."]); the same source also mentions (p. 53) that the earl of Gloucester led his 500 men-at-arms to the battle at his own expense.

[30] A. E. Prince, "The Army and the Navy," in *The English Government at Work, 1327–1336* (New York, 1940), pp. 355–64, describes the system in detail, but its origins date back to the reign of Edward I. For its implementation in 1314, see *Rotuli Scotiae*, vol. I, pp. 114, 120, 124, and especially 130.

[31] Prestwich, *Armies*, p. 98.

[32] Ibid., pp. 344–6.

to arms in 1327, it was the voice of a dying feudalism."[33] From the army
raised in 1334 onward (and probably from 1333), the entire strength of
Edward III's armies consisted of men who received the king's wage.[34]

Campaigning at the head of an army of *soldiers* – the very word derives
from the Old French for pay – had very definite advantages. Although
feudal armies were less rash and undisciplined than usually supposed, commanders could hold paid soldiers and unit leaders to a high standard of
discipline.[35] In particular, troops who received enough remuneration to
meet the expenses incurred in campaigning were under somewhat less pressure than feudal forces to take prisoners for ransom. This made it easier to
demand that they stand in unbroken close-order formation until the enemy
had been completely and decisively defeated (a practice that reduced each
individual's opportunities to take prisoners, but was one of the keys to
English tactical success).[36] Furthermore, the generous (very generous in
some cases) pay that the Plantagenet offered encouraged voluntary military
service, which had obvious advantages for the fighting power of the English
armies. Once the huge profits of the French war started rolling in on top of
the reliable campaign wages offered (typically paid in advance for a quarter
or half a year), participation in Edward's military expeditions became
highly attractive. Many soldiers served in campaign after campaign.[37]

Perhaps the best illustration of this development is the large group of
foreign men-at-arms who sought to join the English army's campaign
through France in 1359:

> knights and esquires began to provide themselves with horses, armor, and all
> sorts of military equipment, and went to Calais to await the arrival of the King
> of England, for each thought to gain so much by accompanying [the king] that

---

33 Ibid., p. 346.
34 There are no pay records for 1333, but Ferriby's wardrobe book shows that by 1334
    even earls were accepting pay. BL, Cottonian MSS, Nero C VIII, fo. 233.
35 Cf. C. T. Allmand, "The War and the Non-Combatant," in Kenneth Fowler, ed., *The
    Hundred Years' War* (London, 1971), pp. 177, 180; Kenneth Fowler, *The King's
    Lieutenant: Henry of Grosmont, First Duke of Lancaster, 1310–1361* (London, 1969),
    pp. 168–71; H. J. Hewitt, *The Organization of War under Edward III* (Manchester,
    1966), p. 105.
36 On the importance of keeping a steady, close-order formation, see Rogers, "The
    Offensive/Defensive in Medieval Strategy," in *From Crécy to Mohács: Warfare in the
    late Middle Ages (1346–1526), Acta of the XXII Colloquium of the International
    Commission of Military History* (Vienna, 1997), pp. 158–60; note also Rogers,
    "Military Revolutions," p. 63, and BN MS Fr. 693, fos. 262v–263.
37 For example see the remarkable career of Sir John Sully, K.G., in Sir N. H. Nicolas,
    ed., *The Controversy between Sir Richard Scrope and Sir Robert Grosvenor in the
    Court of Chivalry* (London, 1832), vol. 2, pp. 240–1; also Matthew Bennett, "The
    Development of Battle Tactics in the Hundred Years' War," in Anne Curry and
    Michael Hughes, eds., *Arms, Armies and Fortifications in the Hundred Years' War*
    (Woodbridge, 1994), p. 2.

he would never be poor . . . even though Edward had not sent for a quarter of them, not even a fifth.[38]

Common soldiers likewise had noteworthy opportunities to enrich themselves with booty collected on *chevauchée*: those who accompanied the Black Prince on his 1355 campaign to Carcassonne found so many valuables that they "took no account of coined silver, nor of goblets . . . only good florins of gold" and rich jewels.[39] This encouraged potential archer-recruits to develop their skills to the highest possible proficiency, so that they would be among those chosen for such potentially profitable service. Military service ceased to be an onerous duty and became a desirable opportunity.[40]

That shift and the administrative and political demands of sustaining war on many fronts (Scotland, Gascony, Picardy, Brittany, Normandy, and elsewhere) for many years greatly changed the recruiting system by which Edward III's government raised its troops. Comparison between the army that suffered the greatest defeat of Edward II's reign with the one that won the most significant victory of Edward III's era (the battle of Poitiers in 1356) best illustrates the development. As already noted, most of Edward II's army at Bannockburn was infantry raised by commissions of array, along with a relatively small proportion – about 15 percent of the army – of heavy cavalry provided by the retinues of the earls and other magnates of the realm, many of whom served at their own expense in response to the king's feudal summons. The paid infantry and men-at-arms of the royal household formed the third major component. The Black Prince's army at Poitiers, by contrast, contained only a small element of true infantry: fully half his soldiers were men-at-arms, and most of the rest of the troops were mounted archers who fought as infantry but rode to the battlefield.[41] The fact that very few, if any, of the soldiers traveled on foot greatly enhanced the army's mobility, making it possible for a large proportion of the troops to disperse over the countryside to pillage and burn while continuing to

---

38 Jean le Bel, *Chronique*, vol. 2, pp. 290–1.
39 Profits: Jean le Bel, *Chronique*, p. 222; see also p. 221. Note also Walsingham's comments, cited in Hewitt, *Organization of War*, p. 108.
40 See Ayton, "English Army," p. 27.
41 The army that fought at Poitiers consisted of around 6,000 troops: 3,000 men-at-arms, 2,000 English archers, and 1,000 "serjaunts," who may or may not have been purely footmen (Bartholomew Burghersh's letter to John Beauchamp, in Froissart, *Oeuvres*, vol. 18, p. 387). The sources do not specify that the English archers were mounted, but this can be presumed with near certainty; the sergeants, too, more likely than not had horses, since they had been selected from a larger group to accompany the *chevauchée*, while others remained behind for the defense of Guienne (Galfridi le Baker de Swynebroke [Geoffrey le Baker], *Chronicon*, ed. E. M. Thompson [Oxford, 1889], pp. 140, 143; Corpus Christi College, Oxford, MS 78, ff. 179–179v.

make steady forward progress. Most common soldiers were volunteers who had enlisted into the retinues of the prince himself or of one of the bannerets who served with him.[42] The prince, the earls and the other English captains in the army had not answered a feudal summons to service. Rather they served the crown according to formal contracts set out in "letters of indenture" which specified the size of their contingents, rates of pay and other compensation, duration of service, and the like. The Gascon lords who brought their contingents to the host apparently served on similar terms.[43]

Some historians have seen these administrative and structural changes as the core of the "Edwardian military revolution." And yet the examples above tend to exaggerate the extent of transformation. Arrayed troops played a much larger role in many other victories of Edward III's reign, including Halidon Hill and the Crécy–Calais campaign, than they did in 1356. And the system of indentures between retinue captains and the crown was, as Andrew Ayton has recently observed, "a mechanism designed to fill the administrative vacuum which appeared when . . . the clerical staff of the royal household were not on hand to supervise the distribution of wages and deal with related matters, such as horse appraisal." When the king himself led the army in the field, as for example in the 1359–60 campaign which ended with the Peace of Brétigny, the army normally did not employ the system.[44] And while these developments and the stunning success of the prince's army on the battlefield may be related, the connections remain tenuous. In the end the Edwardian RMA cannot be understood without an explanation of the English armies' *battlefield* successes – which in turn requires an examination of the changes in English tactical doctrine in the wake of Bannockburn.

TACTICS

The tactical formula employed in the first two battles of Edward's reign, Dupplin Moor and Halidon Hill (where the king himself commanded), proved extraordinarily successful. From then until the mid-fifteenth century, the English almost inevitably fought in more or less the same formation, using what might be called "Dupplin tactics": a central block of close-ordered dismounted men-at-arms using lances like pikes, flanked by two forward-leaning wings of archers positioned to fire into the front and flanks

---

[42] With the exception that some of the archers had been raised by commissions of array in the prince's palatine earldom of Chester or in Wales.

[43] Hewitt, *Black Prince's Expedition*, pp. 16–21, 92; Barber, *Edward, Prince of Wales*, pp. 113–15 (English troops); M. G. A. Vale, "The War in Aquitaine," in Curry and Hughes, eds., *The Hundred Years' War*, pp. 81–2 (Gascons).

[44] Ayton, "English Armies," p. 25.

of any force attacking the men-at-arms.[45] This tactical system, though not fully developed until the 1330s, had its roots in the time of Edward II. It was a part of the broader infantry revolution of the early fourteenth century sparked by the success of the Flemish footmen at Courtrai that had in turn inspired the Scots to fight on foot and win against the English royal host at Bannockburn.[46] That crushing defeat transformed English ideas of warfare; by the end of Edward II's reign it was widely accepted that even knights should generally do battle on foot, "contrary to the ways of their fathers,"[47] reserving mounted shock action for post-battle pursuit and – "if convenient" – for deeds of chivalry.[48]

Aside from border skirmishes and the small "battle" of Boroughbridge in 1322,[49] however, this emerging tactical synthesis was never put to the test until the reign of Edward III, when in 1332 a small group of noble English adventurers with claims in Scotland (and the covert support of Edward III) invaded the northern realm and achieved one of the most dramatic battle-field victories in history at Dupplin Moor. Fifteen hundred Englishmen (500 men-at-arms and 1,000 archers) deployed in the formation described above defeated an enemy force about ten times their strength.[50] Although one contemporary northern chronicle claimed that the Scots were defeated

---

[45] The evidence for this formation is somewhat ambiguous, and for some battles could support A. H. Burne's (and others') interpretation of a series of such formations rather than just one, but on balance the evidence suggests that the usual formation was a central block with two wings only. See the descriptions of Dupplin Moor, Halidon Hill, Crécy and Poitiers in Rogers, *War Cruel and Sharp*, or, for a good overview, Bennett, "Development of Battle Tactics," pp. 1–20.

[46] Infantry revolution: Rogers, "Military Revolutions of the Hundred Years' War," pp. 58–64. Scots following Flemish example: *Scalacronica*, p. 142. Morris argues that the chronicler "is really wrong. Doubtless Bruce knew about Courtrai, but Falkirk was fought four years before that, and if he imitated anyone he imitated Wallace. In truth he had no need to learn even from Wallace . . . A long shaft of wood with an iron head has been used by foot in all ages. It is nature's weapon for poor or untrained men against professional mounted men." Morris misses the point: it may be true that Bruce did not need the Flemings' example on *how* to fight, but he probably did need the inspiration of their victory to give him the confidence to fight at all. Falkirk, after all, had been a severe defeat for the Scots, and might not have inspired imitation were it not for Courtrai.

[47] Geoffrey le Baker, *Chronicon*, p. 51.

[48] Knights fighting on foot: Jean le Bel, *Chronique*, vol. 1, p. 65 (see also p. 53), describing the English battle formation for the 1327 campaign, with three great divisions or "battles" of infantry (including the majority of the men-at-arms on foot and with their spurs removed) flanked by smaller wings of 500 still-mounted men-at-arms rather than by archers. For fighting on foot, but mounting for deeds of chivalry when "convenient," see the story of William Marmion in the *Scalacronica*, pp. 145–6.

[49] See T. F. Tout, "The Tactics of the Battles of Boroughbridge and Morlaix," in *Collected Papers of Thomas Frederick Tout* (Manchester, 1932–34), vol. 2.

[50] English numbers: *Gesta Edwardi de Carnarvan Auctore Canonico Bridlingtonensi*, in W. Stubbs, ed., *Chronicles of the Reigns of Edward I and Edward II*, vol. II (London, 1883), pp. 102–03; *Scalacronica*, p. 159; *Liber Pluscardensis* [Historians of Scotland, vol. VII], ed. Felix J. H. Skene (Edinburgh, 1877), p. 198; *Chronicon de Lanercost*, p. 267;

(continued)

"mainly by the English archers,"[51] this does not do justice to the thin line of men-at-arms that withstood the powerful first onrush of the Scottish pikemen and held them in check until the Scots found themselves assailed by arrows from both flanks, impaled by lances to their front, and relentlessly pressed forward by their own men in the rear. The result was a Cannae-like situation in which the crushed men in the center of the compressed mass could not breathe, much less fight: as later at Crécy and Agincourt, many of the vanquished died of suffocation rather than wounds.[52] The English archers could not have won without the men-at-arms,[53] nor the men-at-arms without the archers. Even the two groups combined could not have prevailed against such heavy odds had they fought with the tactics their fathers[54] had employed at Bannockburn.

Dupplin Moor was almost as decisive strategically as tactically, for Edward Balliol followed it up by seizing the Scottish capital, Perth, having himself crowned King of Scots at Scone, and securing the submission of nearly the entire realm. The next year, a larger English army under Edward III himself used the new tactics to solidify the position of the English king's protégé by destroying another Scottish national host – this time merely twice as large as the English force – at Halidon Hill.[55] The English stuck

(continued)
Wyntoun, *Orygynale Cronykil*, vol. 2, p. 383; Burton, *Chronica Monasterii de Melsa*, vol. 2, p. 362; also Rogers, *War Cruel and Sharp*. Virtually every chronicle, English or Scottish, gives the size of the Scottish host at 40,000 or 30,000. No pay records confirm this, but what appears to be the relics of a retinue roll for the Halidon Hill army indicates a force of about 15,000 men, and this is probably about right for the Dupplin Moor campaign as well. H. C. Hamilton, ed., *Chronicon Domini Walteri de Hemingburgh* (London, 1849), vol. 2, pp. 308–09. Scottish losses at Dupplin Moor were probably around 3,000: John of Fordun, *Chronica Gentis Scotorum*, p. 355; *Liber Pluscardensis*, p. 266; English sources give much higher figures. English losses were reportedly only thirty-five men-at-arms and no archers (*Hemingburgh*, vol. 2, p. 304). The fifth of the five earls (counting Lord Robert Bruce as an earl), the Earl of March, was captured.

51   *Lanercost*, p. 268 ["maxime per saggitarios Anglicorum"]. This is a somewhat odd usage of "*maxime*," and it is possible that the phrase should be rendered "crushingly [*maxime*] defeated by the English archers."
52   For the battle and the campaign that led up to it, see Rogers, *War Cruel and Sharp*; for the suffocation phenomenon, idem, "Offensive/Defensive," p. 160.
53   Bannockburn, where the Scottish cavalry charged the English bowmen and cut them down without mercy (Barbour, *The Bruce*, p. 308), made clear the vulnerability of archers unsupported by men-at-arms.
54   Or, in some cases – Henry Beaumont, for example – they themselves.
55   *Lanercost*, p. 274. Other estimates are higher: 5:1 according to F. W. Brie, ed., *The Brut or the Chronicle of England* (Early English Text Soc., Orig. Ser., 131, 136 [1906–08]), pp. 285, 288; 3:1 according to the *Chronica Monasterii de Melsa*, vol. 2, p. 370). The new Scottish regent and four more earls perished in this fight, along with new thousands of their compatriots. Between the two battles Balliol had been attacked by surprise in time of truce and driven out of Scotland. He then secured Edward III's overt support, after which the two Edwards besieged Berwick in order to draw the Bruce partisans to battle, a strategy which succeeded. For more detail on both battle and campaign, see Rogers, *War Cruel and Sharp*.

to this same tactical system for over a century thereafter, and it brought them victory at Crécy, Poitiers, Verneuil, and Agincourt – among other battles.

STRATEGY

The newfound battlefield prowess of the English appears to suggest that the fourteenth-century English RMA was essentially *tactical* – or, at least, that it was the tactical changes of Edward III's reign that unleashed the latent technological power of the longbow and made it revolutionary rather than merely useful. This thesis, however, would be difficult to sustain. Although the Dupplin tactics succeeded in cutting down enemy armies on battlefield after battlefield, they offered little prospect of success against strong chivalric armies that prudently refrained from making frontal assaults. So long as they were able to retain the tactical defensive, the English could expect to win decisive victories, but it was up to strategy to provide the archers and men-at-arms with the opportunity to face and overcome an adversary's charge.

In an age in which prevailing ideas of strategy generally advised the avoidance of open battle whenever possible,[56] when commanders who were willing to fight usually preferred to remain on the tactical defensive, and when (as in the sixteenth and seventeenth centuries) the relative superiority of fortifications over siege warfare strengthened the strategic defensive,[57] compelling an enemy to attack could be quite difficult. Edward himself discovered this in Scotland in 1334–37 and in France in 1338–45, 1347–55, 1359–60, and again after 1369.

The king and his advisers used two main approaches to resolve the difficulties inherent in attempting to combine an aggressive strategy with a tactical/technological system which dictated a defensive stance on the battlefield.[58] The first method, employed at Berwick in 1333, Cambrai in 1339, Tournai in 1340, and Calais in 1346–47, was to besiege a key city belonging to the enemy until the defenders were on the verge of surrender, so that the opposing field army had to fight unless its leaders were willing to

---

56 John Gillingham, "Richard I and the Science of War in the Middle Ages," in Gillingham and J. C. Holt, eds., *War and Government in the Middle Ages* (Woodbridge, 1984); Prestwich, *Armies*, p. 11 ("the new orthodoxy is that medieval commanders sought to avoid battle wherever possible"); Vegetius (Flavius Vegetius Renatus), *The Earliest English Translation of Vegetius' De Re Militari*, ed. Geoffrey Lester (Heidelberg, 1988), p. 126 ("ffor gode lederes and wise cheuenteynes ne fightith noght bletheliche with open bataille and in open feeld yif there be open drede of perel"); p. 158 ("Gode dukes ne fighteth neuere opounlyche in feeld but thei ben idryue therto by sodeyn hap or grete nede"; note also BN, MS Fr. 693, fo. 155.
57 Rogers, "Military Revolutions," pp. 64, 74.
58 Rogers, "Offensive/Defensive," discusses this issue in a broader context.

see the place fall. In the first instance, that system led to the resounding victory at Halidon Hill, but failed in the second two largely due to financial difficulties which made it impossible to maintain the sieges. In the fourth case, Calais, the gambit failed to induce Philip of Valois to risk a second Crécy, but Edward did gain a key strategic port, which the English retained for two centuries.[59]

The second strategic device employed by Edward III to compel his enemies to give battle on English terms or submit was the *chevauchée*. The "war-ride" served to remind the French or the Scots that the fundamental reason for having an army – or a government – was to defend the commonweal against the ravages of enemy warriors. By riding through enemy territories with torch in hand, creating a zone of destruction thirty miles wide by hundreds long, English armies imposed unbearable penalties on enemies who refused to fight.[60] Unless the invading army allowed itself to be pinned in place and starved, the victims of the *chevauchée* had little choice but to do battle on Edward's terms or suffer the economic and political collapse to which such recurring episodes of devastation generally led.

The technique was not new – ample medieval precedents existed, and Edward's system was essentially similar to Spartan strategy at the outset of the Peloponnesian War. But it was a particularly effective answer to the strategic difficulties that faced the Plantagenets. It was the *chevauchée* strategy that led to the two greatest battlefield triumphs of the reign, Crécy and Poitiers; that forced the Scots to accept Edward's dominion (albeit briefly) in 1335; and that compelled the French to seek peace on his terms in 1360.[61]

LEADERSHIP

The last two paragraphs may have made the triumphs of Edward III's reign seem easy: combine longbowmen and steady men-at-arms fighting in accordance with the close-order infantry tactics employed at Dupplin

---

[59] This interpretation of the siege of Calais is mildly revisionist (see Rogers, *War Cruel and Sharp* for more detail on these sieges).
[60] For the extent of devastation wrought by the *chevauchées*, see Rogers, "By Fire and Sword: *Bellum Hostile* and 'Civilians' in the Hundred Years' War," in Mark Grimsley and Clifford J. Rogers, eds., *Civilians in the Path of War* (University of Nebraska Press, forthcoming); see also Clausewitz, *Vom Kriege*, p. 92 (Book 1, Chapter 1.4): "If the enemy is to be coerced you must put him in a situation that is even more unpleasant than the sacrifice you call on him to make."
[61] There is a general discussion of Edward's use of the *chevauchée* strategy, with particular focus on the Crécy campaign, in Clifford J. Rogers, "Edward III and the Dialectics of Strategy, 1327–1360," *Transactions of the Royal Historical Society*, 6th ser., 4 (1994). Rogers, *War Cruel and Sharp*, covers all these campaigns in detail.

Moor with one or another strategy to force the enemy onto the tactical offensive, and victory is assured. That formulation contains an element of truth, but needs refinement. The Dupplin Moor tactical system was indeed extraordinarily effective, as proven by the simple fact that troops employing it were able to win so many victories, so consistently, against such heavy odds. But it could not *guarantee* victory; many English victories of this period were near-run things. Some of the Scots who fought at Dupplin Moor believed that they would have won the day were it not for a major tactical blunder arising from rivalry between two of their army's leaders.[62] Neville's Cross in 1346 was a long fight, and the Scots twice drove off the English archers. Only the extraordinary determination of the men-at-arms, who fought on even after their wings had broken, and thereby bought time for the light infantry to rally and return to the struggle, enabled the English to prevail.[63] At Poitiers, the English likewise came very close to defeat: "in former times," wrote one chronicler, "people knew which side would win immediately after the third or fourth flight of arrows, or at the latest the sixth, but here one archer loosed a hundred aimed [*cum providentia*] shots and still neither side accepted defeat; nowhere in [histories of] wars or [songs of] deeds does one hear of another fight maintained for such a long time."[64] Although skillful execution of the Dupplin tactics enabled Prince Edward to crush three successive attacks by the French marshals, by the Dauphin, and by part of the division of the Duke of Orléans, such a large force under King John still remained that many of the English thought that their cause was lost.[65] It took the outstanding personal leadership of the prince and of his tough and experienced subordinate commanders to keep the Anglo-Gascon army from collapsing as the final French assault began.

Yet even defensive tenacity was not enough: the English ultimately prevailed only because the prince, at the crisis of the battle, recognized that exceptional circumstances called for exceptional action, and abandoned the tactics that had enabled the English to withstand the repeated attacks of a larger and better-equipped army. Instead of readying his troops to receive yet another charge, he detached a small mobile force under the Captal de Buch, a Gascon baron, to circle the battlefield and strike the French from the rear. The prince, with what remained of his army, simultaneously

---

62 Wyntoun, *Orygynale Cronykil*, vol. 2, p. 388.
63 See Rogers, "Scottish Invasion of 1346," pp. 62–7.
64 *Eulogium historiarum*, ed. F. S. Haydon (London: RS, 1858–63), vol. 2, p. 225: "In antiquo tempore ad tertium vel quartum vel ultimo ad sextum tractum unius sagittae homines scirent continuo quae pars triumpharet, sed ibi unus sagittarius c. emisit cum providentia et adhuc neutra pars cessit alteri; non est auditum in bellis nec in gestis quod aliqua pugna tam diu perseverabat."
65 Le Baker, *Chronicon*, p. 150; Knighton, vol. 2, p. 89.

launched a head-on attack. That desperate gamble crushed the French army; King John himself fell prisoner along with 1,900 men-at-arms in addition to the 2,500 French knights and esquires killed.[66]

The long run of Plantagenet battlefield successes thus owed something to enemy errors, hard-fighting troops, and good leadership as well as a superior tactical system that made maximum use of an advantage in weaponry. Edward III's success in converting tactical victory into strategic success likewise required more than the simple implementation of a formula or set of principles. The fourteenth-century English clearly did possess a set of strategic principles to which they in general adhered; these revolved around the need to ensure that Edward's armies fought battles as often as possible without being forced to take the tactical initiative. That principle was simple, but as Clausewitz notes, in war, "even the simplest thing is difficult." Medieval commanders were well aware of the advantages accruing to the tactical defensive;[67] the fact that Edward's opponents nevertheless took the offensive in every major land battle of his reign – Dupplin Moor, Halidon Hill, Crécy, Neville's Cross, Poitiers, and Nájera, not to mention smaller fights at Morlaix, Mauron, Saintes, and Lunalonge – is an indication of how skilled he and his comrades-in-arms were at controlling the strategic situation. The same campaigns also show remarkable boldness, aggressiveness, determination, and courage among the leaders and men of the Plantagenet armies.

The Poitiers campaign once more provides an excellent example. From the start the 1356 *chevauchée* was a risky operation: it takes a special kind of aggressive and self-confident spirit for an invader to set out for the Ile-de-France, the core of the French kingdom, at the head of an army of only 6,000 men.[68] The prince had to walk a fine line throughout the campaign: he had to keep the French from cutting him off from his base with a large army (which could force him onto the tactical offensive in order to break out of the trap), and yet at the same time he had to give the French the opportunity to close for the defensive battle he sought. He tried to provoke the French into making a premature attack by besieging the castle of Romorantin; when King John refused the gambit, the prince skillfully took up a series of positions along river lines on which he could await an attack while minimizing the risk of an enemy slipping past him to block his line of retreat. Even when John, in one of the most remarkable marches executed by a French commander in the Hundred Years' War, did succeed in getting in between the English army and Gascony, the prince reacted

---

[66] Rogers, *War Cruel and Sharp*, Chapter 16, covers the campaign and the battle.
[67] Clausewitz, *Vom Kriege*, p. 159; Rogers, "Offensive/Defensive," pp. 158–61.
[68] Bartholomew Burghersh's letter to John Beauchamp, in Froissart, *Oeuvres*, vol. 18, pp. 386–7; the prince's letter to the Bishop of Worcester in H. T. Riley, *Memorials of London Life in the XIIIth, XIVth, XVth Centuries* (London, 1868), p. 207.

swiftly and decisively, striking the French rearguard by surprise and once again getting ahead of the Valois army, if only barely.

At that point his situation was very dangerous. The French had superior numbers, were more rested and better supplied, and were on their own ground, fighting for the defense of their homeland under the eyes of their king. "In the ordinary course of things," predicted a veteran captain among King John's advisers, "the English cannot prevail."[69] The French were particularly superior in numbers of men-at-arms, and thus could potentially encircle the English army if it simply formed up and awaited attack according to its usual tactical doctrine.[70] Prince Edward recognized the peril of his situation, but did not let it dishearten him. He and his subordinate leaders arranged a withdrawal so skillful that he drew the French into a premature attack on the strong rearguard he had established under the veteran Earl of Salisbury. That action soon embroiled both armies, but the English were much quicker in sending in reinforcements and forming a full battle line, so that for most of the fight they enjoyed the advantage of the tactical defensive.

Throughout the campaign and in the immediate preliminaries to the battle – as in the battle itself – the English army benefited from the prince's more than competent generalship and the boldness, courage, and determination that he both displayed personally and inspired in his men. Similarly, the battle of Halidon Hill was made possible by the administrative and logistical skills of Edward III and his staff, which enabled them to maintain the siege of Berwick until its defenders reached the verge of starvation, and by the cold resolve with which the king ignored a Scottish attempt to draw him away from the city through an advance against the castle of Bamburgh, where his young wife, Queen Philippa, was lodged. More generally, the king's charisma and political skill – which enabled him to enlist the lasting support of magnates and Commons alike – enabled him to mount the expensive campaigns that gave him the chance to bring his strategic ability and tactical strengths to bear. Finally, Edward possessed the wisdom to listen to the sound advice of the Black Prince and of Henry of Lancaster, who warned him not to be too greedy in his peace terms; the result was the

---

69 Le Baker, *Chronicon*, p. 144. Much the same was said concerning the battle of Crécy: see BN, MS Fr. 693, fo. 164v (selon cours commun des batailles les nostres [i.e. the French] deussent en [i.e. the victory] avoir. Car ilz estoient plus sans comparoison et de meilleur chevalerie que les autres.) The wording of the contemporary sources thus confirms the extraordinary, or revolutionary, nature of the tactical superiority of the English.

70 Froissart, *Oeuvres*, vol. 5, p. 413; vol. 4, pp. 435, 419–20 (au voir dire, il [the English] ne ressongnoient point tant le bataille que il faisoient ce que on ne les tenist en tel estat, ensi que pour asségiés et affamés); cf. M. Villani, *Cronica*, pp. 532–3 (gli ha Iddio ridotti e rinchiusi nelle vostre mani per modo ch'addietro non possono tornare, né a destra né a sinistra si possono allargare. Da vivere hanno poco . . .).

Treaty of Brétigny, which transformed military victory into political success.[71] Edward was in this respect far wiser than some beneficiaries of later military revolutions or revolutions in military affairs such as Napoleon or Hitler.

CONCLUSION

Study of particular cases cannot fully illuminate broader phenomena. Nevertheless, the fourteenth-century English revolution in military affairs suggests a general principle: improvements in weapons and military organization do not consistently win battles unless employed as part of an effective tactical system, and strong tactics do not bring lasting victory unless military leaders first develop and implement strategies that create the right circumstances for their employment, then translate battlefield success into political results. Edward II's use of paid longbowmen did not raise England even to the level of a second-rate power; it took the combination of Dupplin tactics, well-crafted strategy, and the personal contributions of an outstanding group of military leaders to effect Edward III's revolution in military affairs.

[71] See *War Cruel and Sharp*, Chapter 4 [Bamburgh] and Chapter 16 [Brétigny].

3

Forging the Western army in seventeenth-century France

JOHN A. LYNN

The art of war in seventeenth-century Europe passed through a transformation so fundamental that scholars have proclaimed it a "military revolution."[1] Changes in everything from tactics to institutional hierarchies gave armies many of the characteristics now recognized as modern. After initial advances credited to the Dutch and the Swedes, the French led the wave of change during the second half of the century. This essay focuses on French military refinements and innovations in the *grand siècle* in which Louis XIV, renowned as the Sun King, set the style in armies as much as in architecture.

Historical debate on seventeenth-century military development centers on two related issues. The first concerns the pace and character of change, and involves a semantic – but also substantive – dispute between advocates of "revolution" or "evolution"; the simplicity of the dichotomy belies the variety of innovations and changes in existing patterns. The language of revolution satisfies the inherent human desire for drama, but a more evolutionary interpretation fits the evidence better. The second point of contention involves the role of technology in driving the process of change, whatever its pace. Technology seduces all who examine the military past;

---

[1] Important works on the early modern military revolution include Michael Roberts, *The Military Revolution, 1560–1660* (Belfast, 1956); George Clark, *War and Society in the Seventeenth Century* (Cambridge, 1958); Geoffrey Parker, "The 'Military Revolution' 1560–1660 – a Myth?," *Journal of Modern History* 48 (1976), and *The Military Revolution: Military Innovation and the Rise of the West, 1500–1800* (Cambridge, 1988). For criticisms of the Roberts and Parker formulations of the theory see Jeremy Black, *A Military Revolution? Military Change and European Society, 1550–1800* (Atlantic Highlands, NJ, 1991) and *European Warfare, 1660–1815* (New Haven, CT, 1994); and John A. Lynn, "The *trace italienne* and the Growth of Armies: The French Case," *Journal of Military History*, July 1991. Clifford J. Rogers, ed., *The Military Revolution Debate: Readings on the Military Transformation of Early Modern Europe* (Boulder, CO, 1995), offers a useful survey.

hardware promises to explain so much and pretends to be the stuff of revolutionary change. But the transformation this chapter describes nevertheless owed relatively little to technology.

Understanding the timing, causation, and importance of seventeenth-century military change requires analysis of the paths not taken as well as those that contemporaries chose to follow. The first section of the essay considers advances in weaponry that promised but failed to deliver rapid tactical transformation. Then the analysis shifts to the conceptual and institutional innovations that exerted immediate, enduring, and defining influence upon the military traditions of the West.

TECHNOLOGICAL CHANGE WITHOUT REVOLUTION

French military experience under Louis XIV provides two principal examples of technological innovations that fell short of their potentially revolutionary implications for warfare: the adoption of flintlock and bayonet, and the limited use and subsequent rejection of the artillery *de nouvelle invention*.

1. Fusil and bayonet

Jeremy Black has repeatedly claimed that the transition from matchlock musket and pike to flintlock fusil and bayonet brought revolutionary tactical change.[2] But at least for the French, the initial impact of this new "weapons system" was surprisingly modest.[3] At the start of the 1600s the musket was the basic infantry firearm. It fired by means of a lock that ignited the powder charge with a lighted "match," a cord of flax or hemp. A complicated loading procedure limited its rate of fire to one shot per minute, and up to half of all shots misfired.[4] The lighted match was dangerous to the musketeer and to those around him, since it might accidentally ignite his gunpowder supply.[5]

Musketeers lacked shock potential and could not defend themselves effectively against cavalry; for both reasons pikemen joined musketeers in the battalion formations that derived both from French practice and from the Dutch tactical reforms. Pikemen normally occupied the center files of the battalion, flanked on either side by files of musketeers (see Figure 3.1).

---

[2] See both his *A Military Revolution?* and *European Warfare*.
[3] For thorough discussion of the issues raised in this section, see John A. Lynn, *Giant of the Grand Siècle: The French Army, 1610–1715* (Cambridge, 1997), Chapter 14.
[4] David Chandler, *The Art of Warfare in the Age of Marlborough* (New York, 1976), p. 77.
[5] Vauban spoke of "a thousand fire accidents because of the match." Vauban to Louvois, 21 December 1687, in Albert Rochas d'Aiglun, *Vauban, sa famille et ses écrits*, 2 vols. (Paris, 1910), vol. 2, p. 286.

Over time, the proportion of muskets to pikes in the battalion increased, from 1:1 at the start of the 1600s, to 2:1 by mid-century, to 4:1 by 1690. And as the proportion of firearms increased, battalions formed in fewer ranks: formations gradually became thinner and longer. In this system companies were primarily administrative rather than combat units – they contained a mix of musketeers and pikemen, and therefore had to disperse to form the battalion combat formation in which musketeers and pikemen joined their like-armed comrades (Figure 3.1).

The mix within both company and battalion became even more compli-cated as the safer and more reliable flintlock fusil began to elbow aside the

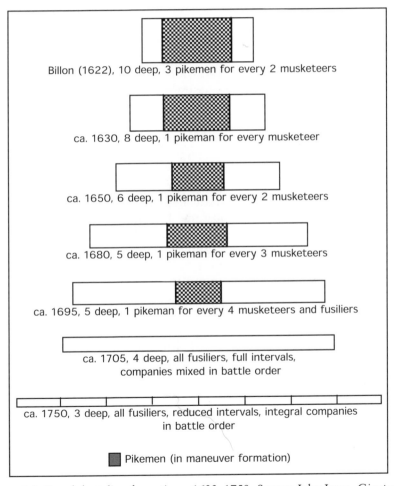

Figure 3.1. French battalion formations, 1622–1750. *Source*: John Lynn, *Giant of the Grand Siècle* (Cambridge, 1997), p. 476.

older musket. Instead of using a lit match to set off the gunpowder in the priming pan, the fusil employed flint striking steel to generate a spark that ignited the charge. Freed from worry about the match, a fusilier could load with a third fewer movements than a matchlock-armed musketeer.[6] He could also prime and load his fusil, set it on half-cock safety, sling or stack the weapon, and still be instantly ready to fire the moment he took it up again. Slowly, by stages, the French army adopted fusils. In 1670 Louis XIV approved the inclusion of four fusiliers in every infantry company, and the weapon soon became standard in the new grenadier companies.[7] Yet as late as 1688 most infantrymen still carried matchlocks.[8] The monarch's unwillingness to pay the bill for converting the army to the new weapons explains the slowness of the transition. Combat in the Nine Years' War (1688–97) nevertheless increased the number of fusils in infantry battalions, and with the return of peace, an ordinance of 1699 prescribed the universal adoption of the fusil.[9]

About the same time that the French finally set aside the matchlock for the fusil, they also discarded the pike for the socket bayonet. The desire to give the musket some shock value for defense and offense by turning it into a short but stout pike had led to the introduction of primitive "plug" bayonets around 1640.[10] These consisted of "straight, double-edged blades a foot long with tapering handles also a foot long" that fit down the barrel of the musket and when fixed, prevented the weapon from being loaded or fired – a noteworthy disadvantage.[11] In 1687 Vauban created a socket bayonet that allowed the weapon to be loaded and fired with bayonet attached. Louvois, at first a skeptic, soon became a convert and in 1689 ordered all musketeers and fusiliers to carry such bayonets.[12] In 1703 the French at last abandoned the pike altogether, and the combination of fusil and bayonet became standard for all infantrymen except a few NCOs and officers.[13]

Until the universal adoption of the fusil/bayonet, the mix of weapons within an infantry battalion dictated its tactical order. Musketeers, fusiliers,

---

6   Corvisier says the number of movements fell from 36 to 23. Philippe Contamine, ed., *Histoire militaire de la France*, vol. 1, series editor André Corvisier (Paris, 1992), p. 409.
7   6 February 1670 ordinance in Camille Rousset, *Histoire de Louvois*, 4 vols. (Paris, 1862–64), vol. 1, p. 191.
8   Service Historique de l'Armée de Terre (SHAT), Archives de Guerre (AG), A[1]807, 23 August 1688, letter to inspectors in Rousset, *Louvois*, vol. 3, p. 329 note.
9   Jean Colin, *L'infanterie au XVIIIe siècle: La tactique* (Paris, 1907), p. 26.
10 Louis André, *Michel Le Tellier et l'organisation de l'armée monarchique* (Paris, 1906), p. 344.
11 Puységur in Chandler, *The Art of Warfare*, p. 83.
12 SHAT, AG, A[1]861, 29 November 1689, Louvois to inspectors, in Rousset, *Louvois*, vol. 3, p. 330 note.
13 Jacques-François de Chastenet de Puységur, *Art de la guerre par règles et principes*, 2 vols. (Paris, 1748), vol. 1, pp. 51, 57; Louis XIV, *Oeuvres de Louis XIV*, eds. Philippe-Henri de Grimoard and Philippe-Antoine Grouvelle, 6 vols. (Paris, 1806), vol. 4, pp. 396–7 note.

and pikemen abandoned their companies to occupy their places within the battalion march formation, and then shifted within the battalion when it approached the enemy. From the 1670s, for example, directives stipulated that pikemen were to group in the center files of the battalion on the march, but at the approach of combat, they were to split into three bodies, one of which remained in the center, while the other two marched off to right and left to provide protection for the battalion's flanks (see Figure 3.2). This evolution required musketeers to close on the center to fill the gaps the departing pikemen had left.

In order to permit all this shifting, large distances separated ranks and files – thirteen feet between ranks and three to six feet between files in marching order, with the distances halved for combat. These ample spaces also protected the battalion from the dangers that arose when musketeers with lighted matches and gunpowder at the ready stood too close together. Since companies lost their integrity when moving into battalion formation, battalions maneuvered in subunits other than their component companies; the only meaningful combat drill was battalion drill.

Adoption of a single weapon for all infantry could have revolutionized this tactical picture. Arming all men alike would eliminate any need to shift men within the battalion. That step and the disappearance of lighted matches from the midst of the formation would have made unnecessary the wide spaces between files and ranks. Closer order might in turn have accelerated a formation's rate of fire, or at least have made firing more efficient. Companies could have retained their integrity in combat, so that company drill would have had a much closer relationship to battlefield movements. The potential of this innovation alone for improving combat performance would have been great, because companies drilled far more frequently than battalions.

But none of this happened during the War of the Spanish Succession (1701–14). Drills and formations inherited from the age of musket and

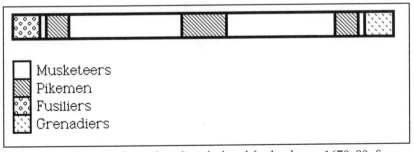

Figure 3.2. A French infantry battalion deployed for battle, ca. 1670–90. *Source*: Diagram based on "Order that the King wants his infantry to observe on the day of combat," AG, Arch. hist., 78, vol. 67.

pike continued into the age of fusil and bayonet. Large gaps remained between files and ranks. Battalions continued to maneuver by manches, demi-manches, and divisions, not by companies, which still dispersed in order to form battalions, even though the need for musketeers, fusiliers, and pikemen to go their separate ways had disappeared. Ranks apparently did not in fact close up until the 1750s. Then and only then did the French army adopt a cadenced marching step in order to prevent men packed tightly together from stepping on each other's heels.

Infantry tactics thus *evolved* at a measured pace during the seventeenth and eighteenth centuries. Battalions already gave battle in linear formations early in the 1600s, and these formations simply became thinner and longer as the decades progressed, as indicated in Figure 3.1. The flintlock/bayonet-armed battalion of 1705 looked surprisingly similar to the musket/pike-armed battalion of 1690. It took several decades before the new infantry armament encouraged a further evolutionary step toward the still-thinner linear orders of the War of the Austrian Succession and Seven Years' War. What might have been a technological earthquake created only a tremor, because the French continued to think and act in ways defined in an earlier age by a different set of circumstances—so fundamental and enduring are habits of the mind.

2. *Cannon* de nouvelle invention

Rigid conceptions of warfare also prevented the French from exploiting the potential of a new artillery system in the late seventeenth century.[14] These guns, the cannon *de nouvelle invention*, possessed many of the key advantages that made the Gribeauval system so valued a century later. But the cannon *de nouvelle invention* remained only a *révolution manquée* because the French were not intellectually ready for such guns in an age dominated by siege warfare.

The chief factor that limited the use of cannon in the early modern era, particularly on the battlefield, was weight. In the 1620s the barrel alone of a 34-pounder weighed 5,600 livres, and the cannon on its carriage required twenty horses to move it and a crew of thirty-five to serve it.[15] Nor did artillery trains possess their own draft animals or teamsters; instead, armies hired civilian drivers and teams to haul cannon. On the day of battle these contractors would drag the heavy pieces into position and prudently with-

---

[14] For details on seventeenth-century French artillery, including the cannon *de nouvelle invention*, see Lynn, *Giant of the Grand Siècle*, Chapter 14.

[15] These figures come from the very interesting and detailed tables in Du Praissac, *Les discours militaires* (Paris, 1622), pp. 112–30. I have called his $33\frac{1}{3}$-pounder a 34-pounder and his $15\frac{1}{4}$-pounder a 16-pounder for convenience.

draw, depriving the army of what little tactical flexibility the weight and bulk of the artillery itself allowed.

By mid-century the French had in essence settled on Sully's system of six calibers; pieces firing balls of 33, 24, 16, 12, 8, and 4 pounds. These cannon *de vielle invention* were heavy regardless of caliber. Their chamber walls were thick enough to accommodate powder charges of two-thirds or more of their projectile weight. Each barrel was about eleven feet long regardless of caliber, from a self-conscious decision to ensure that all cannon be suited to firing through embrasures in fortress walls or siege works; muzzle blast from short barrels damaged embrasures. Fortress guns were thus essentially interchangeable with field guns.

The cannon *de nouvelle invention* resulted from discoveries attributed to Antonio Gonzalès, who first tried to market his system in Spain and after meeting failure there brought it to France in 1679.[16] By reshaping the powder chamber into a spherical form with a larger diameter than the bore, he found that he could achieve acceptable results with powder charges only one-third the weight of the projectile. With less powder, the walls of the bore, if not of the chamber, could be thinner and thus lighter. And he designed the new pieces specifically for field use; they were therefore much shorter than normal cannon. Excluding the cascabel, the knob projecting from the rear of the barrel, a 24-pounder of the old system extended 10 feet 2 inches, while a 24-pounder of the new system was only 6 feet long (see Figure 3.3).[17] The new pieces were thus much lighter than the old; excluding the carriage, the old 16-pounder weighed in at 4,100 livres, while the new came in at 2,220; the respective weights for a 4-pounder were 1,300 livres and 600 livres. Changes in the carriage and the addition of an *avant train* further increased mobility. Such pieces promised many advantages, but the potential economies resulting from the smaller gunpowder charge most attracted Louvois: the war minister saw the new artillery in financial rather than tactical terms. In 1681 he

16 For accounts of cannon *de nouvelle invention* see Ernest Picard and Louis Jouan, *L'artillerie française au XVIIIe siècle* (Paris, 1906), pp. 44–7; Howard Rosen, "The Système Gribeauval: A Study of Technological Development and Institutional Change in Eighteenth-Century France," Ph.D. dissertation, University of Chicago, 1981, pp. 128–33, and Chandler, *The Art of Warfare*, pp. 176–93.

17 Chandler, *The Art of Warfare*, p. 178, gives the contrasting dimensions as 10 feet 10 inches and 6 feet 3 inches. My dimensions come from Denis Diderot et al., *Encyclopédie*, 17 vols. text, 12 vols. plates (Paris, 1751–65), vol. 1 plates, plates V and VI in *art militaire, fortification*. Strictly speaking these plates show a gun *de nouvelle invention* and one of the Vallière system ca. 1732, but the Vallière cannon followed the dimensions of the older models. These plates allow a close comparison that demonstrates how the metal was tapered differently in the cannon *de nouvelle invention* to allow for the force of the charge but still employ thin walls along the bore. All measurements of length and weight are given here in the French system of the *ancien régime*.

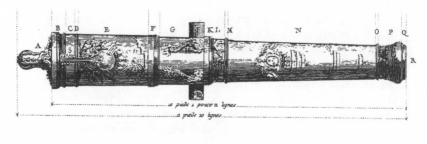

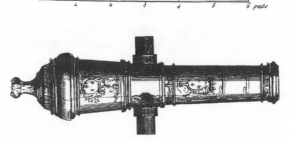

Figure 3.3. 24-pounder French cannon of the Vallière system (top) and *de nouvelle invention* (bottom). *Source*: Diderot's *Encyclopédie*, plates V and VI, *art militaire, fortification*. Image courtesy of the Rare Book and Special Collections Library, University of Illinois at Urbana-Champaign.

ordered models of the lighter guns sent to all French foundries to serve as templates for production.

Cannon *de nouvelle invention* promised a great breakthrough in artillery, but at the same time they suffered from two principal drawbacks that ultimately caused the French to reject them in the early eighteenth century. The spherical chamber, being of greater diameter than the bore, was hard to swab out between rounds; burning residue from the previous shot had a nasty habit of setting off the next charge rammed home. This "produced bad accidents to the cannoneers servicing the pieces, particularly when they were obliged to fire rapidly."[18] And the light cannon fired with a violent jerk that damaged gun carriages, battered embrasures, and hampered accuracy. The guns simply had less mass to dampen their recoil.

It is interesting to compare the ultimate failure of the cannon *de nouvelle invention* with the success of the Gribeauval system adopted in the 1770s (see Table 3.1). Although the Gribeauval guns boasted more precise manufacture and improved powder chambers, the two sys-

[18] For the three criticisms stated here, see Diderot, *Encyclopédie*, vol. 2, p. 613; Picard and Jouan, *L'artillerie française*, pp. 45–6, echo two of them.

Table 3.1. *Barrel and shot weight of French cannon, 1650–1800*

Shot wgt.	Vielle invention (circa 1660)	Nouvelle invention (circa 1680)	Vallière system (1732)	Gribeauval system (1776)
4	1,300 livres	600 livres	1,150 livres	290 kg/638 lbs.
8	1,950 livres	1,000 livres	2,100 livres	580 kg/1,276 lbs.
12	3,400 livres	2,000 livres	3,200 livres	880 kg/1,936 lbs.
16	4,100 livres	2,220 livres	4,200 livres	
24	5,100 livres	3,000 livres	5,400 livres	

tems were of essentially the same weight. The cannon *de nouvelle inven-tion* might thus have made possible the same high level of mobility the Gribeauval pieces later afforded.[19] Yet this potential failed to materia-lize. Why?

The key difference between the two light artillery systems was that the pieces *de nouvelle invention* did not mesh easily with seventeenth- and early eighteenth-century predilections for siege warfare. Because the new pieces jumped vigorously and damaged embrasures, gunners inevitably preferred the heavier designs – familiar, stable, and safe – to the lighter pieces except when mobility on the battlefield was paramount. The politics of gun pro-duction may also have hampered the adoption of the new cannon; the regional lieutenants-general of artillery saw orders to produce the new guns as a challenge to their authority to cast guns as they saw fit.[20] Judged by weight reduction alone, the cannon *de nouvelle invention* equaled the innovations of Gribeauval, and because the former came a century earlier, their improvement was perhaps even more dramatic because so unprecedented. That the cannon *de nouvelle invention* failed to revolutionize the late seventeenth-century battlefield illustrates the point that military technology must fit into a broader conception of warfare to become effective.

The particular cases described should not be read as a blanket dismissal of the role of technology in early modern warfare. In two cases, technolo-gical innovation of the purest kind was a central factor in the late fifteenth and sixteenth centuries. The three-masted caravel-built sailing ship, a pro-duct of late medieval naval architecture, was an absolutely vital addition to the European arsenal – the ultimate transport and weapons platform of its day. Without it, European colonial expansion would have been unthink-able. In addition, fifteenth-century advances in artillery design and produc-tion eventually transformed warfare both at sea and on land. At sea, artillery mounted in sailing vessels assured Europe's worldwide expansion. On land, artillery played an increasingly critical role in siege and field warfare. As Geoffrey Parker has explained so well, artillery also made necessary a new style of fortification, the European artillery fortress, dis-tinctive in its low silhouette, massive oblique walls, bastioned trace, and defensive artillery emplacements. Fortresses built in this style and armed with cannon of European design were of world significance: they allowed the West not only to dominate the seas but to maintain and defend trading

---

[19] See comparative weights in Diderot, *Encyclopédie*, vol. 2, p. 608; Picard and Jouan, *L'artillerie française*, pp. 44–7; Howard Rosen, "The *Système Gribeauval*," p. 130; Matti Lauerma, *L'artillerie de campagne française pendant les guerres de la Révolution* (Helsinki, 1956), pp. 10, 16; and Chandler, *The Art of Warfare*, p. 178.

[20] Rosen argues that the lieutenants-general resisted as political threats efforts to standardize artillery (Rosen, "The *Système Gribeauval*," p. 132).

colonies around the globe.[21] The age of Louis XIV could not boast of technological advances of comparable magnitude.

THREE SEVENTEENTH-CENTURY CHANGES THAT MATTERED

Conceptual and institutional innovation, not technological change, had a decisive impact on seventeenth-century warfare. The first such change was a new and counter-instinctual attitude toward combat losses – an approach described here as the "battle culture of forbearance." The second was an extension of the first: the use of drill to control and sustain troops within this battle culture. The third was the creation of a new form of military community, exemplified by the European regiment of the late seventeenth century. If military revolutions – by semantic license – can take a century or more, then these three changes were genuinely revolutionary in character.

1. The battle culture of forbearance

Louis XIV wrote that "[g]ood order makes us look assured, and it seems enough to look brave, because most often our enemies do not wait for us to approach near enough for us to have to show if we are in fact brave."[22] For Louis XIV, order meant victory; the secret was to appear unshakable. He was not alone. For seventeenth-century generals and military thinkers battle – and infantry combat in particular – had become a test of wills. Victory went to the force that absorbed the worst that the enemy could inflict and still maintained order, rather than the force that inflicted the greatest physical casualties on the other side. Marshal Catinat, a practical soldier, insisted in describing an assault that "[o]ne prepares the soldier to not fire and to realize that it is necessary to suffer the enemy's fire, expecting that the enemy who fires is assuredly beaten when one receives his entire discharge."[23] This emphasis on taking losses stoically was far from the primitive warrior ethos that commanded headlong attack. The surprising truth is that seventeenth-century Europe developed a battle culture based less upon fury than upon forbearance.

The triumph of firepower brought the triumph of suffering; long-range weapons compel armies to endure losses before they can reply. The only effective reply to cannon was to cross the valley of death and kill the

21 See especially his *The Military Revolution*, Chapter 4.
22 Louis XIV, *Mémoires de Louis XIV pour l'instruction du dauphin*, ed. Charles Dreyss, 2 vols. (Paris, 1860), vol. 2, pp. 112–13; for general discussion of the issues raised here, see Lynn, *Giant of the Grand Siècle*, Chapter 15.
23 Catinat in Colin, *L'infanterie au XVIIIe siècle*, p. 25.

gunners. Roman forces confronting the Parthians and French or Scottish troops facing English longbowmen faced a similar problem, but no earlier weapon equaled the range of artillery or could inflict such hideous damage. Muskets were closer to bows in range and in some other characteristics as well. Like the longbow, the musket was above all a defensive weapon, more capable of stopping an enemy assault than in overpowering an enemy in the attack. Yet while longbowmen rarely fought other longbowmen, musketeers and fusiliers regularly confronted forces armed with the same weapons. And even on the offensive, the musket was brought to bear. Losses could be staggering when forces stood at close range and poured volley after volley into one another. But as Louis noted, one side usually broke, ending the duel. As firepower became the norm, the use of armor died out; even the illusion of protection vanished.

Soldiers now received standardized orders to hold fire as long as possible: "until you see the whites of their eyes." In a memoir dedicated to his young king in 1663, the experienced soldier d'Aurignac advised generals that they must above all "command both cavalry and infantry when approaching the enemy to fire only after the enemy had fired first." Vauban put it even more succinctly, "Usually, in man-to-man combat the advantage lies with those who fire last."[24] In an age of inaccurate and slow-loading weapons, it made sense to hold fire until close enough to make it tell, and at close quarters the force that fired first disarmed itself. All that is true. But to hold his fire, the soldier must endure, must hold back the promptings of fear and the instinct to do something, anything, in the face of intolerable and steadily increasing danger. For d'Aurignac, the soldier must exert self-control or his officers must impose control upon him. Even in the charge, the French infantryman of the *grand siècle* had orders not to speak: silence, order, solidity.

It may be tempting to explain the emphasis on forbearance simply with reference to the limitations of fusil and bayonet. But such an explanation can only go so far. With the same weapon, the armies of Revolutionary France developed and applied a very different and far more aggressive battle culture, one that sacrificed order to speed and élan, with the troops advancing to songs and shouts – to the infinite terror of their enemies. The battle culture of the late seventeenth century derived from a specific psychology, not a specific technology.

In a recent volume, the distinguished American military historian Russell Weigley defined the entire 1631–1815 period as "The Age of Battles," a period in which soldiers believed that battle promised decisive

---

[24] Sébastien le Prestre de Vauban, *A Manual of Siegecraft and Fortification*, trans. G. A. Rothrock (Ann Arbor, MI, 1968), p. 123.

results.[25] Battle as an exercise in forbearance does not fit this picture. Within the French battle culture that came to dominate the second half of the *grand siècle*, battle was expected to be costly, and it was. But day-long struggles of attrition also failed to produce war-ending decisions; the great losses suffered in combat merely magnified the crushing expense of conflict that was such a dominant theme in the *grand siècle*.[26] Moreover, chance and the unexpected seemed to rule the battlefield; French commanders, to use current terminology, recognized that battle was non-linear. Worse yet, the presence of numerous fortified towns and the dependence of armies on wholly inadequate logistical systems – bad or nonexistent roads and poorly organized supply services using wagon trains – made it difficult to convert battlefield victories into decisive political results. Given these conditions, battle seemed an unpromising technique. The same king who counseled that good order was enough to gain victory also came to distrust the promise of battle; to Louis XIV and his age siege warfare seemed far more predictable – more linear – and its results more assured.

2. Drill

Order amid chaos in the face of death was far from natural. It had to be learned. Infantry training emphasized obedience and restraint. It was not enough that the soldier should master the tools of war; the soldier himself must be mastered. In later ages, officers came – or found themselves compelled – to trust in the initiative of their troops. But during the *grand siècle* aristocratic commanders assumed a low level of honor and motivation among the rank and file. Self-control had to give way to control by officers. Actions must be automatic and obedience complete, and both must be imposed upon recruits. What Michael Roberts has termed the "revolution in drill" was the key.[27]

During the first half of the seventeenth century, Dutch and then Swedish armies employed new linear formations that contrasted with the heavy infantry squares that the Spaniards had made famous. The intricacies of linear tactics demanded a high level of skill from the troops, and drill first developed to impart that skill. The adoption of Dutch and

---

25   Russell F. Weigley, *The Age of Battles: The Quest for Decisive Warfare from Brietenfeld to Waterloo* (Bloomington, IN, 1991).
26   John Keegan believes that battle was intrinsically indecisive because of equilibrium of weapons, but this seems an ill-considered argument, for there was relative equality of weaponry even at the most decisive battles, such as Blenheim (Keegan, *A History of Warfare* [New York, 1993], p. 345).
27   Roberts, *The Military Revolution*, p. 10; on seventeenth-century drill, see particularly Lynn, *Giant of the Grand Siècle*, Chapter 15.

Swedish infantry formations by the French was evolutionary, not revolutionary; the imported tactics were consistent with earlier native French development.[28] Yet to deny a radical impact to Dutch and Swedish linear order is not to argue that the drill they created in order to use their new formations was anything short of revolutionary. Quite the contrary, from the French perspective: the creation of drill was an absolutely crucial innovation with profound implications. The drill developed by Maurice of Nassau and further extended by Gustavus Adolphus made possible speedy maneuver and a hitherto unknown rate of fire; this promise of tactical effectiveness lured French officers to the Netherlands and northern Germany.

Louis XIII first imported Dutch and Swedish techniques, but no French monarch surpassed Louis XIV's intense interest in drill. He was convinced that "many more battles are won by good march order and by good bearing [*contenance*] than by sword blows and musketry . . . This habit of marching well and of keeping order can only be acquired by drill."[29] Here again he repeated the theme that order, not bloody combat, wins battles. Louis XIV was such a believer that he personally drilled his troops, and attended exercises whenever possible. Louis confessed that he "often employed [his] leisure hours in having drilled before [him] a body of troops, sometimes one, sometimes another, and sometimes several together."[30] This passion was not simply a royal eccentricity; the king hoped thereby to set an example: "I continue to drill carefully the troops which are close to my person in order that, by my example, the other individual military chiefs will learn to take the same care with those that are under their command."[31] He advised his heir without apology that "this application in drilling the troops is one of the things in which I counsel you to imitate me the most."[32]

The behavior required of infantry in battle and learned through drill seemed so unnatural, so counter-instinctual, that contemporaries viewed the level of skill expected of foot soldiers as higher than that demanded of mounted troops. Chamlay wrote that "five or six years were necessary to create a regiment of infantry and it required only a year to make a good cavalry regiment."[33] This might come as a surprise to historians familiar with late eighteenth-century views that it took far longer to train cavalry. By the French Revolution the emphasis on mechanical discipline was wan-

28 See especially John A. Lynn, "Tactical Evolution in the French Army, 1560–1660," *French Historical Studies* 7:4 (1985).
29 Louis XIV, *Mémoires*, vol. 2, pp. 112–13.
30 Louis XIV, *Mémoires*, vol. 2, p. 125.
31 Louis XIV, *Mémoires*, vol. 1, p. 237 note.
32 Louis XIV, *Oeuvres*, vol. 2, pp. 113–14.
33 Chamlay in Jean Bérenger, *Turenne* (Paris, 1987), pp. 384–5.

ing, and infantry skills came to appear more easily mastered; Napoleon himself later commented that three months sufficed to prepare a recruit for battle if he was with an experienced unit.[34]

Early in his personal reign, Louis attempted to make up for inadequacies in French training through a series of ordinances and directives that set the pattern for the remainder of the *grand siècle*. An ordinance of 1661 increased the training burden:

> In order to maintain the said infantry troops in military order and discipline, to teach the soldiers the handling of their weapons and evolutions, and to instruct them in the form and manner of fighting, the sergeants-major of the towns and fortresses will cause general drills to be conducted for the infantry troops who are in garrison once each month; and the chiefs and officers of the said troops will have the soldiers of their companies who are not on guard perform [drill] at least two times each week; and those soldiers who neglect to instruct themselves and do not drill well will be broken.[35]

Similar orders appeared again and again.

In the second half of the century, the purposes of drill altered perceptibly, from imparting skill to engendering a psychology. In *Keeping Together in Time*, William McNeill argues that communal physical movement in dance or drill enhances group cohesion through "muscular bonding."[36] Few doubt that drill encourages group cohesion, and research demonstrates the importance of that cohesion in supporting soldiers in combat and holding them to their tasks.[37] For McNeill the unavoidable product of drill was and is *esprit de corps*, the forging of group identity.

In addition to the creation of positive feelings through muscular bonding, the aspect that McNeill stresses, drill ensured effective battlefield performance in other ways. Drillmasters taught soldiers to fear the consequences of disobedience. When Frederick the Great stated that he wanted his troops to be more afraid of their officers than of the dangers they faced on the

34 During the Revolution, General Wimpfen said that infantry could be ready in six weeks, whereas cavalry took three to four years and artillery seven or eight years to train properly (Address by General Felix Wimpfen in the National Assembly, 15 December 1789, *Archives Parlementaires de 1789 à 1860*, première série [Paris, 1867–1980], vol. 10, p. 587); Napoleon in Jean Morvan, *Le soldat impérial*, 2 vols. (Paris, 1904), vol. 1, p. 282.

35 Ordinance of 12 October 1661, art. 19, in André, *Le Tellier*, p. 557 note.

36 William H. McNeill, *Keeping Together in Time: Dance and Drill in Human History* (Cambridge, MA, 1995).

37 There is a large literature on primary group cohesion. See in particular S. L. A. Marshall, *Men Against Fire* (Gloucester, MA, 1947 [1978]), Samuel A. Stouffer et al., *The American Soldier: Combat and Its Aftermath* (Princeton, NJ, 1949), and Anthony Kellett, *Combat Motivation* (Boston, MA, 1982). For a consideration of primary group cohesion in the early modern French army see John A. Lynn, *Bayonets of the Republic: Motivation and Tactics in the Army of Revolutionary France, 1791–94* (Boulder, CO, 2nd ed., 1996).

battlefield, the warrior-king was driving at precisely that point.[38] Fear balanced fear; the consequence was greater steadiness under fire. In addition, the mechanical actions that drill demanded distracted the soldier from the impulse to hide or flee. It was not enough to simply practice the necessary movements of musket-loading or pike-handling; these had to become so automatic that troops performed their duties regardless of danger. Drill was thus essential to the physical and psychological control that the battle culture of forbearance demanded.

3. The creation of a modern military community

As conceptions of the battlefield altered in the course of the century, a new form of military community emerged: the regiment.[39] That organization, which by the late 1600s had become typical of the French and other European armies, possessed a number of hitherto unusual characteristics: it was standardized, permanent, and male. While it was not the first military formation to serve as the focus of life and devotion for its members, the European regiment fostered a new intensity and direction of loyalty. And in addition to being an organization of soldiers, the regiment was both product and creature of the modern state.

The earliest roots of the regiment may be more Spanish than French, but the French form of regiment had the greatest impact on seventeenth-century military development. The first French regiments were picked infantry formations of the late sixteenth century with names such as Champagne, Piedmont, and Navarre. But while royal guard units continued to exist, the line infantry regiments of the sixteenth century virtually disappeared during the demobilization that followed the return of peace after 1598. Infantry regiments were effectively reborn as the French entered the Thirty Years' War in 1635. The army first organized its cavalry into regiments at this time, although mounted regiments did not truly become a permanent part of the French standing army until the 1670s.

The regiment was a regular, standardized unit of a defined size that included one or more battalions subdivided into a set number of companies. Although some regiments contained several battalions, it was the regiment, not the battalion, that became the essence of the new military community – the regiment was no mere organization, but rather a focus of identity. Companies were also standardized, with a prescribed strength. And even if they often fell short of that strength in the field, they were never-

---

[38] J. F. C. Fuller, *A Military History of the Western World*, vol. 2 (New York, 1955), p. 196.
[39] For the development, organization, and hierarchy of the regiment, see Lynn, *Giant of the Grand Siècle*, Chapters 7, 9, and 14.

theless very unlike the ad hoc and irregular assemblages of the past. The notion of companies established by regulation, like that of regiments, predates the seventeenth century; in the French case it goes back to the *compagnies d'ordonnance* of 1445. But that earlier institution concerned only a part of the army, whereas the regimental principle became universal.

In addition to formal requirements for numbers of companies and of soldiers, regiments possessed an officially prescribed cadre of officers with clearly defined ranks and functions. The regimental chain of command, an institution for which only limited precedents existed, established and enforced the reality and concept of military hierarchy. Military rank, not social prestige or personal bonds, defined the obedience that became the operative principle of the modern army. Military institutions still employ the titles, categories, and relationships established in the seventeenth-century regiment.

The regiment was also in theory permanent, with a life beyond a particular campaign, war, or commander. In reality, mobilization for war repeatedly led to the creation of new regiments that did not survive the end of the conflict. But even these temporary creations were patterned after the truly permanent regiments, many of which claim to exist even to this day in the forces of the Fifth Republic. The long life of these formations allowed the creation of a regimental culture typified by strong unit identity and intense devotion. If McNeill is right, muscular bonding and *esprit de corps* engendered by the new drill aided significantly in forging these new military communities.

A coincident and absolutely integral development was the exclusion of the vast majority of women and children from the military community. Armies of the sixteenth and early seventeenth century included huge numbers of camp followers. Geoffrey Parker describes a body of 5,300 veteran Spanish soldiers who marched from the Netherlands in 1577 accompanied by 14,700 non-combatants.[40] Herbert Langer mentions a 40,000-man imperial army in Germany during the Thirty Years' War accompanied by 100,000 camp followers, many if not most of them women.[41] Soldiers took the field with wives, concubines, and children. In the field, women often assisted the soldiers and were thus an integral part of earlier military communities even though only men stood in the line of battle. Sir James Turner described the soldiers' wives of the early seventeenth century as "their husbands' mules" and noted that during the siege of Breda (1624–25), "the married soldiers fared better, looked more vigorously, and were able

---

[40] Geoffrey Parker, *The Army of Flanders and the Spanish Road, 1567–1659: The Logistics of Spanish Victory and Defeat in the Low Countries Wars* (Cambridge, 1972), p. 87.

[41] Langer in Barton Hacker, "Women and Military Institutions in Early Modern Europe: A Reconnaissance," *Signs* 6:4 (1981), p. 648.

to do more duty than the bachelors."[42]

Then, in the name of efficiency and morality, the French army under Louis XIV eliminated these masses of non-combatants from its line of march. It permitted a modest number of peddlers, the *vivandiers*, to serve the troops, and perhaps as many as twenty women of good repute still marched with their husbands to serve as regimental washerwomen, seamstresses, and nurses. But the great crowds of camp followers disappeared. For example, woodcuts of sixteenth-century armies show women tending cooking pots for the troops, but late seventeenth-century camp diagrams show neat rows of cooking fires serving squads of men who prepared their own food and ate in prescribed mess groups. The regiment had become an essentially male community that isolated men from other bonds and obligations and focused their loyalties on the unit. It seems likely that the implications of this change for motivation, morale, and professionalism were profound. And along with women, idleness disappeared from the regiment. The same sixteenth-century scenes that display numerous women in camp also show soldiers lying about. But drill and work details ensured that the soldiers of Louis's regiments had little time to themselves; the army now consumed with its own internal routines the hours that its soldiers had once spent upon women, drink, and mischief.

The creation of the regimental community was but one part of an important seventeenth-century organizational change: the shift from the aggregate contract army to the state commission army.[43] In the first, princes concluded their contracts for military service not with individual soldiers, but with the leaders of soldier bands epitomized by the military entrepreneurs who supplied foreign troops. And princes also relied upon "private armies" raised by their own grandees. Units hired or incorporated in this fashion were "off the shelf," they arrived already officered, armed, trained, and organized for battle. When the princely paymaster had no further need of them, he simply paid them off and put them back on the shelf. That happened frequently at the close of a campaign, and almost invariably at the close of a war; only skeletal forces survived between conflicts.

The state commission army emerged in the seventeenth century. At the opening of his war with Spain in 1635, Louis XIII decided to rely neither upon foreign mercenary bands – with the unique and final exception of Bernard of Saxe-Weimar – nor upon private French forces. The king

---

[42] Sir James Turner, *Pallas Armata* (London, 1683) in Hacker, "Women and Military Institutions," pp. 653–4.

[43] The evolution of army style is dealt with briefly in Lynn, *Giant of the Grand Siècle*, Chapter 1. For a more complete discussion of the aggregate contract army and the state commission army see Lynn, "The Evolution of Army Style in the Modern West, 800–2000," *International History Review* 18:3 (August 1996).

instead issued commissions to individuals who raised regiments for the king's service under strict monarchical authority and supervision. Regimental mobilization became more intricately defined and more completely supervised under Louis XIV. Most regiments were French in composition, but even when they were composed of foreign soldiers, their pattern was that of state-commissioned forces rather than of the old "off the shelf" bands. The new regiments took longer to raise, but were more controllable, more loyal, and arguably more expert. The requirement for ever-higher levels of technical expertise, far larger armies, and peacetime forces for both military and political reasons made the state commission army the universal standard by the end of the century. The emergence of the regiment and that of the centralized bureaucratic modern state were part of the same process.

SEVENTEENTH-CENTURY MILITARY CHANGE, "THE WESTERN WAY OF WAR," AND SOUTH ASIA

These innovations shaped the development of warfare; they defined the *ancien régime* army and with it much future military practice. But their impact stretched even further, as part of the formula that made possible a new wave of European overseas military expansion from the mid-eighteenth century onward. Until roughly 1750, European colonial domination outside the New World largely ended at the high-water mark; the guns and sails – in Carlo Cipolla's formula – of fifteenth-century innovation had ensured European control of the seas but little else. Technology, conviction, and luck had allowed Spanish and Portuguese to conquer huge empires in Mexico, central, and south America, crushing civilizations with Stone Age weapons and populations decimated by the diseases the Europeans brought. But in Asia, relatively modern native technology, far larger populations than those of Europe itself, the immunities common to the inhabitants of the Eurasian land mass and the tropical diseases that killed numerous Europeans all confined Western power to the range of fleet cannon.[44]

Then, in the mid-eighteenth century, a power vacuum in South Asia and British–French rivalry there and in the wider world inaugurated a struggle for control of the subcontinent. The British won: they defeated the French and their native allies, crushed a series of native states and peoples, and established the hegemony of the East India Company over all of India. That

---

[44] Carlo M. Cipolla, *Guns, Sails and Empires: Technological Innovation and the Early Phases of European Expansion 1400–1700* (New York, 1965).

new stage of imperial expansion demonstrated that the Europeans had moved far beyond their earlier command of the outer seas: they had now transformed land warfare in Asia as well.

That transformation owed a good deal to technology. The conversion to flintlock and bayonet and the creation of tactics that took full advantage of the new weapons multiplied the firepower of European armies beyond seventeenth-century levels. Late eighteenth-century improvements in artillery such as the Gribeauval and Liechtenstein artillery reforms in Europe further increased that technological edge. But technological explanations go only so far. South Asians borrowed and copied European weaponry without great difficulty, nor were firearms and artillery strangers to the subcontinent in any case: Babur had used artillery to crush his opponents at Panipat in 1526 and found the Mughal Empire. So good were cannon of native manufacture that the future Duke of Wellington, serving in India around 1800, declared Maratha guns the equal of British cannon and worth incorporating into his own artillery train.[45] Certainly the British enjoyed technological superiority at the outset, but that was a temporary and not insurmountable advantage.

Britain's decisive superiority lay in a cultural and institutional approach to war that its native foes could not imitate with the same ease with which they could fire – or manufacture – fusils. European attitudes toward combat ran wholly counter to native Mongol notions of horse-archer warfare, which stressed individual prowess and minimal casualties. The battle culture of forbearance was counter-instinctual, a product of long experience on the gunpowder battlefield. Once acquired, it had to be taught and replicated through relentless drill. Traditions of this kind were wholly alien to the states of South and East Asia – although the British found that they could impose their system upon South Asian troops through rigorous training.

Some current explanations of European colonial expansion ascribe it to a "Western Way of War" that conferred particular advantages in the organization of violence.[46] In John Keegan's extreme formulation, the Greeks fashioned a Western Way that then remained essentially immu-

---

[45] Bruce Lenman, "The Transition to European Military Ascendancy in India, 1600–1800," in John A. Lynn, ed., *Tools of War* (Urbana, IL, 1990), p. 120.

[46] On the Western Way of War, see Victor Davis Hanson, *The Western Way of War: Infantry Battle in Classical Greece* (New York, 1989); Keegan, *A History of Warfare*; and the introduction to Geoffrey Parker, ed., *The Cambridge Illustrated History of Warfare* (Cambridge, 1995). By implication, McNeill, *Keeping Together in Time*, stresses change and the need for a revival of classical methods of drill, and revival implies discontinuity with the past, thus the need at one point to bring back old, unused, methods.

table through subsequent ages, a particularly aggressive form of warfare aimed at decisive results even at the price of high casualties. Was the battle culture of forbearance therefore merely a variation upon an essentially unchanging Western tradition, or was it situational and temporary? The evidence suggests the second alternative. Classical texts influenced early modern European military practice, but no unbroken Western pattern linked ancients to moderns. Willingness to accept losses might make the seventeenth-century battle line seem a lineal descendant of the Greek hoplite army or the Macedonian phalanx, but those formations aimed at striking down the enemy rather than passively accepting losses. And in any case, as Chapter 2 suggests, the discontinuity between the ancient and the late medieval–early modern worlds extended to combat styles; the hoplites of Marathon shared little with the archers of Agincourt.

All military cultures must teach the acceptance of losses. But attitudes toward casualties vary across time and culture. Commanders throughout the first years of the First World War remained as willing to see their own men drop in droves as any combat leader from Breitenfeld and Malplaquet to Gettysburg and Port Arthur. But by 1917–18 hard experience on the industrialized battlefield had taught the wisdom that Patton later formulated so memorably: "It is not your duty to die for your country, but to make the other poor dumb bastard die for his." Now that the Cold War is over, Western societies sometimes resist passionately even the second half of Patton's injunction. The battle culture of forbearance seems best described as a time-specific *ancien régime* or absolutist phenomenon, dominant from the mid-seventeenth century through the late eighteenth century.

Yet even if Keegan's notion of an enduring Western battlefield superiority over two millennia is a myth, the British did enjoy distinct military advantages in South Asia by the mid-eighteenth century. Their superiority rested at first on battle culture and drill but ultimately depended more upon importing the regiment – another early modern Western invention that owed little to ancient precedent. The regiment provided the foundation for a permanent British/sepoy military establishment in India that defeated the great native state of Mysore, the Maratha warrior confederacy, and ultimately even the tenacious Sikhs. The regiment turned into a highly effective repository for indigenous cultural values that tapped native codes of personal and community honor in ways that temporary or irregular native military units could not. Within a generation, despite its European structure, the sepoy regiment had taken on a fundamentally Indian character. Whereas the European regiment separated the soldier from civil society and isolated him from family in a male military community, the sepoy regiment integrated the civil and military communities and thereby reinforced personal codes of honor, *izzat*, with the very strong local community codes of honor, *rasuq*.[47] The European male regiment thus became an Indian institution that often reincorporated women and children back into the life of the army. In a society dominated unconditionally by caste, the sepoy soon constituted a new *jati*, a hereditary professional group with its own distinct ethos and privileges.

However great the advantages derived from imported European military concepts, techniques, and institutions, the British would have failed had not their East India Company learned to function as an Indian power – and had not the internal situation on the subcontinent favored it. Company soldiers learned to campaign under South Asian logistical and climatic conditions. They also mastered Indian politics. British battlefield success may have been European, but British success in negotiation was quintessentially Indian in character.[48] Finally, the decay of the Mughal Empire and the decline of the Marathas made possible the Company's expansion; either Indian power at its height could probably have checked the British.

The implications for world history of this second, eighteenth-century, wave of imperial expansion are very great, though rarely acknowledged except by British or South Asian historians. Without the conquest of the South Asian subcontinent and the consequent harnessing of its manpower and wealth, nineteenth-century British imperialism would have been far slower to refashion the globe.

This excursion into world military history should not distract the reader from the important cultural and institutional innovations of seventeenth-century Europe. It suggests rather the lasting and fundamental importance of the military changes born while the Sun King stood high in the continental firmament. In this particular case, concepts and institutions, far more than technology, served as the engines of change. That insight should serve as a caution to RMA enthusiasts who exult in the sophistication of modern weapons, communications, and information technology. The culture of technological gullibility invites defeat by ignoring the unchanging reality of war as the domain of chance, violence, and politics.

---

[47] For example, see the stress placed on *izzat* and *rasuq* in Pradeep Dhillon, *Multiple Identities: A Phenomenology of Multicultural Communication* (Frankfurt, 1994). In contrast, McNeill, *Keeping Together in Time*, p. 135, sees sepoys as developing European *esprit de corps* when exposed to Western drill, but this conclusion misses the point. While native regiments certainly developed *esprit de corps*, this took a very South Asian flavor for very South Asian reasons.

[48] Pradeep Barua argues convincingly that the East India Company became proficient at Indian logistics and politics in his "Military Developments in India, 1750–1850," *Journal of Military History* 58 (October 1994).

4

Mass politics and nationalism as military revolution:
The French Revolution and after

MACGREGOR KNOX

[W]ar . . . again became the affair of the people as a whole, and took on an entirely different character, or rather approached its true character, its absolute perfection.[1]

—Carl von Clausewitz

The revolution of industrial capitalism and of science and technology is the greatest transformation in human existence since the coming of agriculture. It began in the late eighteenth century and its end is not in sight. It has given such immense power to the societies that pioneered it or adopted it that it has obscured a fundamental truth: military revolutions are changes in the nature and purposes of war itself. They are normally the military outcome of underlying processes – ideological, political, social, economic, and demographic – far deeper and broader than the advent of a particular technology or cluster of technologies.

While the Industrial Revolution was achieving – for the first time in human history – self-sustaining and seemingly limitless growth in Britain's textile mills, mines, and foundries, a political revolution with consequences almost as great erupted across the Channel. The upheaval of 1788–94 was not merely a revolution in France. It marked the beginning of the exceedingly violent end, first in France and then throughout Europe, of an entire social, political, and international order.

The events in France brought mass politics and mass warfare to Europe, and ultimately to the world. The Revolution represented the political breakthrough of the notion, increasingly widespread among the pre-1789 French

---

[1] *On War*, eds. and trans. Michael Howard and Peter Paret (Princeton, NJ, 1976), p. 593. This essay owes a great deal to Paret's *Yorck and the Era of Prussian Reform* (Princeton, NJ, 1966), *Clausewitz and the State* (Oxford, 1976), and *Understanding War* (Princeton, NJ, 1992), and to a wonderful lecture by Tim Blanning on "Nationalism and the French Revolution" delivered at Princeton University on 21 April 1989.

intelligentsia, that France was not a dynastic unit but an ethnic–linguistic identity, *la nation*. Revolution swept away the old nation of king, nobles, and Church, and created with startling bloodshed a new nation of *citizens* theoretically free and equal under the law and the guillotine. Asserting equality within and sovereignty without plunged the new nation into war with most of Europe and forced the decapitation of the king – and of the old society he had personified – in January 1793. The war of 1792 to 1814/ 15 thus became – first unilaterally by France and then by the belated and usually hesitant response of France's victims – the first modern war, the first war between *nations*.[2] Far more than the religious struggles before 1648 it was a type of war potentially unlimited in both aims and methods, for nations by their very nature recognize no higher power. As the foremost theorist of the Revolution, the Abbé Sieyès, proclaimed in 1789, "the nation exists before everything; it is at the origin of everything; its will is always legal, it is the law itself."[3]

BEFORE THE REVOLUTION

The military revolution that emerged in and from the Revolution's wars was a *political–ideological* revolution that remade warfare from top to bottom, from strategy, to operations and logistics, to tactics. Understanding its origins and consequences requires a brief backward glance at the framework of Old Regime politics and war.

The state system that emerged after 1648 from the wars of religion rested, with a few exceptions or partial exceptions that included England and the Dutch Republic, on rigidly hierarchical societies divided into occupational groups or castes that for the most part traced their origins back to the Middle Ages. All below the monarch in these "societies of orders" were subjects, not citizens, with all the subordination and lack of initiative and independent will the word implies. Politics was almost exclusively the affair of monarchs and ministers. Under their aegis, the centralizing administrative and legal reforms characteristic of the eighteenth century remodeled the society of orders in the name of enlightenment – a word almost synonymous in practice with massive increases in state power over the individual.

---

[2] The genuine novelty of warfare between *nations* compared to that between territorial princes, traditional agrarian monarchies and empires, and tribes offers of course only one possible means of defining "modern" war. The sophisticated analysis of Jonathan B. A. Bailey in Chapter 8 of this work, and the apparent suggestion of Hew Strachan ("On Total War and Modern War," *International History Review* 17:2 [2000], especially pp. 350–1) that modern war is simply industrial warfare offer essentially military-technical and technological definitions. Yet ideology – unfortunately for humanity – has at least as good a claim as technology to be modernity's defining characteristic.

[3] Emmanuel Sieyès, *Qu'est-ce que le Tiers état?* (Geneva, 1970 [1789]), p. 180.

Even republics – the Dutch and the free cities of the Holy Roman Empire – or parliamentary regimes such as England were in both theory and practice ruled by narrow oligarchies of merchants or landowners. The occasional riot and the carefully circumscribed roles allotted to consultative assemblies largely defined popular participation in politics. Foreign policy and war were and remained the central functions of states which resisted popular interference with the utmost jealousy. And consciousness of belonging to a broader unit than the village, region, and estate was limited. Even in France, the largest and most economically advanced society of continental western Europe, literacy was confined to perhaps a third of the population, and overwhelmingly to town-dwellers.

The military implications of these conditions were many, but are swiftly summed up: social and political forces drastically curtailed both the aims and the methods of the contenders in the Old Regime's many wars. War aims that required efforts or summoned up risks that might imperil internal order and the exclusive control of politics by king and ministers were rare indeed. Exceptions did exist: fanatics such as Charles XII of Sweden or icy gamblers such as Frederick the Great might risk the very existence of their states on the battlefield. Occasionally, as in the coalition of France, Austria, and Russia against Prussia in the Seven Years' War or the collusion of Austria, Prussia, and Russia in the partition of Poland, powers might aim at the total destruction of other powers. But no state seriously entertained the notion of arming its subjects irrespective of their estate. The greatest tactical theorist of the Old Regime, the comte François de Guibert, scornfully and accurately summed up in 1772 the normal pattern of warfare:

> States have neither treasure nor surplus population. Their expenditure outstrips their revenues even in peace. Nevertheless they declare war. They take the field with armies they can neither recruit nor pay. Victors and vanquished alike are exhausted. The mass of the national debt increases. Credit falls. Money grows scarce. Fleets are at a loss for sailors and armies for soldiers. The ministers on both sides feel it is time to negotiate. Peace is made. A few colonies or provinces change masters. Often the source of the quarrels is not dried up, and each side sits on its shattered remains while it attempts to pay its debts and sharpen its weapons.[4]

Both the imperative of maintaining political control and the relative lack of military means – despite the increasing centralization and efficiency of Europe's states – kept aims limited. The military art of the Old Regime suffered from interlocking and crippling constraints on mass, mobility, and decisiveness that were irremediable within its social and political order. Almost all these limits stemmed not from technological constraints

---

[4] Quoted in David Chandler, *The Campaigns of Napoleon* (New York, 1966), p. 140.

overcome in the revolutionary era, but from social and military-organiza-
tional bottlenecks in the recruitment, nature, and motivation of the individual soldier on the one hand and in the system of command and control on
the other.

The soldiers of the Old Regime were the product of military institutions
inextricable from the society of orders that they defended. In France, the
sweepings of the taverns of cities and market towns predominated, along
with Swiss and other foreign mercenaries; in Russia, the state snatched serfs
from their villages for twenty-five years of service; in Prussia from the
1730s, peasant conscription as well as voluntary and foreign recruitment
filled the ranks of the line infantry.

A few far-seeing contemporaries understood fully the military consequences of this situation, and Guibert was predictably scathing:

> Today all the armies of Europe, with small differences, have the same char-
> acter, that is an imperfect one, that poorly exploits the available means, and
> that rests neither on honor nor on patriotism. All armies are composed of the
> lowest [*la plus vile*] and most pitiful segment of the citizens, [and] of foreigners,
> of vagabonds, of men who, for the slightest cause, [such as] personal interests
> or discontents, are ready to desert. These are the armies of *governments*, not
> those of *nations*.[5]

They were also armies largely devoid of command articulation. Control-
mania was the foremost characteristic of the eighteenth century's philoso-
phy of command. The ideal was the great Frederick sternly directing the
machinelike advance of his battalions from a low hill, the *Feldherrenhügel*,
that commanded a view of the entire battlefield. Only around mid-century
did French theorists such as Guibert and Pierre de Bourcet pioneer the
notion of self-contained infantry–artillery and all-arms divisions, urge supply by plunder rather than wagon train, and propose concentration during
rather than before battle.[6]

Four principal factors thus frustrated attempts to assemble and move
large masses of men. First, in all these societies the higher and middle
estates along with virtually all gainfully employed townspeople enjoyed
exemptions from service ordained by custom or law, and by the state's
pressing interest in tax revenue. That deprived the armies of significant
numbers and of much of the state's stock of talent.

Second, the prevailing tactical and disciplinary system further restricted
numbers. States recognized that domestic enlistees and foreign mercenaries
were exceedingly expensive and time-consuming to train in the "battle

---

5 *Essai général de tactique* (Liège, 1773), vol. 1, pp. 13–14 (emphasis supplied).
6 See especially Guibert, *Essai*, vol. 1, pp. xii, lxv–lxvii, vol. 2, pp. 24–9, 73–4, 184, and
   Agar Gat, *The Origins of Military Thought: From the Enlightenment to Clausewitz*
   (Oxford, 1989), pp. 43–53.

culture of forbearance," and even more expensive and difficult to maintain. The troops' lack of inner motivation other than compulsory *esprit de corps* required – or was thought to require – the inculcation of *Kadavergehorsam* – "corpse-obedience" – as the Prussian service jestingly described the conditioned reflexes designed to keep even the dead in line, advancing and discharging ordered volleys. And the punishments required – or believed to be required – to convert the lower orders into automatons, to prevent their subsequent escape, and to keep them rigidly in line on the battlefield were drastic and frequent. Frederick summed up the prevailing command view in 1768 in a much-quoted remark: the troops must

> fear their officers more than all the dangers to which they may be exposed. Otherwise no one will be able to lead them to the attack in the face of three hundred muskets thundering at them. Good will can never induce the common man to defy such dangers; fear must therefore do the job.[7]

Fear without propaganda – of which the Old Regime was incapable – required the sacrifice of most other forms of motivation, and thus curtailed further the meager manpower resources available to the state.

Third, the tendency of the troops to desert if unsupervised by officers or NCOs restricted the size and mobility of armies. Commanders could not allow their line infantry to forage; operations remained tied to regular supply by wagon trains from magazines. That laborious technique could not support, even in the few areas of western Europe with roads that were not mud-wallows, armies larger than perhaps 70,000 men. It also drastically limited operational movement, for fifty to seventy miles was the furthest from a magazine that an army could move without losing its supply links, and the decisive importance of those same links made armies fatally vulnerable to flank attack. Logistical inadequacy also magnified the importance of manmade bottlenecks – the many fortresses controlling road or river junctions around which much of eighteenth century warfare revolved. Finally, the absence of divisional organization and of adequate staffs for the theater commander further reinforced the logistical constraints on operations, for even had larger armies been available, operational control would scarcely have been possible.

These limits made Old Regime warfare profoundly indecisive. At the strategic level, limited aims – "a few colonies or provinces" – did not warrant great risks or any rethinking of the domestic order. Troops were too expensive and difficult to procure and train to hazard lightheartedly on the battlefield. And the brittleness of armies held together largely by coercion

---

7 Testament of 1768, quoted in Reinhard Höhn, *Scharnhorsts Vermächtnis* (Frankfurt a. M., 2nd ed., 1972), p. 193.

argued powerfully against seeking a decision at all costs, a precept only the most skilled and ruthless of Old Regime commanders – Marlborough and Frederick the Great – dared to disregard.

Operationally, unalterable restrictions likewise condemned combatants to protracted and indecisive struggle. The logistical restraints on field army size limited commanders' chances of outflanking or trapping the enemy. Armies dared not outrun their supply trains. Even small threats to their communications immobilized them. Movement required foresight and planning to avoid the confusion that might offer the troops yet more opportunities to desert. Dispersed movement was difficult or impossible, given the character of the troops and the lack of divisional organization and specialized staffs. Reconnaissance was available only to the few armies well-provided with reliable light cavalry or light infantry whose primary motivation was loyalty rather than fear.

Finally, decision at the tactical level was unusually difficult. Fear of desertion and control-mania crippled tactical reconnaissance and delayed or prevented the introduction – except for specially trained picked troops – of open-order combat or skirmishing. The relative absence of skirmishers in turn drastically reduced the effectiveness of the attack. It prevented major actions in broken terrain except in exceptional circumstances, it restricted the firefight largely to frontally delivered volleys, and it deprived commanders seeking decision of the surprise in the strength and direction of the attack that screens of skirmishers alone could provide. Night attacks risked loss of tactical and disciplinary control even more than did skirmishing, and were correspondingly rare. Finally and most decisively, the kind of pursuit needed to destroy beaten enemies and convert battlefield success into strategically binding decision offered too great a risk of chaos to be practical for most eighteenth-century armies.

These restraints on what Clausewitz later described as war's true nature were social, political, and organizational rather than technological. With the sole important exception of the French royal army's mobile field artillery, a significant but evolutionary change dating from the reforms of the comte de Gribeauval in the 1770s, the powers fought the great war of 1792–1815 with the technology of the wars of Frederick the Great. What changed was ideas and politics.

THE REVOLUTION AT WAR

A quarter of a century before the revolution that was to give his tactical, operational, and strategic ideas full scope, Guibert dedicated his *General Essay on Tactics* to his Fatherland (*Patrie*). The king was for him still the father of the *Patrie*; the people of France were its children – an image that anticipated the famous first line of the Marseillaise. Guibert's fondest hope was that "one could return to this term *Patrie* all its significance and energy, [and] make it the cry of the nation."

That was a hope widely shared in the advanced and fashionable Paris circles in which Guibert's book enjoyed – precisely because it invoked the *Patrie* – a success unprecedented for a military–technical work. The monarchy's subsequent downfall was in large part a delayed consequence of the offense that royal military and fiscal incompetence had given to the exalted sense of the nation that the educated and enlightened held.[8] The monarchy's prestige never recovered from stinging defeat at Frederick's hands at Rossbach in 1757, and the catastrophic effect of the Seven Years' War and the War of the American Revolution on its finances were the root of its political and administrative collapse in 1787–89.

The inability of king and ministers to translate into policy the revolutionaries' lofty view of the dignity of the fatherland unhinged from the beginning the disastrous experiment of constitutional monarchy in 1789–92. Nationalist fanaticism, egalitarian zeal, revolutionary paranoia inflamed by the king's failed flight and continuing contacts with the émigré nobility, and cold political calculation led the Legislative Assembly of 1791–92 to challenge all of Europe.[9]

From the fall of 1791 onward the Girondin wing of the revolutionaries proclaimed openly to the Assembly that "this war will be a true blessing; a national blessing; and the only calamity France has to fear is *not* to have war." The national interest "required war, for the nation must will its dignity, its majesty, its security, and its credit, and can only reconquer them at sword-point."[10] The new France was incompatible with the old system of dynastic interstate relations: "the treaties of princes cannot govern the rights of nations."[11] The new France was "invincible if it remained united"; "With 400,000 slaves Louis XIV could defy all the powers of Europe: should we, with our millions of armed men, fear them?"[12] And the new France had a cosmic mission: "The French have become the most noteworthy people in the universe; their conduct must now correspond to their new destiny."[13]

8 Blanning, "Nationalism and the French Revolution."
9 T. C. W. Blanning, *The Origin of the French Revolutionary Wars* (London, 1986) offers a brilliant introduction, despite perhaps excessive emphasis on the extent to which Austrians and Prussians also helped to precipitate war.
10 Brissot, 29 December 1791, *Archives Parlementaires de 1789 à 1860*, première série (Paris, 1867–1980), vol. 36, pp. 607, 608; see also (among other similar remarks) Gensonné, ibid., vol. 37, p. 412 (14 January 1792).
11 Merlin de Douai, 28 October 1790, ibid., vol. 20, p. 83.
12 Isnard, 5 January 1792, ibid., vol. 37, p. 85; Dubois-Du Bais, 22 October 1791, ibid., vol. 34, p. 348.
13 Brissot, 29 December 1791, ibid., vol. 35, p. 441.

Externally, war would be "the salvation both of France and of the human race," a world revolutionary war of "peoples against kings"; "the French people only had to cry out, and all other peoples would answer its call and the earth would fill with fighting men; and, at a single blow, the enemies of equality would be expunged from the rolls of the living."[14]

War would be total: "the French are lions, and would defend themselves in a manner that would leave no man alive nor tree standing; they would bury themselves under the ruin of their great houses and peasant hovels. . . . The soil of France would be enslaved, but [the French] would die free, together with [their] wives, [their] children, and [their] flocks [applause]."[15]

And war would also be internal, against the "snares and perfidy" of the Revolution's enemies: "no citizen, priest, general, minister, king or anyone else shall deceive us with impunity; the die is cast; we resolve on equality even if we are to find it only in the grave – yet before we descend there ourselves, we shall hurl down into it all the traitors."[16] This war – as the two principal orators and leaders of the Girondins both summed it up – was simultaneously foreign and domestic. War was "indispensable for consummating the revolution."[17]

The collective wisdom of the industrial democracies at the turn of the twenty-first century tends to discount heroic oratory of the kind quoted above. Advertising for the masses and post-modernism for the elite have between them devalued "rhetoric" or "discourse" – life is all TV. But in 1792–94 the more perceptive officers of the Prussian and Austrian armies soon recognized that French rhetoric dictated battlefield reality. Clausewitz, who first saw action in 1793 at the age of twelve, had little doubt about the nature of the connection: "the colossal weight of the whole French people, *unhinged by political fanaticism*, came crashing down upon us."[18]

In this first great conflict of the era of mass politics, fanaticism abolished all theoretical limits on the aims and methods of warfare. The Revolution's practice and its development by Napoleon were the living models for Clausewitz's Kantian abstract notion of absolute war: "war is an act of force, and there is no logical limit to the application of that force."[19] The revolutionary government's aim of world revolution ordained an empire

---

[14] Cloots, 13 December 1791; Isnard, 29 November and 5 January 1792, ibid., vol. 35, p. 412, vol. 37, p. 87.
[15] Cloots, 13 December 1791, ibid., vol. 36, p. 79.
[16] Isnard, 6 March, 20 January 1792, ibid., vol. 39, p. 416, vol. 37, p. 547.
[17] Isnard, 5 January 1792; Brissot, 17 January 1792 ("la guerre . . . consomme la révolution"), ibid., vol. 37, pp. 85, 471. For the future of this concept, see MacGregor Knox, *Common Destiny: Dictatorship, Foreign Policy, and War in Fascist Italy and Nazi Germany* (Cambridge, 2000), especially pp. 1–4 and Chapter 2.
[18] *On War*, p. 518 (emphasis added).
[19] *On War*, pp. 582–4, 75–7; also 217, 592–3.

that stretched to the Rhine and beyond. The passing of the wave of revolutionary enthusiasm in 1794 had no moderating effect, and Bonaparte's growing thirst for universal domination after 1799 was simply a personalization, in the name of a shared *Patrie*, of the revolutionaries' mission of saving the human race through sacred violence by the French nation.

The new politics abolished, along with the society of orders, all theoretical limits on the state's actions. Individual lives and property were unconditionally at the nation's service. Pervasive police surveillance, persecution and extermination of real and imagined enemies on a scale and with a brutality unseen again in Europe until 1917–45, and quasi-universal military service became the order of the day. Abroad as at home, the revolutionaries acknowledged no limits either of custom or pity; they turned swiftly and savagely on all of France's neighbors who obtusely "refuse[d] to accept liberty and equality, and renouncing it, might wish to preserve, recall, or negotiate with their prince or privileged castes." By September 1793 France had solemnly "renounc[ed] from henceforth every philanthropic idea previously adopted by the French people for the purpose of making foreign nations appreciate the value and the benefits of liberty." France, as Guibert had preached – invoking Cato the Elder – would henceforth "nourish war by war."[20] The French state asserted an unlimited right of conquest and officially proclaimed plunder as its system of logistics.

Finally, the Revolution abolished the limits on warfare embodied in the character of the Old Regime's armies. The troops were now not social outcasts but "our friends, fellows, citizens, and soldiers of the *Patrie*." Revolutionary nationalist propaganda built around the defense and international self-assertion of that *Patrie* and resting on ideological terror powerfully motivated the troops. The aim, in the words of the Revolution's minister of war, was thinking obedience, "not the obedience of slaves, but that of free men."[21] Once in the field, the new soldiers deserted less than their Old Regime counterparts – and desertion mattered less, for men were now plentiful and cheap. They faced the enemy willingly and fought inventively and tenaciously. And their leaders were also new men, for the collapse of the society of orders in 1789–90 and the increasing radicalization of the Revolution had entailed the emigration of the vast majority of the old army's aristocratic officer corps. The resulting vacuum, the ideology of equality, and the revolutionary fervor and paranoia that prompted the execution of seventeen generals in 1793 and sixty-seven in

[20] National Convention decrees, 15 December 1792 and 15 September 1793, *Archives parlementaires*, vol. 55, pp. 74–6 and vol. 74, p. 231; Guibert, *Essai*, vol. 1, p. xiii, vol. 2, p. 184.

[21] Camille Desmoulins and Jean-Baptiste Bouchotte, quoted in John A. Lynn, *Bayonets of the Republic: Motivation and Tactics in the Army of Revolutionary France, 1791–94* (Champaign, IL, 1984), pp. 64, 100.

1794 brought the "career open to talent" in warfare – and general officers who a few years before had been privates, or sergeants, or (like Bonaparte) lieutenants. Almost half of the officer corps of summer 1794 had not served even as private soldiers under the Old Regime.[22] The prospect of further promotion combined powerfully with devotion to France and fear of the guillotine – "sword of equality" – to drive them and their men forward into battle.

Strategically, the Revolution's unlimited aims and growing means – 750,000 men in the field by mid-1794 – demanded the destruction of the enemy armies by battle. And the new French armies soon proved they had the cohesion even in defeat to warrant taking extreme risks for victory. Operationally, the new soldier made unprecedented movement possible. Nationalism made the logistics of plunder practical; troops foraged merrily but usually did not desert.[23] That freed armies to move dispersed and bypass the many fortresses built to stalemate the hesitant forces of the Old Regime. Commanders no longer tied to fixed bases and supply lines could swiftly change the direction and speed of large units, and move great distances into an unsuspecting enemy's rear. Confusion on the march was no longer a prelude to disintegration; broken country no longer a deterrent. And the new logistics, when combined with the brigade and divisional organization systematized in the Army Regulations of 1791 and in war after 1792, allowed dispersed movement and concentration on the field of battle itself.

Tactically, the new soldiers gave us the modern battlefield, peopled increasingly – as firepower intensified – by dispersed *individuals* rather than close-order *formations*. At first largely from improvisation, then by design, the French armies of 1792–95 preceded their advance with clouds of skirmishers. Behind them came the *ordre mixte* of column for swift movement and line for the firefight outlined by Guibert and enshrined in the great Regulations of 1791. Commanders could freely alternate skirmishers, column, or line depending on terrain and situation. The mobile artillery of Gribeauval offered close support, and the infantry was trustworthy enough for the pursuit that could alone transform enemy defeat into rout and total destruction.

NAPOLEONIC SYNTHESIS, PRUSSIAN RESPONSE

The Revolution had transformed war; war also transformed the Revolution. By the late 1790s the immense prestige of victory and the delights of plunder had made the army rather than the politicians the motor of French expansion and the embodiment of French nationalism.

[22]   Lynn, *Bayonets*, p. 75.
[23]   See the figures for the Armée du Nord in Lynn, *Bayonets*, pp. 110–13.

Its most striking figure, the young General Bonaparte, added only a few personal touches to his political, organizational, and doctrinal inheritance after seizing supreme power in 1799. As an artilleryman, he privileged his branch and used it lavishly to make up for the growing lack of tactical subtlety of his infantry as years passed and losses mounted. He perfected the divisional system by grouping divisions and other units flexibly, according to the task at hand, into all-arms army corps. Huge armies of 150,000 to 500,000 men divided into corps could thus move dispersed a day's or two day's marches apart, linked by screening cavalry and couriers. Each corps was small enough to avoid logistical embarrassment but by design strong enough to face an enemy army for a day or two, until the remaining French corps, under Napoleon's fierce urging, could close on the enemy flank or rear. To control these widely dispersed formations Napoleon created a staff system and headquarters that despite a lack of decision-making power and many structural deficiencies was of a size and complexity never before seen; by 1812 it numbered 3,500 officers and 10,000 men including escort troops. Finally, the emperor provided a degree of unity of command in the field and at the summit of the state only equaled in recent memory by Frederick the Great, and a fertility in operational expedients, a driving energy, and a speed of execution all his own.[24]

From 1800 onward he routinized and made permanent the mass recruitment and nationalist passion of the revolutionary armies. The dichotomy sometimes drawn between the nation-in-arms of 1793 moved by revolutionary enthusiasm and the professional soldiers of the late 1790s and the Napoleonic Empire moved solely or primarily by honors and *esprit de corps* is implausible.[25] The amateurs of '93 were professional enough to defeat the best troops of the Old Regime through skill as well as enthusiasm. The professionals of Austerlitz and Jena–Auerstädt and after were recruited overwhelmingly by the quasi-universal annual conscription authorized by General Jourdan's law of 1798 and so expanded by Napoleon that the army raised two million troops between 1800 and 1814.[26] The Emperor himself had no doubt about the system's central importance to France: "Without conscription," he wrote in 1804, "neither national power nor national independence is possible . . . our success and the strength of our position depend on our having a national army; we must take care to preserve this advantage."[27]

---

[24] See the excellent summaries in Chandler, *Campaigns*, pp. 133–201 (operations), 332–78 (tactics and command technique).

[25] See Lynn, "Army of Honor," especially pp. 159–60; Jean-Paul Bertaud, *La vie quotidienne des soldats de la Révolution 1789–1799* (Paris, 1985), p. 115.

[26] For the figure, Lynn, "Army of Honor," p. 158.

[27] Quoted in Marcel Baldet, *La vie quotidienne dans les armeés de Napoléon* (Paris, 1964), p. 32.

Knox

The soldiers of this army went into battle for France as well as for their units, leaders, and emperor, and for the honors and rewards he offered. Napoleon for his part strengthened his always precarious legitimacy by the continued invocation of patriotic–revolutionary symbols; he had the "*Chant du départ*," most famous of the fighting songs of the early 1790s besides the Marseillaise, played to fire the troops on the morning of Austerlitz.[28] Clausewitz's description of the Napoleonic army as "this juggernaut of war, based on the strength of the entire people" was not verbal excess.[29]

Napoleon's most lasting achievement was twofold: to make the French army the army of the *nation* on a permanent basis, and to thereby durably if partially militarize that same nation. The peasantry inevitably resisted, and the state grudgingly conceded exemptions for those wealthy enough to pay a tax and a substitute. But evasion of conscription gradually diminished, reaching remarkably low levels in 1811–13.[30] The emperor had "rendered honorable, because compulsory, the calling of the private soldier."[31] Nor did Napoleon have any intention of allowing wealth to escape. With the enthusiastic backing of the army, he sought to make the officer corps the dominant component of France's post-revolutionary elite, and to lure or compel the sons of France's notables to serve in it.

Astonishingly high pay and lavish perquisites, rising to stratospheric heights for generals and marshals, was one element in this program of social engineering. Another was military precedence in ceremonial protocol at all levels, from the village, to the prefecture, to Paris itself. Soldiers and officers predominated crushingly among those awarded the Legion of Honor. By imperial order, high school students paraded in uniform; "war was in, and the drum muffled in my ear the voices of the schoolmasters," as Alfred de Vigny later recalled.[32] First the Revolution and then Napoleon – his victories, institutions, and memories – made France, for the next century and more, a military nation as it had never been under the Old Regime.[33]

Its adversaries inevitably responded in kind – but only one took up the challenge fully in the revolutionary era itself. "Peoples' war" as practiced against the French invaders by Calabrian *banditi*, Spanish guerrillas,

---

28 Numbers: Jean Morvan, *Le soldat impérial* (Paris, 1904), vol. 1, p. 120; Imperial motivation by revolutionary–patriotic song: Maurice Choury, *Les grognards et Napoléon* (Paris, 1968), pp. 145–6.

29 *On War*, p. 592.

30 See Isser Woloch, "Napoleonic Conscription: State Power and Civil Society," *Past and Present* 111 (1986), pp. 122–5.

31 Morvan, *Le soldat impérial*, vol. 1, p. 120.

32 *Servitudes et grandeurs militaires* (Paris, 1959 [1835]), p. 26.

33 On the militarization of society, see especially Jean-Paul Bertaud, *La Révolution armée: les soldats-citoyens et la Révolution française* (Paris, 1979), pp. 342–5, and "Napoleon's Officers," *Past and Present* 112 (1986) pp. 91–111.

Tyrolese mountaineers, and Russian serfs and Cossacks was not modern. Austria, despite its invocation of the "German nation" in 1809, was structurally incapable of following the French example very far, even had the Archduke Charles, its most perceptive and successful military leader, so wished.[34] Britain's staggering level of manpower mobilization by 1812–14 and its outstripping of French military and naval expenditure by a factor of perhaps five helped create a fragile sense of nationhood among its disparate peoples. But that effort did not require revolutionary changes, either political or military, to an Old Regime that survives to the present.[35] Only one power – indeed one institution – took up the French challenge with almost Jacobin zeal: the army of Prussia.

Prussia's transformation followed Napoleon's crushing defeat of its army at Jena–Auerstädt in October 1806, and was in part a consequence of Prussian peculiarities. War was Prussia's reason for existence, and even the most timid or recalcitrant of its conservative–noble military caste perceived after 1806 that Prussia must learn to win battles again, or cease to exist. But Prussia's transformation was also a consequence of the dynamics of nationalism. France had led the way – and the German-speaking lands had been its first victim. The armed hordes of the French had brutalized a people whose intelligentsia, for all the cosmopolitanism sometimes ascribed to it, contributed as much to the theory of nationalism as the French themselves. Modern German literature, born as the eighteenth century wore on among the small Protestant middle class of pastors and bureaucrats, was in part a reaction to the aping of French letters and manners by the aristocracy of western Germany. "Spew out the ugly slime of the Seine / Speak German, O you German!" thundered Friedrich Gottlieb Herder, the virtual inventor both of the theory of ethnic–linguistic nationalism and of nationalism's German variant.[36]

French conquest of Germany's borders in the 1790s and of its central core in 1800–06 transformed literary movement into political religion. The prophets of the German nation, from writers of patriotic verse such as Arndt, to philosophers such as Fichte, to dramatists such as Heinrich von Kleist, created a national cult that rested on the Protestant apocalypse, highly colored fantasies of the Germanic–tribal and medieval–imperial past, the French revolutionaries' Rousseauvian vision of a regenerated

---

34 See especially Gunther E. Rothenberg, "The Archduke Charles and the Question of Popular Participation in War," *Consortium on Revolutionary Europe Proceedings* (1982), pp. 214–24.

35 On the creation of the British "nation," see especially Linda Colley, *Britons: Forging the Nation, 1707–1837* (New Haven, CT, 1992); on the war effort, Chapter 10 of Geoffrey Best, *War and Society in Revolutionary Europe* (London, 1982) remains an excellent summary.

36 Quoted in Elie Kedourie, *Nationalism* (London, 1966), p. 59.

nation of citizens rendered incapable of disobeying the general will, and a
sense of world mission that made the Jacobins seem tame. Pitiless hostility
to the French was the lowest common denominator; Kleist, in his blood-
thirsty verse drama on Arminius' destruction of the Roman invaders in
9 A.D., summed up the general sentiment when he commanded the extermination of the enemy in biblical tones: "Strike him dead: the Last Judgment
will not ask your reasons!"[37]

These ideas fused, perceptibly if as yet imperfectly, with the traditions of
the Prussian army and state after 1806–07. Their bearers were the cadre of
reformers, many of them neither Prussian nor noble by origin, to whom
King Frederick William III grudgingly turned after Jena: Heinrich von und
zum Stein for the civilians, and for the army Gerhard von Scharnhorst,
August von Gneisenau, Hermann von Boyen, Karl von Grolman, and (as
Scharnhorst's assistant) Carl von Clausewitz.[38]

The military reformers had two revolutionary answers to Napoleon: the
thinking combatants that only universal military service could provide, and
a thinking officer corps and staff system honed by *Bildung* – systematic
professional study and the cultivation of decision-making skill. To make
universal service possible, the reformers proposed something wholly new
and alien to Prussian absolutism: an "alliance of government and people."[39] The state decreed the abolition of serfdom in 1807, and the army
ended corporal punishment in 1808. In 1813, after Napoleon's defeat in
Russia allowed Prussia to break with France, the reformers organized militia formations and volunteer light infantry units for the middle classes
alongside the infantry of the line.[40] The following year, after a revived
Prussian army of almost 300,000 men had helped drive Napoleon from
Germany and his throne, they promulgated Europe's first genuine universal
service law, the *Wehrgesetz*. The law, which after radical increases in scope
in 1860–67 remained in essence in effect until 1918, proclaimed the militarization of society with a thoroughness that had escaped even Napoleon:
the new army was to be the "chief school of the nation for war."

Unlike France, Prussia barely flinched at middle-class distaste for service
in the ranks. Not substitution, but a one-year term of service and opportunity to become a reserve officer or NCO was Prussia's principal conces-

[37] See Gordon Craig, "German Intellectuals in Politics, 1789–1815: The Case of Heinrich
von Kleist," *Central European History* 2:1 (March, 1969), pp. 8–10.
[38] The nationalism of the reformers, although inevitably exaggerated by later German
nationalists, was genuine and operative. See for instance Clausewitz's passionate and
chaotic "Profession of Faith" (Bekenntnisdenkschrift) of February 1812, in Carl von
Clausewitz, *Schriften–Aufsätze–Studien–Briefe*, ed. Werner Hahlweg (Göttingen, 1966),
especially Clausewitz's almost Fichtean disparagement of the French, p. 735.
[39] See Höhn, *Scharnhorsts Vermächtnis*, pp. 181ff.
[40] See especially Dennis E. Showalter, "The Prussian *Landwehr* and its Critics, 1813–
1819," *Central European History* 14:3 (1971), pp. 4–12.

sion to wealth and status, and that concession promised and ultimately
delivered the most military-minded middle classes in the world. The officer
corps changed as much as the troops. To expunge defeat and open the way
for talent, the reformers carried through a purge that surpassed in rigor any
such measure ever inflicted upon itself by a sizable modern military–bureaucratic institution; Napoleon helped by demanding a massive reduction in
the army's size. In the end, barely over half the officer corps of 1806 fought
in the wars of 1813–15.[41] Simultaneously, the reformers ended the jealous
noble quasi-monopoly of the officer corps upon which the great Frederick
had insisted; from August 1808 the officer caste was open to all possessing
"knowledge and education [*Bildung*] in peacetime . . . and in war outstanding bravery and military judgment." Prospective officers now entered
the ranks as officer candidates, and had to pass competitive written exam-
inations before being coopted, subject to royal approval, by the officers of
their regiment.[42]

Bildung was at the root of the new operational methods and tactics that
combined the distilled essence of the best in French practice with the results
of analysis and experiment, and made the Prussian army of 1813–15 at last
equal or superior to its enemy in movement, flexibility, inventiveness, and
fighting power. The Regulations of 1812, endpoint of the army's retraining
after Jena, made light infantry tactics the common property of all infantry
units, which now trained in the swift and interchangeable employment of
skirmishing, line, and column and the use of artillery and cavalry support.[43]

Bildung was also at the center of a fourth great reform, after the revolutions in recruitment, officer selection, and operational and tactical technique: that of the high command. Scharnhorst's reflections on Napoleon's
campaigns and his first-hand experience of Prussia's floundering without a
Frederick the Great in 1806 had persuaded him that the army must find a
way to do without genius at the top.[44] His answer was a reformed staff
system based on specialized military education for the very brightest junior
and middle-level officers. The center of that education was critical thought

---

41 Rainer Wohlfeil, "Vom stehenden Heer des Absolutismus zur allgemeinen Wehrpflicht
    (1789–1814)," Militärgeschichtliches Forschungsamt, *Handbuch der deutschen
    Militärgeschichte 1648–1939* (Frankfurt am Main and Munich, 1964–81), vol. 2, p. 141
    gives the most balanced account of the purge; 1,791 (or 23 percent) of the 7,096
    officers of 1806 remained active by September 1808, and only 3,898 (or 54 percent) of
    the officers of 1806 fought in 1813–15.
42 Ernst Rudolf Huber, *Deutsche Verfassungsgeschichte seit 1789* (Stuttgart, 1957–90),
    vol. 1, pp. 232–8.
43 See especially Paret, *Yorck*, pp. 181–9, and Dennis E. Showalter, "Manifestation of
    Reform: The Rearmament of the Prussian Infantry, 1806–1813," *Journal of Modern
    History* 44:4 (1972), pp. 364–80.
44 For the genesis of this notion long before Jena, see among other sources Charles
    Edward White, *The Enlightened Soldier: Scharnhorst and the Militärische Gesellschaft
    in Berlin, 1801–1805* (New York, 1989), pp. 64ff.

resting on thorough professional and military–historical understanding; its aim was aptitude and eagerness for independent action. Scharnhorst aimed to make staff officers not merely assistants to commanders, but a sort of central nervous system for strategic planning and operational control that would harness the *collective* wisdom of the best minds the army could recruit. The mass armies created in the French military revolution thus secured a reliable mechanism, independent of individual genius, for ensuring that hundreds of thousands of men would "fight in the right place at the right time."[45]

CONCLUSION: TO 1941 AND BEYOND

The victors of 1814–15 failed to suppress for long either nationalist revolution or the military revolution it had launched. No one could "disinvent" mass politics or mass warfare. Governments and armies ignored the pressing need for thinking warriors at their peril; the storm of steel of the Industrial Revolution increasingly emptied the battlefield of formations, reducing even junior leaders' span of control to the few men they could reach by crawling. And demographic expansion continually increased the size of armies and the necessity of ever more sophisticated mechanisms of command and control – which only some approximation of the Prussian staff system could provide.

Scharnhorst and his colleagues had remolded the Prussian army-state for the age of mass politics. Perhaps contrary to their partly liberal intentions, they and their less liberal successors produced Europe's most perfectly militarized society and most professional mass army. German nationalism's peculiarly violent character and limitless aspirations then combined with the new-won military self-assurance of the German people to carry strategic–ideological lunacy far beyond the high standards that the Girondins, Jacobins, and Bonaparte had set. The final lineal descendant of the reformed Prussian army of 1813–15 was the "National Socialist people's army" of 1939–45, which fought the greatest war in history to consummate a racist world revolution, and realized the Prussian reformers' career open to talent in ways that would have filled them with horror.[46]

The increasingly automated firepower of the permanent revolution of science and technology is at last ending the age of the armed horde that began in 1792–94. But the political religion of the nation-state remains

45 Clausewitz on the aim of "the whole of military activity," *On War*, p. 95.
46 See particularly Knox, "The 'Prussian Idea of Freedom' and the Career Open to Talent: Battlefield Initiative and Social Ascent from Prussian Reform to Nazi Revolution, 1807–1944," in Knox, *Common Destiny*; also Knox, "1 October 1942: Adolf Hitler, *Wehrmacht* Officer Policy, and Social Revolution," *The Historical Journal* 43:3 (2000), pp. 801–25.

mighty on Europe's fringes and among the rising powers of East Asia. The German Revolution's terrifying combination of professional military organization and technological mastery with mass fanaticism – *Panzerdivisionen*, V-2s, and racial–ideological extermination – should warn against overestimating the military decisiveness of technology alone, or its ability to define the nature of warfare.

5

Surviving military revolution: The U.S. Civil War

MARK GRIMSLEY

Commanders seek control, the more absolute the better. The best way to achieve it is to obtain a crushing, unanswerable advantage. Clausewitz put it with his habitual pithiness: "The best strategy," he wrote, "is always to be very strong."[1] Warring states greedily seize and ruthlessly exploit any weapon, method, or technology that offers crushing advantage. Supremacy is the Holy Grail of warfare.

Yet despite ceaseless search, advantages that produce lasting victory have appeared only rarely in the history of war. When they have, their most cherished attribute, *asymmetry* – the fact that one side has them while the other does not – has been fleeting. Belligerents adopt innovations with a conviction proportionate to their fear; new developments spread so swiftly that battlefield imbalances are usually brief. Genuine earthquakes in warfare are of a different nature entirely, and are largely independent of purely military factors. It is rather political, social, and economic changes, like the movement of vast tectonic plates, that most readily revolutionize war in all its aspects, from weapons and tactics, to methods of raising manpower, to the fundamental purposes the state pursues through war. Changes of that magnitude are truly military revolutions, and have little in common with the predictable, domesticated technological asymmetries that Pentagon commentators, with some conceptual help from Soviet theorists, have designated as "revolutions in military affairs." Individuals or groups do not control military revolutions: they merely seek to survive them.

The U.S. Civil War exemplifies – unlike the Prusso-German wars of 1866 and 1870–71, which it dwarfed in both duration and magnitude of effort –

---

[1] Carl von Clausewitz, *On War*, eds. and trans. Michael Howard and Peter Paret (Princeton, NJ, 1976), p. 204 [book 3, Chapter 11].

a military revolution. It took place within the context of two nonmilitary revolutions, both of which fostered revolutionary changes in the nature and purposes of war. Neither the Union nor the Confederacy fully understood these changes. Like Lincoln in Stephen Vincent Benét's epic poem, *John Brown's Body*, the people of the North and South could truly say:

> I have not once controlled the circumstances.
> They have controlled me. But with that control
> They made me grow or die. And I have grown.[2]

The Civil War combined the mass politics and passions of the Wars of the French Revolution with the technology, productive capacity, and managerial style of the emerging Industrial Revolution. The result, foreseen by Lincoln in December 1861, was a "remorseless, revolutionary struggle" that prefigured the First World War, and similarly beggared the ability of contemporaries to imagine its sweep, duration, and consequences.[3]

The Union and Confederacy fielded armies that dwarfed all military formations previously seen in the New World. They supplied these vast hosts with food, munitions, and equipment shipped by railroad and steamship. They connected units hundreds of miles apart with webs of telegraph lines and motivated soldiers and civilians with ceaseless propaganda. When necessary they repressed dissent through intimidation, arbitrary arrest, and the occasional murder. Before the war was half over, both sides had abandoned cherished notions of individual liberty and had conscripted men for military service for the first time in American history. In their quest to finance the struggle, they trampled venerable traditions of limited taxation and fiscal rectitude. And by the war's third year they had begun to accept attacks upon enemy civilians and property as necessary and even virtuous. They mobilized their resources and populations to the utmost extent of their nineteenth-century ability and, when they reached the end of that ability, strove for ways to extend it. The Union and Confederate armies, in short, waged a total war: one in which both sides pitted their full destructive energies against each other.[4]

---

2 Stephen Vincent Benét, *John Brown's Body* (New York, 1990 [1928]), p. 191.
3 "Annual Message to Congress," 3 December 1861, Roy P. Basler, ed., *The Collected Works of Abraham Lincoln*, 8 vols. (New Brunswick, 1953), vol. 5, p. 49.
4 "Total war" is an elastic, unsatisfactory term that requires qualification. It is generally used in one of two ways: to indicate a no-holds-barred conflict that targets civilians as readily as soldiers, or to describe a war in which one side or both mobilize their populations and economies to a high degree and conduct large-scale attacks on their opponent's war resources. The American Civil War fits the second definition but not the first. Its destructiveness, though massive, did not extend to the widespread killing of civilians. For a review of the relevant historiography, see Mark Grimsley, "Modern War/Total War," in Steven E. Woodworth, ed., *The American Civil War: A Handbook of Literature and Research* (Westport, CT, 1996), pp. 379–89.

These key dynamics go far beyond the hoary, college-survey notion that the Civil War was a revolutionary conflict by virtue of its technology or tactics. Such a notion is misleading and sometimes flatly wrong. The text-books tell us, for example, that the new rifled muskets greatly extended the range and killing power of the infantry and that this innovation revolutionized the battlefield.[5] In fact, a survey of the ranges of engagement in all major battles between First Bull Run (21 July 1861) and the battle of the Wilderness (5–6 May 1864) reveals that the average infantry unit opened fire on its opponent at a distance of 116 yards – an improvement over the 80-100 yards characteristic of smoothbore warfare, but at best an incremental improvement.[6] The same was true of breech-loading repeating carbines. Such weapons were revolutionary in their potential, but while both sides possessed them, only the Union deployed breech-loaders in quantities massive enough to have significant battlefield impact. An infantry brigade equipped with Spencer repeaters, such as John T. Wilder's famous "Lightning Brigade," wielded the firepower of a reinforced division, while Union cavalry with single-shot breech-loaders could hold off far stronger opponents, as John Buford's dismounted troopers proved on the first day at Gettysburg.[7] But the Union army never distributed these weapons widely enough to achieve an asymmetrical advantage. Like the rifled

5 See for instance the sidebar "Why Did So Many Soldiers Die?," in James L. Roark et al., *The American Promise: A History of the United States* (Boston, MA, 1997), p. 594. The best study to allege the revolutionary impact of the rifled musket on Civil War combat is Grady McWhiney and Perry D. Jamieson, *Attack and Die: Civil War Military Tactics and the Southern Heritage* (Tuscaloosa, AL, 1982).

6 This sample was created using the keyword "yards" in a computer word search of *War of the Rebellion: A Compilation of the Official Records of the Union and Confederate Armies*, 128 vols. (Washington, DC, 1880–1901) (henceforth OR) on *The Civil War CD-ROM 1.0* (Carmel, IN, 1997). The search yielded numerous references to ranges of engagements. The battles examined were First Bull Run (2 unequivocal range references), Second Bull Run (8), Antietam (21), Fredericksburg (10), Chancellorsville (16), Gettysburg (25), Bristoe Station and Mine Run (7 combined). If anything the actual ranges were somewhat shorter, since five of the longest ranges are from attackers' estimates of the distance at which they first received musketry and artillery fire. (It is uncertain that they could have detected the difference between the two types of fire.) In any case, the findings corroborate those of Paddy Griffith, *Battle Tactics of the Civil War* (New Haven, CT, 1987), pp. 144–150. From his own survey of Civil War ranges of engagement, Griffith concluded that the average range for musketry fire was 127 yards. One explanation for the relatively short range is that most Civil War commanders preferred the shock effect of a single close-range volley to the firepower advantage of several volleys delivered at longer range.

7 Peter Cozzens, *This Terrible Sound: The Battle of Chickamauga* (Urbana, IL, 1992), p. 393, offers a vivid impression of the impact of the firepower generated by Wilder's brigade: "So heavy was the fire from Wilder's Spencers that [Confederate General James] Longstreet, hearing the clatter from nearly half a mile off, thought for a moment that a fresh Federal corps had come crashing down on his left." For Buford's defense of the ridges west of Gettysburg, see especially David G. Martin, *Gettysburg, July 1* (Conshohocken, PA, 1995), pp. 59–88.

musket, the breech-loader's impact on combat was incremental rather than absolute.[8]

A second "modern" feature of the Civil War was the use of ironclad warships, steam and rail transportation, the telegraph, and other artifacts of the Industrial Revolution that had spread from Great Britain to parts of the continent and was fast gaining a grip upon antebellum America. This observation comes closer to the mark, for it touches upon one of the two nonmilitary revolutions mentioned above. But since both sides made extensive use of these new technologies, the prized asymmetry of the Pentagon-style RMA was not in evidence. The technologies were mere epiphenomena; the crucial innovation, as will become clear below, lay elsewhere.

A third "modern" feature, the deliberate, large-scale destruction of property with the aim of robbing the enemy of resources and demoralizing his civilian population, was very old. The massive raids of William T. Sherman and Philip H. Sheridan through Georgia, the Carolinas, and the Shenandoah Valley seem to anticipate the "total wars" of the twentieth century. In fact, they were comparatively well-behaved cousins of the horrific *chevauchées* conducted by the English armies during the Hundred Years' War, the scarcely less terrible devastation of the Palatinate by the soldiers of Louis XIV in 1688–89, and the lethal "feedfights" inflicted by the white American colonists on the Native Americans who sought to oppose them. Sherman, a student of military history, knew as much.[9]

Each of these elements – the rifled musket, breech-loading carbine, emergent industrial technologies, and destructive raids – were prominent features of the North's ultimate victory over the Confederacy. But so were two more protean factors: the volatile politics of mass democracy and the first great stirrings of the corporatist order – the symbiosis of private enterprise and public administration – that dominated American society during the twentieth century. If the secret of Northern triumph lies anywhere, it was in the Union's superior ability to harness these two factors. Yet exploiting them was far from easy; the North took three years to wring from them the asymmetric advantage required to overwhelm the South.

The nature of the underlying military revolution is perhaps best appreciated by exploring a single episode of the Civil War. An appropriate choice is the Overland Campaign, the first encounter between the rival sides' most successful commanders, Ulysses S. Grant and Robert E. Lee, and the cam-

8 These matters are well addressed in Carl L. Davis, *Arming the Union: Small Arms in the Civil War* (Port Washington, NY, 1973); see also Robert V. Bruce, *Lincoln and the Tools of War* (Indianapolis, IN, 1956).
9 On this point, see Mark Grimsley, *The Hard Hand of War: Union Military Policy Toward Southern Civilians, 1861–1865* (Cambridge, 1995).

paign on which both sides pinned their principal hopes for victory.[10] By the time it opened in May 1864, the revolutionary elements of the Civil War were in full play. The incidents of this campaign illuminate the burdens and frustrations of those elements quite as much as their advantages.

Mass politics, for example, ensured that Grant began the campaign enjoying a comfortable numerical superiority. In the eastern theater, some 165,000 troops were available for field duty as opposed to the 90,000 the Confederacy could muster.[11] This advantage was not meaningfully asymmetrical (indeed the white South mobilized a higher percentage of its military population than the North). Nevertheless, only mass political participation could have created armies of such size, for neither Union nor Confederates possessed the organization or coercive strength to build large armies in any other way. Until 1860, the United States government had been a modest affair, "little more," writes one political scientist, "than an arena in which contending forces and coalitions in the national political economy competed over decisions related to continental government and foreign policy."[12] Although it met the minimum conditions of a "state," the government lacked both an appreciable bureaucracy and a "state elite" with interests distinct from the other classes and interest groups within American society. The Confederate States exhibited the same shortcomings – of necessity to an even higher degree – when they established their own government in February 1861.

As a result, both Union and Confederacy relied from the outset upon their component states to organize the armies required to fight the Civil War, and upon volunteerism to fill those armies. That was the traditional American method and the only one thinkable in societies that venerated individual liberty and unobtrusive government. The Union and Confederate War Departments simply asked state governors to raise quotas of regiments. The governors, in turn, actually found, organized, and equipped the necessary recruits – by turning to community leaders, men of established standing who could persuade others to enlist under their command. The exact details varied widely but were always in keeping with the loose-jointed, localistic nature of American society.

The results were staggering. The Union and Confederate armies fielded at least 2.1 million and 880,000 troops respectively, and nearly half of those

---

10   See Brooks D. Simpson, "Great Expectations: Ulysses S. Grant, the Northern Press, and the Opening of the Wilderness Campaign," and Gary W. Gallagher," 'Our Hearts Are Full of Hope': The Army of Northern Virginia in the Spring of 1864," both in Gallagher, ed., *The Wilderness Campaign* (Chapel Hill, NC, 1997), pp. 1–35, 36–65.
11   These estimates derive from numerous abstracts of returns in OR, vols. 33 and 36/1.
12   Richard Franklin Bensel, *Yankee Leviathan: The Origins of Central State Authority in America, 1859–1877* (Cambridge, 1990), p. 2.

troops joined the ranks in the first two years of the war.[13] In the North, a July 1861 call for three-year volunteers produced 658,000 soldiers; a subsequent call the following August yielded 421,000 more. Lesser calls resulted in another 145,000 enlistments for terms of service ranging between three months and two years.[14] The South's track record was no less impressive.[15] Nearly five times the number of Americans served in the Civil War as in *all previous American wars combined.*[16]

In their homespun way, Americans were harnessing the same thing that had fired the American Revolution: popular sovereignty, the notion that the people themselves form the ultimate source of political authority and legitimacy. Nowhere in the nineteenth-century world was this idea more potent than in America. Because of it, both Northerners and Southerners felt a profound identification with the goals of their respective governments. That identification produced an outpouring of intelligent, politically aware, highly motivated volunteers willing to endure hardship, disease, and combat conditions as lethal as any that Americans have ever faced.[17]

That flood of dedicated soldiers came at a cost. The same democratic ethos that bound them to their nation's cause made them reject passive acquiescence and blind obedience. As virtuous citizens temporarily in uniform, they often mocked regular army discipline, insisted on electing their own officers, and disputed policies with which they disagreed. In the war's first fifteen months, for example, while the Union government earnestly

13 James M. McPherson, *Battle Cry of Freedom: The Civil War Era* (Oxford, 1988), pp. 306–07 note, arrives at these figures after a concise review of available data.
14 This estimate omits the 92,000 90-day volunteers raised under the April 1861 call for troops because most of these extended their enlistments for two or three years, and to include them would have resulted in a misleadingly large sum. The other enlistment figures also contain overlaps, as a number of men enlisted for one term of service later reenlisted for another, but the resultant distortion is not nearly so great.
15 The destruction of many Confederate records make army strength impossible to determine with precision. However, on 1 March 1862 the Confederate Adjutant-General reported his army as having a strength of 340,250 men; three months later its aggregate strength was 328,049, according to a "consolidated abstract from returns of the Confederate forces on or about June 30, 1862," compiled by the U.S. War Department and published in OR, Series IV, vol. 1, p. 1126. Since the compilers could not locate returns for three major commands, and since a number of bloody battles took place between March and June even as additional recruits flowed into the army, it seems safe to conclude that the number enlisted by June 1862 was significantly higher.
16 Participation in the Revolutionary War, War of 1812, and Mexican War totaled about 603,000, according to Allan R. Millett and Peter Maslowski, *For the Common Defense: A Military History of the United States of America* (New York, rev. ed., 1994), p. 653. The Civil War figures used by Millett and Maslowski differ slightly from McPherson's: 2 million plus for the Union, 750,000 for the Confederacy.
17 The literature on this subject is extensive and growing, but see especially Earl J. Hess, *The Union Soldier in Battle: Enduring the Ordeal of Combat* (Lawrence, KS, 1997); James M. McPherson, *For Cause and Comrades: Why Men Fought in the Civil War* (Oxford, 1997); and Joseph Allen Frank, *With Ballot and Bayonet: The Political Socialization of American Civil War Soldiers* (Athens, GA, 1998).

pursued a policy of respect for the constitutional rights of disloyal Southerners and protection to their property, including slaves, Northern soldiers widely rejected this "kid glove" approach, stealing fence rails and foodstuffs from Southern civilians despite all efforts to stop them.[18] Their opinions on the delicate issue of emancipation caused the government no end of headaches. Some regiments harbored runaway slaves at a time when official policy called for the continued enforcement of the Fugitive Slave Act. Others protested when the Lincoln administration issued the Emancipation Proclamation. At least one outfit, the 128th Illinois, deserted en masse.[19]

The recruitment of African American troops, for its part, caused widespread resentment. Many white soldiers regarded it as a mortal insult to have black men foisted on them as comrades-in-arms. The fact that blacks served in segregated regiments scarcely mollified the whites, who vocally questioned the government's wisdom in putting racial "inferiors" in positions of trust and responsibility. (Grant himself was something of a skeptic about the use of black troops. During the Overland Campaign, at a time he needed every available man in the line of battle, an entire division of U.S. Colored Troops – 4,000 men – did little save guard communications.)

The touchiness of the resulting citizen-soldiers was not the sole drawback of mass politics. Keeping them in the field once their terms of service expired was likewise problematic. Although the Confederacy retained its veteran troops by unilaterally extending their enlistments for the duration of the war, the Union government found this course a political nonstarter. It felt obliged to honor the enlistment contracts of its troops, and entered 1864 fully aware that the three-year terms of its 1861 volunteers – the most experienced troops in the Federal army – were due to expire in the coming months. A combination of patriotic appeals, bonuses and 30-day furloughs persuaded 136,000 veterans to reenlist (including 27,000 in the Army of the Potomac), but even more chose to go home. The government let them go. As a result, whole regiments marched off the field during the Overland Campaign, as one unit after another reached the expiration of its service. So massive was this exodus that at one point, Robert E. Lee warned a corps commander not to mistake the impending departure of the Pennsylvania Reserves, which he had read about in the Philadelphia newspapers, for an enemy ruse.[20]

---

18 Grimsley, *The Hard Hand of War*, pp. 39–46.
19 James M. McPherson, *What They Fought For, 1861–1865* (Baton Rouge, LA, 1994), pp. 47–70; Bruce Catton, *Glory Road: The Bloody Route From Fredericksburg to Gettysburg* (Garden City, NY, 1952), p. 227.
20 Charles Marshall [Lee's aide-de-camp] to Richard S. Ewell, 7 May 1864, OR vol. 36, part 2, p. 67.

Both sides attempted to supplement their volunteer-based armies with conscripts, but political ideology – the notion that a man might choose to serve his government but that no man should be coerced – was scarcely conducive to conscription. At first, the draft functioned mainly as a spur to volunteers. The Confederate conscription law, passed in April 1862, conceded that soldiers enlisted for twelve months could soon go home. But if they did, they were liable to the draft without any choice of where they would serve. If they stayed on voluntarily, they could remain with their friends and comrades in their present units. Over time, the Confederacy moved toward more direct forms of compulsion, but even so the system produced only 11 percent of the army's manpower needs, while doing enormous damage to popular support for the government.

The Federal government stuck with the carrot-and-stick approach much longer. Though willing to draft men as a last resort, it preferred to threaten conscription as a means of spurring communities to redouble their efforts to recruit volunteers. State and local governments soon offered cash bounties of up to $1,000 to men willing to enlist. This had the effect of increasing the flow of volunteers, but it also created the "bounty jumper," a con artist who enlisted, took the bounty, and deserted at the first opportunity. Even those who remained gambled, stole, malingered, and disgusted the volunteers. Bounty men had to be watched like hawks to keep them in the army. They could not be trusted to perform any job that required them to work unsupervised. Sentry or outpost duty was unthinkable. "If those fellows are trusted on picket," groused a Massachusetts soldier, "the army will soon be in hell."[21] Most veterans considered the bounty men a curse rather than a source of additional fighting strength. The Army of the Potomac embarked on the Overland Campaign with thousands of such men in the ranks, as well as "substitutes" – men legally hired by draftees to serve in their place. The troops viewed substitutes with nearly as much suspicion as they did bounty men.

The drawbacks of untrammeled democracy did not end there. Contrary to the historical myth that holds that Lincoln, having at last "found a general" in Ulysses S. Grant, permitted him to fight the war without political interference, the demands of mass politics dominated the Overland Campaign more than any other major operation of the Civil War. The campaign's very name is significant. It derived from Grant's effort to attack Richmond via the "overland" route from northern Virginia rather than by landing an army near the Confederate capital, as the navigable James River estuary and the formidable Northern advantage in sea power would readily

---

21 Charles E. Davis, Jr., *Three Years in the Army: The Story of the 13th Massachusetts Volunteers* (Boston, MA, 1893), p. 270. See also Martin T. McMahon, "From Gettysburg to the Coming of Grant," in Clarence C. Buel and Robert U. Johnson, eds., *Battles and Leaders of the Civil War*, 4 vols. (New York, 1887), vol. 4, pp. 91–3.

have permitted. Left to his own judgment, Grant would not have selected the overland route. His original preference was for an army-sized raid from the North Carolina coast against the railroads linking the Southern heartland with Richmond and its defenders, the Army of Northern Virginia under Robert E. Lee. Political considerations – not for the last time – thwarted Grant. The year 1864 was an election year in the North, and the Lincoln administration could not afford the risk of yet another of Lee's strategically questionable but politically damaging raids into Northern soil, even if 60,000 Federals were simultaneously savaging Lee's line of communication with the Deep South. The administration therefore insisted that Grant keep the Army of the Potomac squarely between Washington and the Confederate army, thus forcing him to embrace the overland route.[22]

Politics constrained Grant in other ways. In a decision that endeared him to Lincoln, Grant organized two subordinate expeditions to support his main offensive south across the Rapidan River. The president, noted Lincoln's personal secretary, had for years implored Grant's predecessors to adopt a policy of simultaneous attacks in separate theaters "so as to bring into action to our advantage our great superiority in numbers." Delighted that a top commander was at last implementing this concept, the president earthily captured the key idea: "Those not skinning can hold a leg."[23] Lincoln's delight, however, did not prevent him from quietly insisting that Grant permit two political generals to grip the key legs in Virginia, an offensive in the Shenandoah Valley and an amphibious landing at Bermuda Hundred on the James River, about fifteen miles south of Richmond. German expatriate Franz Sigel received the former assignment because his influence among fellow German immigrants would ensure that Lincoln got their support.[24] Benjamin F. Butler got the even more critical Bermuda Hundred expedition because he was a major power broker and potential presidential candidate whose quest for martial glory Lincoln could not afford to thwart.

The Overland Campaign and its subsidiary offensives jumped off in early May. The Army of the Potomac, 120,000 men, crossed the Rapidan River on 4 May; Butler with 25,000 landed at Bermuda Hundred the following day. Following an unopposed staging march to Strasburg, Virginia, Sigel

22 Grant to Halleck, 19 January 1864, OR, vol. 33, p. 394; Halleck to Grant, 17 February 1864, OR, vol. 22, part 2, p. 412. See also Brooks D. Simpson, *Let Us Have Peace: Ulysses S. Grant and the Politics of War and Reconstruction, 1861–1868* (Chapel Hill, NC, 1991), pp. 54–5.
23 Entry for 30 April 1864, Michael Burlingame and John R. Turner Ettlinger, eds., *Inside Lincoln's White House: The Complete Civil War Diary of John Hay* (Carbondale, IL, 1997), pp. 193–4.
24 Stephen D. Engle, *Yankee Dutchman: The Life of Franz Sigel* (Fayetteville, AR), pp. 169–70.

launched his own offensive on 9 May. All seemed well for ι
weeks. Grant and Lee wrestled inconclusively in the Wilder,
Spotsylvania Court House, but Grant believed his army had
hand. In any event, he fought Lee secure in the knowledge that
presented by Sigel and Butler were starving the hard-pressed ʌɪmy of
Northern Virginia of reinforcements, while his own army was receiving a
steady stream of replacements to offset its heavy losses. Attrition alone
would soon wear down Lee's army even in the absence of striking operational successes. That logic underpinned Grant's famous pledge "to fight it
out on this line if it takes all summer."[25]

On 18 May the roof abruptly caved in. A tart dispatch from the Union
army's chief of staff, Henry W. Halleck, announced the collapse of Grant's
operational design. "[Sigel] is already in full retreat on Strasburg," he
wrote. "If you expect anything from him you will be mistaken. He will
do nothing but run. He never did anything else. . . . Butler has fallen back
to-day. Do not rely on him."[26] The political generals had failed – and failed
so ruinously that they now posed no threat to the Confederates whatever.

The implications of this news were obvious. "Lee," Grant told his staff,
"will undoubtedly reinforce his army largely by bringing . . . troops from
Richmond, now that Butler has been driven back, and will call in troops
from the valley since Sigel's defeated forces have retreated." He met the
new situation with the calm resolve for which he was famous, at once
drafting an order for the Army of the Potomac to leave Spotsylvania.
There was no point in staying if Lee were about to be reinforced. Instead
the Federals would swing around Lee's right flank and seek battle on better
ground.[27]

This was the second time Grant had issued such an order – the first had
come after the stalemated battle in the Wilderness – and in the next three
weeks he executed the same maneuver twice more. Four navigable rivers
cut the Virginia shore: the Potomac, Rappahannock, York, and James.
Thanks to the North's advantage in sea power, Grant could use any of
these rivers as a secure line of communication; at one time or another he
used them all. Scarcely had the battle of the Wilderness ended than Grant
abandoned his initial supply line by way of the Orange and Alexandria
Railroad and ordered a new base established at Belle Plain on the
Potomac River. For ten days this sleepy river landing became one of the
busiest ports in the world, as a continuous stream of ships arrived with
rations and ammunition for over 100,000 men, and around 15,000 reinforcements. Departing vessels took with them at least 14,000 wounded

[25] Grant to Halleck, 11 May 1864, OR, vol. 36, part 2, p. 627.
[26] Halleck to Grant, 17 May 1864, OR, vol. 36, part 2, pp. 840–1.
[27] Horace Porter, *Campaigning With Grant* (Bloomington, IN, 1961 [1897]), p. 124.

soldiers and 7,000 Confederate prisoners of war. Then Grant moved on, Belle Plain quickly regained its anonymity, and a new, equally bustling hub arose at Port Royal on the Rappahannock; White House Landing on the Pamunkey (an arm of the York) and City Point on the James followed. The last remained Grant's base for the rest of the war.

As a logistical achievement this was impressive, but the fiscal achievement that underpinned it was nothing short of brilliant. Wars, after all, must be paid for. Each time Grant turned the Confederate flank, he relied not just on the North's impressive ability to move men and supplies by water, but also on the Federal government's ability to pay for the ships and cargo required. Here the Union *was* able to generate an asymmetric advantage over the Confederacy. Although mass political participation tapped the manpower reservoirs of both North and South, the North alone discovered how to mobilize its material resources without ruinous political and economic consequences.

Like the rifled musket, the North's material edge over the South is a set piece of conventional analyses of the Civil War. The North began the war with a population of 22.1 million whites and 344,000 free blacks against 5.4 million white Southerners, 3.5 million slaves, and 133,000 free blacks. In 1860 the North had over 110,000 manufacturing establishments, the South 18,000. The North produced 94 percent of the country's iron, 97 percent of its coal, and 97 percent of its firearms. It owned 90 percent of the country's merchant ship tonnage and contained 22,000 miles of railroad, compared with the South's 9,280 miles. The North outperformed the South agriculturally as well, accounting for 75 percent of the country's farm acreage, 60 percent of its livestock, 67 percent of its corn, and 81 percent of its wheat. All in all, the North held 75 percent of the nation's taxable wealth.[28]

These were important advantages, but they were also *latent* ones that did not translate directly into military power. "The spreading factories and the burdened busy trains and the limitless fields of wheat," observed historian Bruce Catton, "were not going to appear on the firing line, and it was on the firing line that this [war] must finally be settled." Catton went on to write that the war was ultimately won by "thousands of obscure young men in dirty, sweat-stained uniforms."[29] Fair enough. But the glamourless truth is that it also took the efforts of well-fed, splendidly manicured politicos, lawyers, financiers, industrialists, and contractors to harness those factories, trains, and wheatfields smoothly to the war effort, and not infrequently to make piles of money for themselves.

---

28 These and other statistics are conveniently available in E. B. Long, *The Civil War Day By Day: An Almanac, 1861–1865* (Garden City, NY, 1971), pp. 721–6.
29 Catton, *Glory Road*, p. 242.

Antebellum America had a strongly established tradition of low taxes. Aside from a few excise duties on alcohol, tobacco, and a handful of similar items, the population had been free of direct Federal taxation for over forty years. It was equally free from Federal regulation of the money supply, for the nation had tried and discarded a central Bank of the United States not once but twice. Although many deplored the absence of such a bank – most notably the Whig party, until its abrupt demise in the mid-1850s – most Americans shared Andrew Jackson's suspicions of such institutions because they appeared to benefit plutocrats at the expense of the common man. As a result, the Federal government handled its finances in a fashion not unlike a miser squirreling away gold coins under the mattress. It carried out all its transactions with specie; deposits went into a notional Independent Treasury that in practice consisted of a number of sub-treasuries scattered about the country. These deposits might be physically located in a bank safe for ease of protection, but did not constitute part of the bank's assets. They earned no interest and it was a serious felony to use them for any purpose other than the payment of government obligations. Bray Hammond, a distinguished historian of American finance, aptly remarked that this was the equivalent of requiring government property to be hauled solely by ox-team, for official travel to be made solely on horseback, or for government offices to be lit solely by candle-light. "To keep relations between the government and the economy 'pure' and wholesome," he continued, "tons of gold had to be hauled to and fro in dray-loads, with horses and heavers doing by the hour what bookkeepers could do in a moment."[30]

Although everyone knew that the war would require some departure from this peacetime norm, the predominant outlook remained staunchly conservative. The conventional financial wisdom from Jeffersonian days onward held that governments should meet normal expenses through taxation and pay for war largely through borrowing. The Federal government had financed the Mexican War in this way with little difficulty, although as a small-scale, brief, and highly successful conflict it was of limited relevance to larger, more protracted struggles. A closer analogy to the Civil War was the War of 1812. The Madison administration had also relied on borrowing, although in 1813 it had inaugurated a program of internal taxation that brought in $11.5 million by the close of the conflict. That sum was 12 percent larger than total government revenues in 1812 – yet it represented a mere 8 percent of the war's total cost. Customs duties, sales of public land, and miscellaneous receipts covered about 12 percent; the remaining $120 million came from loans, often on unfavorable terms. Although far from

---

30   Bray Hammond, *Sovereignty and an Empty Purse* (Princeton, NJ, 1970), p. 23.

optimal, these financial policies had worked; both Union and Confederacy began the Civil War with similar systems.

The fiscal program of the Confederate government was particularly conservative. For the first two years of the conflict it restricted taxation to two sources: a modest tariff and a 0.5 percent tax on real and personal property. The Federal blockade prevented the tariff from generating more than $3.5 million, while the tax on real and personal property, for debatable constitutional reasons, exempted the South's two preeminent forms of wealth, land and slaves. In addition, the Confederate Congress required the states to collect the tax – and only South Carolina actually did so. Texas seized property owned by Northern citizens to pay it; most other states either borrowed the amount of their assessment or else printed enough state notes to cover it. The tax ultimately brought in a mere $17.5 million by mid-1863.[31]

The Confederate regime tried to finance its war effort chiefly through the sale of bonds, but with equally meager success. An initial offering of $5 million sold quickly, but after that cash-poor Southerners shunned the bonds, even after the government offered them in exchange for crops – including crops not yet harvested. The Confederacy sold $115 million in bonds but realized only a fraction of that amount in specie or in kind; most buyers purchased the bonds with Treasury notes.

Faced with the tremendous expense of prosecuting the war and unable to pay for it in any other way, the Confederate government quickly turned to printing those same notes, which functioned as currency without being legal tender – a creditor could not be forced to accept them as payment. They were, in effect, merely a transferable government IOU promising to pay the note's face value in specie within two years of the conclusion of peace between the Confederacy and the United States. By the end of 1861, the Confederate Treasury had already issued $311 million of these notes. A year later this total had risen to $580 million, and on the eve of the Overland Campaign it stood at $1.1 billion, of which $851.6 million was still in circulation. Even if the Confederacy had won the war, this staggering sum was far more than it could ever have redeemed in specie; if it lost the war the notes would be utterly worthless. The inevitable consequence was galloping inflation. A Confederate dollar was worth ninety-one cents in gold in May 1861. Three years later it had fallen to five cents and was still dropping.

[31] The discussion in this and succeeding paragraphs is based on Douglas B. Ball, *Financial Failure and Confederate Defeat* (Urbana, IL, 1991); Paul A. C. Koistinen, *Beating Plowshares into Swords: The Political Economy of American Warfare, 1606–1865* (Lawrence, KS, 1996); McPherson, *Battle Cry of Freedom*, pp. 437–42, 615–17; Emory M. Thomas, *The Confederate Nation: 1861–1865* (New York, 1979); and Richard C. Tod, *Confederate Finance* (Athens, GA, 1954).

In the spring of 1863, faced with a rate of inflation that crippled its economy, impoverished its population, and sparked widespread resentment, the Confederate government sought to force holders of Treasury notes to exchange them for bonds and to institute a more comprehensive tax program. The new law called for a graduated income tax, a number of excise taxes, and a 10 percent "tax in kind" on crops and livestock. This seemingly forceful program had three crippling weaknesses: it still exempted land and slaves (assets not finally taxed until February 1864); the income and excise taxes were hard to enforce; and the tax in kind was wildly unpopular. None of these measures arrested inflation, which was running at 600 percent by the end of 1863, but rather fed a climate of unrest in the Confederacy that triggered bread riots in several cities, led farmers to grow fewer crops, and encouraged desertion from the Confederate armies.

The Federal government at first followed a similar path. For the fiscal year ending 30 June 1861, revenue receipts totaled $41.5 million, 95 percent of which came from customs duties. The budget that Treasury secretary Salmon P. Chase submitted for fiscal 1862 envisaged a modest increase in taxes to a hoped-for $80 million (actually yielding far less), and planned to issue $240 million in bonds to finance the war. Congress actually authorized $250 million, and the Treasury issued $50 million in noninterest-bearing demand notes and $200 million in bonds, $150 million of them sold to major northeastern banks that resold them to private investors. The banks had to buy them at par value and pay for them in specie. The most sensible policy would have been for the government to let the banks hold the $150 million and to write checks against it as required, but in good "hard money" fashion, Chase insisted that they fork over the full amount in a few large installments. That was not a move well-calculated to create demand for the bonds, which were slow to sell, and it had the effect of weakening the banks that purchased them by severely reducing their credit reserves. When a diplomatic crisis in December 1861, the *Trent* affair, triggered fears of war with Great Britain, nervous customers rushed to withdraw their deposits, forcing banks to suspend specie payments. Still worse, the expense of fighting the Confederacy, already understood to be enormous, proved even greater than expected, while revenues fell short. By New Year's Day, 1862, the government was broke, and a few days later Lincoln mourned to Montgomery C. Meigs, the army's quartermaster general: "General, what shall I do? The people are impatient; Chase has no money and he tells me he can raise no more . . . The bottom is out of the tub."[32]

---

[32] "General M. C. Meigs on the Conduct of the Civil War," *American Historical Review* 26 (January 1921), p. 292.

Mending the tub again required fresh ideas. If Chase lacked them, others did not. An exceptional group of businessmen, bankers, and attorneys, well-acquainted with the emergent financial and industrial order, stepped forward with advice, and both Congress and Chase paid heed. The result, one analyst has written, was "a fiscal–military revolution" based on a sophisticated balance between loans, currency, and internal taxation.[33]

The strategy of borrowing to meet the demands of the war had foundered on the requirement that the government must pay for most of its expenses either in specie or paper redeemable in specie. The Legal Tender Act of February 1862 removed the difficulty by authorizing the issuance of $150 million in Treasury notes. Despite its superficial similarity to Confederate expedients, the measure *compelled* acceptance of the notes for *all* debts, public or private, with two exceptions: customs duties and interest on government bonds. The first exception guaranteed a continuous flow of specie to the government; the second made Federal bonds a far more attractive investment than their Confederate counterpart.

The bonds sold briskly thereafter, and not merely to banks and wealthy investors. Ordinary citizens could purchase them in denominations as low as $50, and an unprecedented mass marketing machine ensured that they did. The campaign was the brainchild of Jay Cooke, a thirty-one-year-old investor who personally sold 20 percent of all bonds marketed in 1861 and became the general and sole government agent for their sale in October 1862. Cooke set up an organization of 2,500 subagents that reached into every nook and cranny of the Union; by January 1864 his firm had sold $362 million in bonds and had earned a net profit of $220,000.

Even so, payment of war expenses required further issues of paper money – $450 million by early 1863. A National Banking Act, passed that April, helped regulate the currency, but the sweeping new internal tax program that became law in July 1862 was the most effective counter to the inflationary pressures of war. The program imposed a spectrum of excise, luxury, inheritance, and value-added taxes while greatly revising a modest income tax passed in August 1861. The new schedule exempted incomes under $600 but assessed 3 percent of incomes between $600 and $10,000 and 5 percent on higher incomes – rates raised in 1864 to 5 percent of incomes between $600 and $5,000, 7.5 percent of incomes between $5,000 and $10,000, and 10 percent of all higher incomes. The exemption reflected a desire to place the income tax burden upon those who could best afford it – and were least likely to serve in person in the army. The other taxes likewise targeted the affluent.

---

[33] Bruce D. Porter, *War and the Rise of the State: The Military Foundations of Modern Politics* (New York, 1994), p. 258.

Equitable distribution and consistent enforcement made the Internal Revenue Act of 1862 politically palatable and financially sound. Internal revenue jumped from virtually nothing in fiscal 1862 to $3.7 million in fiscal 1863 and almost $11 million in fiscal 1864. By the end of the war, it accounted for 63 percent of Federal income and met 16 percent of expenses – and it enabled the U.S. government to pay for the war effort without ruinous inflation. By the end of the Civil War, prices stood a mere 80 percent above their 1861 levels, compared with increases of 84 percent in the First World War and 70 percent in its sequel. Life in the North during the war years was no picnic – price increases outstripped wages, fueling resentments among the workers and provoking strikes and occasional riots – but it bore little resemblance to the privations most Southerners experienced. Indeed, the North's financial policies on balance increased rather than eroded support for the war effort. An Ohio mechanic earning 6 percent interest from a government bond had a different perspective than a Georgia farmer watching the arrival of Confederate tax-in-kind agents. It was easier to hum "The Battle Hymn of the Republic" while making a profit than to whistle "Dixie" while the government confiscated a tenth of one's cows.

The contrast between the North's smooth management of its wartime economy and the Richmond government's wretched handling of its own finances was telling. It is probably too much to claim, as has one recent analyst, that the Confederacy lost the war because of its clumsy fiscal policies, but it is certain that those policies exacerbated difficulties in the Confederate armed forces while radically increasing tensions within Confederate society. Perceived differences in the burdens shouldered by the planter and yeoman classes, argues Paul D. Escott, a distinguished historian of the South, resulted in "a kind of quiet rebellion" of the common people – a withdrawal of support – that helped to cripple the Confederate war effort.[34] "Wrongheaded wartime financing," concludes political economist Paul Koistinen, "may have been the single most important cause of Confederate defeat."[35]

Grant could certainly see the contrast when he compared his well-clad, well-equipped, well-fed soldiers with the ragged, half-emaciated forms of Confederate prisoners. Lee could see it when he wrestled with the unyield-

---

34 Paul D. Escott, *After Secession: Jefferson Davis and the Failure of Southern Nationalism* (Baton Rouge, LA, 1978), p. 104.

35 Koistinen, *Beating Plowshares into Swords*, p. 265. Charles W. Ramsdell called its financial policy "the single greatest weakness of the Confederacy" (*Behind the Lines in the Confederacy* [Baton Rouge, LA, 1944], p. 85). Douglas B. Ball has argued that it was an avoidable weakness: "The Confederate government had it well within its power to prolong its resistance to the point where independence or at least a compromise peace might have been achieved." In his view, the failure to do so reflected a culpable failure of leadership. (Ball, *Financial Failure and Confederate Defeat*, p. 17.)

ing problem of keeping his army fed, or fretted over increases in desertion – on the eve of the Overland Campaign he informed Jefferson Davis that 5,500 men, a tenth of his force, were absent without leave.[36] Lee's correspondence during the winter of 1863–64 is one long lament about the dearth of supplies, a matter of a seriousness he could not underscore forcefully enough. In part the lack of sufficient food and forage was the consequence of mismanagement by Lieutenant Colonel Lucius Northrop, the Confederacy's notoriously incompetent commissary-general, who blandly urged Lee to make up deficiencies through impressment, a military variant on the tax in kind. But Lee believed that requisitioning goods by force only exacerbated the problem. "Wholesale impressments will give us present relief, but I fear it will injure our future supplies," for it would encourage farmers to hide their crops – or refuse to plant them: "Already I hear of land in Virginia lying idle from this cause."[37]

Yet for all its difficulties, the Army of Northern Virginia gave as good as it got during the Overland Campaign, repeatedly giving the lie to Grant's overconfident belief – based on the Confederates' ever more frequent use of fieldworks – that "Lee's army is really whipped."[38] Its fierce resistance resulted in over 50,000 Union casualties by the end of the campaign, and mirrored similarly strong Southern resistance on other fronts. No one in 1861 could have imagined bloodshed on a scale that seemed out of all proportion to any rational political aim. "If that scene could have been presented to me before the war," admitted Massachusetts' staunchly abolitionist Senator Henry Wilson, "anxious as I was for the preservation of the Union, I should have said: 'The cost is too great; erring sisters, go in peace.'"[39]

The fact that Americans inflicted and absorbed such losses for four years was arguably the greatest single manifestation of the revolutionary nature of the conflict. The regional differences between the North and South had been evident since the nation's founding, and American statesmen had argued about the place of slavery in the United States as far back as the Continental Congress. Yet until 1860 they had always found ways to resolve their disputes within the political system, through the proud and effective American tradition of compromise. What had shattered that tradition?

---

[36] Lee to Davis, 13 April 1864, Douglas Southall Freeman, ed., *Lee's Dispatches: Unpublished Letters of General Robert E. Lee, C.S.A. to Jefferson Davis and the War Department of the Confederate States of America, 1862–1865* (Baton Rouge, LA, 1994 [1915]), pp. 156–7.

[37] Lee to James L. Kemper, 29 January 1864, OR, vol. 33, p. 1128.

[38] Grant to Halleck, 26 May 1864, OR, vol. 36, part 3, p. 206.

[39] Quoted in Allan Nevins, *The War for the Union*, vol. 4, *The Organized War to Victory, 1864–1865* (New York, 1971), p. 23.

In his prize-winning 1991 book, *The Destructive War*, Charles Royster has argued that the Civil War's extraordinary violence was the expression of a changing political culture. The rise of Jacksonian democracy created a society increasingly intolerant of limits:

> Antebellum America was pervaded by an uncompromising insistence on personal autonomy [and] . . . a growing impatience with restraints on the ambitions of individuals or of groups. These tendencies to reject limitations and to defy unwelcome authority knew no certain means to resolve competing demands other than violence. Parties and the mechanics of government thrived on confrontation and on winner-take-all outcomes, but were far less suited to restrain them than to agitate. People so determined to have their own way and so certain of possessing right and power could not readily stop short of war or stop war, once convinced that they were threatened on matters they deemed crucial. All professing to be Americans, they found that America did not keep them together but told them to kill Americans who sought to control them. By so doing they could make history accede to their ethos.[40]

Most Americans shared the profound surprise at the war's destructiveness that Henry Wilson had voiced. They felt caught up in an event far larger than themselves. Northerners and Southerners alike had gone to war to preserve a republic they recognized and understood against a perceived threat from other Americans. They consequently accepted, in the name of military necessity, government measures that would previously have seemed unthinkable. Both sides swallowed conscription and massively increased taxation, whether direct, in-kind, or in the form of monetary inflation, because enough citizens on both sides believed enough in their respective causes to legitimize those measures. They created armies without precedent in American history, composed of men willing to die in unprecedented numbers because the continued life of the nation they fought for seemed more important than their own lives. The story of the Civil War is fundamentally a story about learning to ride the whirlwind. Each side rode as well as it could, and suffered the consequences even while attempting to inflict them upon the enemy. And instead of preserving the old America – however the two sides defined it – the whirlwind radically reshaped the nation's political, economic, and social contours. By the time it ended, the original American republic was gone forever.

---

[40] Charles Royster, *The Destructive War: William Tecumseh Sherman, Stonewall Jackson, and the Americans* (New York, 1991), p. 191.

6

The Prusso-German RMA, 1840–1871

DENNIS E. SHOWALTER

From colonial times Americans have sought force multipliers against an unforgiving physical environment.[1] The man who masters the machine, Hank Morgan rather than John Henry, is a dominant archetype. The Western hero combines moral force and technical proficiency: righteousness sustained by a six-gun in expert hands.[2] The heady visions of supremacy through technology found throughout U.S. policy and military–professional literature through the 1990s and beyond derive both their substance and their persuasiveness from this underlying cultural predisposition.

American analysts have in consequence defined revolutions in military affairs as technological–organizational asymmetries between combatants, usually embracing three distinct but interrelated areas. The first and most obvious is straight-line improvement in the capacity to destroy targets. Second is an "information edge" generated through exponential and synergistic increases in the ability to collect, process, and distribute information. The third decisive aspect of the American-style RMA is the provision of doctrines, skills, and force structures necessary to optimize the potential of new materiel. The fate of French armor in 1940 and of the Arab air forces in 1967 demonstrates the uselessness of hardware without appropriate concepts for its use and competent personnel effectively organized to implement those concepts.

The Prussian army from the 1840s onward provides an almost classic model of technological innovation that acted as catalyst for radical changes in tactics, operations, military organization, and state policy. Those changes in turn allowed Prussia between 1866 and 1871 to alter the very

---

[1] Leo Marx, *The Machine in the Garden* (New York, 1964), remains a useful overview of this concept – and of its ambivalent consequences.

[2] See particularly Richard Slotkin, *Gunfighter Nation: The Myth of the Frontier in Twentieth-Century America* (New York, 1992).

structure of the European state system. The "Prussian RMA" thus fits neatly – at first glance – into the American conceptual framework. But it also entails a stern warning: within twenty-five years all other European great powers except Britain had adopted its chief technological and organizational features and had nullified any asymmetric German advantage. Above all, the other powers also had a *strategic* answer to the "semi-hegemonial" great power that German violence had created in their midst: defensive alliances to blunt the offensive power of the swift "German sword."[3] The collision in 1914 between the conceptual, technological, and organizational traditions founded in the Prussian RMA and the resistance of Germany's belatedly but similarly equipped neighbors produced a cataclysm: a four-and-a-half-year *Weltkrieg* – on the pattern of the U.S. Civil War – that ended in German defeat.

PEACETIME INNOVATION: NEEDLE-GUN AND RAILROAD

Revolutions in military affairs are most likely to occur in peacetime through the efforts of armed forces that perceive themselves as laggards under the existing rules of the game. It was not accidental that in the early 1980s the Soviets began addressing their future prospects in an arms race driven by technologies they could not match without denying the essence of their regime.[4] Prussia in the decades after 1815 faced a similar riddle. But it involved personnel rather than materiel.

The staggering successes of the French revolutionary armies make the decision by Europe's generals and politicians after 1815 to "reprofessionalize" their armed forces appear anomalous. The common explanation for Britain's continuing pattern of long-service enlistment and the use by France, Russia, and Austria of troops conscripted for periods from five to twenty-five years is political. Rulers ostensibly prized soldiers so recruited for their dynastic and regimental loyalties, their relative lack of susceptibility to radical ideas, and their willingness to shoot down adherents of those ideas when duly ordered.[5]

---

3 "Semi-hegemonial": Ludwig Dehio, *Deutschland und die Weltpolitik im 20. Jahrhundert* (Munich, 1955), p. 15.
4 See among others Jacob W. Kipp, "The Nature of Future Wars: Russian Military Forecasting and the Revolution in Military Affairs: A Case of the Oracle of Delphi or Cassandra?," *Journal of Slavic Military Studies* 9 (1996); the essays in Stephen J. Blank and Jacob W. Kipp, eds., *The Soviet Military and the Future* (Westport, CT, 1992); and Kimberly Martin Zisk, *Organization Theory and Soviet Military Integration, 1955–1991* (Princeton, NJ, 1993).
5 See for instance Geoffrey Best, *War and Society in Revolutionary Europe, 1770–1870* (New York, 1986), pp. 204–22.

That interpretation is only partially valid. The French military system that had called the tune for Europe from 1793 to 1815 had depended heavily on mass. It had also shown a disconcerting tendency to outgrow its nervous system. Even under the emperor's hand, the conscript masses of Borodino or Leipzig had proved significantly less effective than the relatively lean striking forces of Lodi, Marengo, and Austerlitz. In the post-Waterloo era, a wide range of military figures who included some of Napoleon's own marshals advocated a return to smaller forces susceptible to precise control: quality rather than quantity. The increasingly demanding tasks of nineteenth-century warfare on a battlefield ever more swept by fire demanded men who had served long enough to become thoroughly proficient.[6]

That was the pattern established in the armies of the great powers and defended by most contemporary military theorists. It was in that context that Prussia after 1815 found itself in the position of a short-money player in a table-stakes game. Even before Napoleon crushed the Frederician army at Jena and Auerstädt, Scharnhorst and Gneisenau had argued for fundamental changes in the relationship between army and society, an "alliance between government and people" that would allow Prussia to remain a great power. The reformers' initial aim of creating citizen-soldiers swiftly evolved into the notion that military service was the essence of citizenship itself. The years in uniform, whether in war or peace, became the defining element of a man's public identity.[7]

The resulting mass army depended heavily on popular enthusiasm; it passed the test of war in 1813-15. But the possessor of such a force risked inheriting Napoleonic France's position as an objective threat to European order. That position Prussia had neither the will nor the capacity to sustain. After 1815 Prussia was concerned instead with maintaining and aggrandizing itself within the stable continental and regional environment created by the Congress of Vienna and the German Confederation. Its national strategy in these years depended on what would now be called crisis management: modest initiatives employing a mixture of negotiation and compromise, underwritten by the credible threat of controlled force for limited objectives.[8]

---

[6] See Paddy Griffith, *Military Thought in the French Army, 1815–1850* (Manchester, 1989), and Gary Cox, *The Halt in the Mud: French Strategic Planning from Waterloo to Sedan* (Boulder, CO, 1994).

[7] On the central role of military service in the reform movement, see among others Heinz Stübig, *Armee und Nation: Die pädagogische–patriotische Motive der preussische Heeresreform 1807–1814* (Frankfurt, 1971), and Bernd von Münchow-Pohl, *Zwischen Reform und Krieg: Untersuchungen zur Bewusstseinslage in Preussen 1809–1812* (Göttingen, 1987).

[8] See generally Lawrence J. Baack, *Christian Bernstoff and Prussia, 1818–1832* (New Brunswick, NJ, 1980) and the case study of Jürgen Angelow, "Die 'belgische–luxemburgische Krise' von 1830–32 und der deutsche Bund: Zur geplanten Bundesintervention in Luxemburg," *Militärgeschichtliche Mitteilungen* 50 (1991), pp. 61–80.

Prussia's economy in any case could not support the kind of army that post-Napoleonic France developed: a force ready for war from a standing start, emphasizing quality, yet large enough to give its possessor great-power status. The Prussian army depended on men recalled from civilian life. It had divided the kingdom into military districts, each responsible for mobilizing a wartime army corps. In its final Biedermeyer form each corps consisted of two divisions, each division of two brigades, and each brigade of two regiments. But only one of the regiments was an active army formation, and its peacetime strength even on paper was little over half its wartime establishment. The *Landwehr*, a citizen militia improvised in 1813 and placed on an equal footing with line units by the army's fundamental law, the *Wehrgesetz* of 1814, provided the remaining regiment.[9]

That structure, similar to if more drastic than the U.S. Army's post-Vietnam "roundout" system, made it virtually impossible for Prussia to wage anything save general war. Even active regiments required large infusions of reservists in order to take the field. Far more significant for operational purposes, Prussia's military organization assumed, indeed required, the equal efficiency of the active and *Landwehr* formations: their missions were identical. But the natural increase in the population after 1815 combined with cuts in the military budget made impossible the financing of a full term of active service for every able-bodied man except at the expense of basic requirements such as barracks, uniforms, and weapons, and the reconstructed network of fortresses deemed vital to Prussia's security.[10] The army therefore ended up with a system analogous to the Selective Service machinery employed in the United States from Korea through Vietnam. The principle of universal military obligation enshrined in the *Wehrgesetz* remained a principle; in practice the army frequently reduced its three-year term of service, assigned more and more untrained conscripts to the *Landwehr*, and left an ever-larger segment of the male population untapped.

The resulting "*Landwehr* recruits" were often worse than useless. Post-1815 experience showed that the army's drillmasters could teach a mass of several hundred men the rudiments of company drill in a few weeks if they worked the recruits to exhaustion. The recruits might also receive some

9 The best overview is Manfred Messerschmidt, "Die politische Geschichte der preussisch-deutschen Armee," in *Handbuch der deutschen Militärgeschichte*, 9 vols. (Frankfurt a. M., Munich, 1964–81), vol. 4, part 2, pp. 59–84; see also Heinz Stübig, "Die Wehrverfassung Preussens in der Reformzeit: Wehrpflicht im Spannungsfeld von Restauration und Revolution, 1815–1860," in Roland G. Foerster, ed., *Die Wehrpflicht: Entstehung, Erscheinungsform und politisch-militärische Wirkung* (Munich, 1994).

10 That was the position of even the most deeply committed military reformers, such as Hermann von Boyen (war minister, 1814–19): Friedrich Meinecke, *Das Leben des Generalfeldmarschalls Hermann von Boyen*, 2 vols. (Stuttgart, 1895–99), vol. 2, pp. 223–4.

sense of group identity and of the meaning of military order. But they were destined to remain ignorant of skirmishing, fieldcraft, marksmanship, and the other essential skills that modern war and the Prussian drill regulations demanded.

The *Landwehr*'s creators had expected that popular enthusiasm would ensure participation in its drills and exercises. But in the long peace after Waterloo the *Landwehr* lost its novelty. Socially or martially ambitious young men no longer sought its commissions. No public eager to watch the show and buy drinks afterward for its brave defenders attended its drills. The civic zeal the reformers had postulated as the basis of the Prussian military system proved difficult to sustain within a political system that even in 1813–15 had never abandoned its deep suspicion of public enthusiasm.[11]

By the 1840s Prussia thus had the worst of both worlds. The state's international position called for a front-loaded army able to deter potential rivals and to undertake swift and decisive operations for clearly defined objectives, yet the institutional legacy of the reform movement was a ponderous blunt instrument ill-suited to policy wars of any sort. Moreover, the reliability and efficiency of that instrument were open to serious doubt.

The revolutions of 1848 and subsequent lesser crises evidenced sullen compliance rather than patriotic eagerness among the reservists and *Landwehr* men summoned to active duty. Discontent tended to be personal rather than principled. Family men in their thirties, forced to abandon farm, shop, or profession for a long-discarded uniform, were likely to feel anything but happy when cheered on their way to glory by bachelors ten years younger who had been omitted from the call-up list. Prussia's semi-willing warriors hardly seemed the raw material of glorious victory in future conflicts.[12]

One possible solution involved using technology as a force multiplier. The impact of industrialization frequently appalled Prussia's officer corps, which long remained suspicious of the social, political, and environmental consequences of the factory system and uncertain of the appropriate degree of state involvement in the process of economic development. The vitalist

[11] See Dennis E. Showalter, "The Prussian Landwehr and its Critics, 1813–1819," *Central European History* 4 (1971); Dorothea Schmidt, *Die preussische Landwehr: Ein Beitrag zur Geschichte der allgemeinen Wehrpflicht in Preussen zwischen 1813 and 1830* (Berlin, 1981); Alf Lüdtke, *Police and State in Prussia, 1813–1850* (Cambridge, 1989). Eckhard Trox, *Militärischer Konservatismus 1815 und 1848/1849* (Stuttgart, 1990) makes a convincing argument for a higher level of popular militarism than has been previously been assumed, but does not show how this translated into actual enthusiasm for wearing the uniform.

[12] See Walther Hubatsch, "Abrüstung und Heeresreform in Preussen von 1807–1861," in Heinrich Bodensieck, ed., *Preussen, Deutschland und der Westen: Auseinandersetzungen und Beziehungen seit 1789* (Göttingen, 1980).

heritage of the French Revolution and of the military reform movement – the emphasis on enthusiasm and willpower as the key to victory – also limited the army's eagerness to exploit new technologies.[13]

The artillery, a logical focus for innovation, improved by stages. The cast-steel breech-loading rifles that Alfred Krupp developed and the army adopted in 1859 represented an incremental rather than an exponential improvement. Early cast steel was not self-evidently superior to the traditional bronze. Nor, in an era of fixed gun carriages, did breech-loading offer a significant increase in artillery firepower. By the time a cannon was hauled back into firing position after recoil, a reasonably efficient gun crew could have it reloaded from either end. And like all continental armies in the 1850s, the Prussians were uncertain whether the definitive field gun of the future would be a long-ranged rifle or a large-caliber smoothbore best able to fire shell, shrapnel, and canister at short and medium ranges: the Napoleon of Civil War fame. Until after 1866 Prussian field batteries were armed with both types of gun in a fifty–fifty ratio.[14]

The Prussian RMA instead began with the rearmament of the infantry.[15] So many stories surround the breech-loading needle-gun that it has been long forgotten that the rifle was designed around its cartridge. The percussion caps that replaced flints in the first quarter of the nineteenth century had a nasty habit of spraying fulminate and metal fragments into the shooter's face when struck by the musket hammer. A German gunsmith, Johann Nikolaus von Dreyse, proposed instead to insert the explosive into the base of the bullet itself and detonate it with a firing pin long enough to drive through cartridge paper and gunpowder.

Dreyse originally used this early approximation of a safety cartridge in a muzzle-loading smoothbore that the Prussian army adopted in small numbers in 1833. These first needle-guns were dangerous to load: premature discharges were inevitable when ramming a paper cartridge onto a firing pin. Powder gases rapidly corroded the firing pin, and replacing a broken pin was difficult. The obvious answer was to develop a breech-loading mechanism. Sporting weapons had been employing such systems for years, but existing designs were too fragile or complex for military use.

What kept Dreyse going was connections. Regimental officers were interested in the potential of his design, and – above all – the Crown Prince, the

---

13 Eric Dorn Brose, *The Politics of Technological Change in Prussia: Out of the Shadow of Antiquity, 1809–1848* (Princeton, NJ, 1993).

14 Dennis E. Showalter, *Railroads and Rifles: Soldiers, Technology, and the Unification of Germany* (Hamden, CT, 1975), pp. 152–82.

15 The following account is based on ibid., pp. 77–90, and Rolf Wirtgen, *Das Zündnadelgewehr: Eine militärtechnische Revolution im 19. Jahrhundert* (Herford, 1991); Heinrich von Loebell's contemporary account, *Des Zündnadelgewehrs Geschichte und Konkurrenten* (Berlin, 1867), remains useful.

future King Frederick William IV, and his brother Prince William directly
supported Dreyse's efforts. Without that personal element and the institutional momentum that the adoption of a few hundred of Dreyse's original
muzzle-loaders had created, the needle-gun might well have been no more
than a footnote to military history like its American contemporary, the Hall
rifle. Instead, Dreyse was able by 1836 to offer a working model of a
breech-loader for consideration – a breech-loader with a rifled barrel.[16]

For four years the army tested the rifle for accuracy, reliability, and
durability under all possible conditions. One of the needle-gun's advocates
declared that with 60,000 men armed with this weapon, the king of Prussia
would be able to determine his frontiers unilaterally. The official testing
commission praised the rifle as a gift of providence and recommended that
it be kept secret until "a great historical moment."[17] The 60,000 needle-
guns ordered on 4 December 1840 were stored in arsenals until enough
were available for the whole army or until a major emergency – whichever
came first.

Dreyse's breech-loader combined a rate of fire higher than that of a
smoothbore musket with the accuracy of a rifle. Its user could reload and
fire lying down – no small advantage for skirmishers. Breech-loading also
eliminated the danger of ramming charges on top of one another in case of a
misfire, and soldiers no longer had to have a certain number of teeth in a
certain position to bite the cartridges. Yet doubts persisted. In the Prussian
army, rifles had been long-range, precision weapons used by an elite corps
of specialists: the *Jäger*. Over decades they had developed their own version
of what has been called a "gravel-belly" mentality.[18] The *Jäger* wanted a
rifle that could hit small targets at a thousand paces and more. Yet the
front-to-back combustion of the needle-gun's cartridge confined its effective
range to seven hundred paces at best. It also produced an irregular trajectory that lowered the range scores of even the best marksmen. For the rest
of the Prussian infantry, the extraordinary demands it placed on fire discipline were the primary stumbling-block to the needle-gun's acceptance.
Fear of introducing a weapon because it uses too much ammunition is an
easy target for ridicule. At the dawn of the twenty-first century, many
combat-arms officers have come to regard logistics as a religious experience: prayer into the radio causes supplies to appear from heaven! But
under mid-nineteenth-century conditions it was difficult if not impossible
to refill even cartridge boxes in battle. The needle-gun's ease of operation

---

16 For Dreyse's vivid account of one of the tests, see Sigurd Rabe, *Das Zündnadelgewehr
    greift an* (Leipzig, 1938), pp. 23–6.
17 Werner Eckardt and Otto Morawietz, *Die Handwaffen des brandenburgisch-
    preussisch–deutschen Heeres, 1640–1945* (Hamburg, 1957), pp. 104–05.
18 The phrase is a leitmotif of William Hallahan's *Misfire: The History of How America's
    Small Arms Have Failed our Military* (New York, 1994).

seemed to invite an automatic reflex of loading and pulling the trigger that could end in terrified flight when an empty cartridge box recalled the shooter to reality.

The revolutions of 1848 forced the army to move from theory to practice: the storming of the Berlin Arsenal on 15 June put a number of Prussia's carefully guarded secret weapons into rebel hands. The army then issued them to units assigned to counterinsurgency operations, and the needle-gun repeatedly proved its worth both in street fighting and the open field. Its virtues were moral as well as material: even inexperienced troops armed with the new rifle were firmly convinced of its superiority, and by extension of their own. In 1851 the government ordered that Dreyse's breech-loaders be used to fill all future requirements for infantry small arms.

The limited operations of 1848–49 highlighted the importance of training. Men carrying needle-guns did in fact tend to open fire at excessive ranges and fire off their ammunition almost randomly. The new rifle's firepower also highlighted a problem already of deep concern to the Prussian army: the conduct of the tactical offensive in the face of modern weapons such as the shell-firing cannon and the Minié rifles sighted to a thousand yards that Europe's armies began introducing in the 1850s.[19]

The resulting exponential expansion of killing zones and killing power, demonstrated in the Crimea in 1854 and northern Italy in 1859, jolted the Prussian army in a way essentially different from its counterparts. All available evidence indicated that Prussia's active regiments, to say nothing of the *Landwehr*, were probably incapable of sophisticated tactical movements, especially in the early stages of a war. Skirmishing against modern rifles might well prove wholly beyond the skills of reservists and especially of *Landwehr* troops. Avoiding long firefights and coming to close quarters with the enemy as rapidly as possible seemed the wave of the future or at least the most promising option.[20]

Yet the popular lack of enthusiasm for military service mentioned earlier was an unspoken argument against the practical prospects of headlong attacks. Prussians committed to such an operation were likely to be neither well-trained nor well-disciplined. They might indeed charge like hell out of temporary exaltation. But no one could predict the direction and duration of their movement or assume that many of them would live

19 See generally Georg Ortenburg, *Waffen und Waffengebrauch im Zeit der Einigungskriege* (Koblenz, 1990); Paddy Griffith, *Forward into Battle: Fighting Tactics from Waterloo to the Near Future* (Novato, CA, rev. ed., 1991), pp. 62–6; and the excellent overview in Hew Strachan, *European Armies and the Conduct of War* (London, 1983), pp. 111–24.
20 See among others "Das gezogene Gewehr als Hauptwaffe der Infanterie," *Allgemeine Militärische Zeitung* (1856), Nos. 25–32; and Prince Friedrich Charles, *Eine Militärische Denkschrift (über die Kampfweise der Franzosen)* (Frankfurt a. M., 1860).

long enough to run away. Nor could the Prussian army base its doctrine and training on defensive tactics. In principle it was clearly preferable to maneuver the enemy into attacking. But in practice, Prussia's infantry would in the end have to advance against modern firepower. The question was not whether it could advance, but how to do so without crippling losses, and how to convince the troops to attack for a second or third time.[21]

The Prussian army tested skirmish lines organized into small squads under the direct control of a noncommissioned officer. The 250-man company column increasingly replaced the massed battalion during field exercises. The army expected companies to make up in flexibility and firepower what they lacked in mass.[22] But all these innovations highlighted a structural problem. The army's trainers faced persistent difficulties in implementing the new methods. Fire discipline, unit cohesion, and battlefield control remained deficient. Through the 1850s critics – by no means all of them anonymous reactionaries – wondered whether breech-loading rifles might not be leading Prussia down a blind alley to military disaster.[23] The Prussian army's annual exercises, never a showpiece, became an embarrassing joke. A French observer declared one performance so bad as to compromise the whole profession of arms.[24]

Clearly the needle-gun by itself could not serve as the fulcrum of military revolution. A possible alternative involved developing innovations that offered strategic and operational opportunities rather than tactical ones. Railroads had made their first appearance in Prussia in the early 1830s. Their promoters, men like Friedrich Harkort and Ludolf Camphausen, had argued for the military potential of steam transportation. The army's initial reaction was more positive than often recognized.[25] But planners and com-

21 This dilemma is well expressed in the writings of Helmuth von Moltke, appointed chief of the Prussian general staff in 1857. See "Bemerkungen von 12. Juli 1858 über Veränderungen in der Taktik infolge der verbesserten Infanteriegewehrs," und "Bemerkungen vom 5. Januar 1860 zu einem Bericht des Oberstleutnant Ollech über die französische Armee," in his *Militärische Werke*, II. Abt., *Die Thaetigkeit als Chefs der Generalstabes der Armee im Frieden*, 3 vols. (Berlin, 1892–1906), pp. 7, 16–24.

22 See among others Franz Georg von Waldersee, *Die Methode zur kriegsgemässen Ausbildung der Infanterie und ihrer Führer im Felddienste* (Berlin, 1861); "Das System der Compagnie-Colonne als Grundlage der Elementärtaktik," *Allgemeine Militär-Zeitung* (1861), No. 5; and the army's green book," *Allerhöchsten verordnungen über den grossen Truppenübungen* (Berlin, 1861).

23 See for example Eduard Pönitz, "Zum Zündnadelgewehr," *Allgemeine Militär-Zeitung* (1856), Nos. 33–4; and Paul Sauer, "Das Württembergischen Heer in der Zeit des Deutschen Bundes," Dissertation, Freiburg University, 1956, pp. 260–1.

24 Quoted in Werner Bigge, *Feldmarschall Graf Moltke. Ein Militärisches Lebensbild*, 2 vols. (Munich, 1901), vol. 2, p. 106.

25 Brose, *The Politics of Technological Change in Prussia*, pp. 224–8, corrects Showalter, *Railroads and Rifles*, pp. 24–35, in this respect. James M. Brophy, *Capitalism, Politics, and Railroads in Prussia, 1830–1870* (Columbus, OH, 1998) offers a recent analysis stressing the multiple synergies between public and private initiative.

mentators nevertheless feared that railroads might facilitate enemy invasion, and warned against neglecting the construction of a paved highway network in favor of a new and untried innovation. The limited carrying capacity of early railroads also sharply restricted their ability to move troops and materiel except in token amounts. As late as 1836, a pamphlet accurately demonstrated that a full-strength Prussian corps on foot could cover in sixteen days a distance that would require twenty by rail.[26] Nor were railroads without potentially serious consequences for state policy. Hermann von Boyen, the reform era hero reappointed as war minister in 1841, believed firmly that the widespread use of railroads might make mobilization plans dangerously rigid and mechanical. The army could find itself wrongly concentrated and the state forced into war through railroad time-tables.[27]

Despite growing military pressure for nationalizing or subsidizing the railroads, or at least for requiring private companies to conform to military requirements in particular cases, commercial factors largely determined Prussia's routes and track systems. Even the *Ostbahn*, built after 1848 at government expense to cover the six hundred kilometers from Berlin to the Russian border, served economic and political rather than strategic purposes.[28] Nevertheless the growth of track mileage and the steady improvement of rails and rolling stock on the private lines significantly enhanced the military potential of the railroad. During the revolution of 1848 the railroads allowed the army to deploy swiftly mobile reaction forces of a few battalions to actual or potential trouble spots. In the spring of 1850 Moltke, then chief of staff of the Rhineland-based VIII Corps, used local railroads in field exercises. In May 1850, when steadily worsening relations with Austria led Prussia to order mobilization, the army recalled almost half a million men to the colors in the expectation that the railroads would move them to the frontier.

Prussia had intended a classic exercise in deterrence: a show of force that would convince Austria to modify its position rather than escalate. The result wavered between tragedy and farce. No significant plans for using the railroads existed. Loading and scheduling was haphazard, and frequently separated equipment and the units to which it belonged. Men, animals, and supplies piled up at loading centers and shuttled randomly from station to station. Food, water, and sanitary facilities were all lacking. Prussian chaos contrasted sharply with Austria's relatively troublefree movement of 25,000 men into Bohemia by rail within less than four

---

26 *Über die militärische Benutzung der Eisenbahnen* (Berlin, 1836).
27 Meinecke, *Boyen*, vol. 2, pp. 530-4.
28 See Brose, *The Politics of Technological Change in Prussia*, pp. 230–45, and Showalter, *Railroads and Rifles*, pp. 28–35.

weeks – an achievement long-forgotten but legitimately described as "the birth hour of modern military transportation."[29]

In the aftermath of the 1850 fiasco the Prussian general staff began to develop systems for the large-scale transport of men and supplies by rail. But the thrust of expert opinion still perceived the railroad as a defensive tool through which to reinforce threatened sectors and maintain communications between the fortresses deemed vital to Prussia's security. Railroads only became part of an RMA in 1857, when Helmuth von Moltke became chief of staff.

Along with an increasing number of his contemporaries, Moltke had drawn three conclusions about railroads. Their effective use for military purposes required detailed planning of a scope, and on a scale, unprecedented in Prussian history. The temptation to bring the largest forces to the largest railroad junctions posed logistical risks as well. The horse transport connecting railroad-fed supply dumps with the cartridge boxes, haversacks, and nosebags of units at the front limited the force that could be supplied by a single major road to 30,000 or so men. Nor did an army a hundred thousand strong really march: it inched across country, using every possible dirt track and cowpath to move the food and forage on which it depended. Finally – a point frequently overlooked by contemporary RMA enthusiasts – machinery made its own laws. Appeals to patriotism and threats of punishment alike were futile in the face of broken axles or hotboxes, and tracks leading to operationally undesirable destinations.[30]

These factors in combination made calculation and preparation the keys to the successful use of railroads in war. The Prussian army of the late 1850s was hardly capable of managing its mobilization and concentration through a Teutonic counterpart to France's national tradition of genial improvisation, the *"système D"*; Prussia needed every initial advantage that its best brains could secure. The general staff had existed in embryo even before the war of 1806. But no one had a clear idea of its functions or its authority. After Waterloo the army formalized its structure, but its spheres of influence and control remained limited. Mapmaking, war-gam-

[29] Julius von der Osten-Sacken, *Preussens Heer von seinen Anfängen bis zur Gegenwart*, 3 vols. (Berlin, 1911–13), vol. 2, pp. 320–1, 370–1, and Hermann Rahne, *Mobilmachung* (Berlin, 1983), pp. 16–18 summarize the resulting fiascos. On the Olmütz crisis, see Hans Julius Schoeps, *Von Olmütz nach Dresden 1850/1851: Ein Beitrag zur Geschichte der Reformen am Deutschen Bund* (Cologne, 1970) and Roy Austensen, "The Making of Austria's Prussian Policy, 1848–1852," *The Historical Journal* 27 (1984), pp. 861–76. Quotation: Joachim Niemeyer, *Das österreichische Militärwesen im Umbruch: Untersuchungen zum Kriegsbild zwischen 1830 und 1866* (Osnabrück, 1979), p. 162.

[30] See Michael Salewski, "Moltke, Schlieffen, und die Eisenbahn," in Roland G. Foerster, ed., *Generalfeldmarschall von Moltke: Bedeutung und Wirkung* (Munich, 1992), pp. 89–102, and Moltke's "1869 Instructions for Large Unit Commanders," in Daniel J. Hughes, ed., *Moltke on the Art of War* (Novato, CA, 1993), pp. 171–224.

ing, and historical research were the everyday stuff of general staff routine; the institution only developed into its modern form in response to railroad technology.

The general staff started down the technocratic road by reconfiguring one of its principal departments to deal with mobilization, and creating a railroad section. Planning thenceforth depended on machines. Mobilization orders went out by telegraph, reducing notification time from five days to one. Formations were to remain intact: each train would carry a battalion, squadron, or battery from initial loading point to final destination. Loading and unloading boxcars became part of the army's training schedule. As early as the summer of 1859, V Prussian Corps completed a practice mobilization in twenty-nine days – no small feat given its location in Posen, an eastern province that lacked a developed communications network. Prussian railroads passed their first major administrative test in 1864, against Denmark, when they successfully moved most of an expeditionary force to Schleswig-Holstein, supplied it there, and brought it home after victory.[31]

The challenges of 1866 were more complicated. Prussia fought the Seven Weeks' War in widely separated theaters, Bohemia and central Germany. Austria began its mobilization and concentration weeks before Prussia. French intervention was a significant possibility. But Prussia held the trump cards: five railroad lines leading to the main theater of war. Moltke and his subordinates used those lines to move the bulk of the army to Bohemia in less than a month and to supply three separate maneuver armies as they moved forward to concentrate on the battlefield at Königgrätz on 3 July.[32]

Events in 1870 followed a similar pattern. As late as 1867 the army of the new North German Confederation required over a month to concentrate in the West for a projected war with France. By 1870 a constantly updated movement plan had cut that time to twenty days. When implemented at the outbreak of war it functioned so smoothly that Albrecht von Roon, the minister of war, jovially complained he had too little to do! Swift and well-organized strategic concentration gave Prussia's forces a decisive initial edge over a French army that in its own way was at least as modern as its enemy.[33]

---

31 See Arden Bucholz, *Moltke, Schlieffen and Prussian War Planning* (New York, 1991), pp. 21–44; Showalter, *Railroads and Rifles*, pp. 42–51; and Rahne, *Mobilmachung*, pp. 24–45.
32 Dennis E. Showalter, "Mass Multiplied by Impulsion: The Influence of Railroads on Prussian Planning for the Seven Weeks' War," *Military Affairs* 38 (1974), pp. 62–6.
33 Rahne, *Mobilmachung*, pp. 51–66, and Wolfgang Petter, "Die Logistik des deutschen Heeres im deutsch-französischen Krieg von 1870–1871," in Militärgeschichtliches Forschungsamt, *Die Bedeutung der Logistik für die militärische Führung von der Antike bis in die Neuzeit* (Bonn, 1986), pp. 109–33.

The Prussian army's adaptation to the railroad is an example of what has become known as the "Boyd cycle" – the ability to analyze, decide, and act faster than an opponent.[34] Moltke succeeded twice in presenting Prussia's adversaries with innovations to which they could not adapt in time to prevent Prussia from setting the rules of the conflict. The Austrians had expected to win their wars on the battlefield, and had correspondingly limited strategic research and development. They had spent on fortresses money not wasted on pensions and sinecures for a bloated officer corps and an inefficient military administration. France had more rolling stock and more double-tracked lines than the North German Confederation. Its trains were faster and its loading facilities larger. Extensive government involvement in railroad construction had ensured a much higher degree of concern for strategic considerations than in Prussia. What was absent was a concept for the effective use of these advantages.

The French had been committed since the 1820s to making war from a standing start, and prefigured the German and Japanese armed forces of the Second World War in regarding logistics and administration as the concern of bureaucrats rather than warriors. France and Austria were the defining military powers of mid-century Europe, and their inability to anticipate or counter Prussia's unique approach to railroad warfare suggests the nature and magnitude of the Prussian RMA.[35]

THE PRUSSIAN SYNTHESIS: MOLTKE AND ROON

By 1860 the technological components of an RMA were clearly present in the Prussian army. The railroad could move troops and supplies exponentially faster and in exponentially greater mass than any land transportation system in human history. The breech-loading rapid-firing, medium-ranged needle-gun had far more in common with the modern assault rifle than with the smoothbores it replaced or the Miniés that were its contemporaries. But as yet these innovations remained within a traditional framework. Prussia's revolution in military affairs moved to its second stage only when Moltke began developing new strategic and operational concepts and Roon began changing the army's institutional structures in order to maximize the potential of the new hardware.

---

[34] "Observation, orientation, decision, action": see Barry D. Watts, *The Foundations of U.S. Air Doctrine: The Problem of Friction in War* (Maxwell Air Force Base, AL, 1984), pp. 114–15 and 127 note 45.

[35] See most recently Geoffrey Wawro, *The Austro-Prussian War; Austria's War with Prussia and Italy in 1866* (Cambridge, 1996), pp. 25–35; Thomas J. Adriance, *The Last Gaiter Button: A Study of the Mobilization and Concentration of the French Army in the War of 1870* (Westport, CT, 1987); and Richard Holmes, *The Road to Sedan: The French Army, 1866–1870* (London, 1984).

Two factors influenced Moltke's perspective on strategic planning. He recognized Prussia's need for short, decisive conflicts. That was hardly an original insight: it dated back at least to Frederick the Great. Carl von Clausewitz had argued as early as the 1820s that limited war was not a degenerate cousin of the Kantian ideal of "absolute war" illustrated in the wars of the Revolution and Empire. It was rather a valid form in its own right: violence that expressed rather than replaced diplomacy.

An approach to strategy focused on control and limitation was particularly congenial to a military system that since the first decade of the century had stressed the importance of education. After 1815 the Prussian War Academy had become the chief point of entry to high command. Between Waterloo and Königgrätz the war ministry and the general staff developed as organizations whose main purpose was the taming of Bellona: organizing the most efficient use of Prussia's limited resources for the greatest number of contingencies without destabilizing the society that the army existed to serve.

Moltke was convinced that the swift decision Prussia required was most likely in a war's early stages. It was best achieved by seizing the initiative and forcing opponents to react to Prussian moves. But the battlefield itself offered increasingly limited prospects for decision, particularly given the nature of the Prussian army. The flank attacks and encircling movements that Moltke perceived as the best counters to modern firepower were tactically demanding. Napoleon had repeatedly demonstrated the use of operational maneuver, but an army on the Prussian model was not likely to match the skills of Napoleon's veterans – or even of their French and Austrian contemporaries. Maneuver must therefore begin before the war started: envelopment was a strategic problem.

Railroads were decisive in the execution of this concept. Prussia lay without natural frontiers in the midst of powerful and potentially hostile neighbors: time was all-important. Railroads could buy time. They could counterbalance geography. They made possible a new approach to concentration by deploying forces simultaneously to widely separated areas outside the projected theater of operations, then moving them forward into enemy territory. Moltke's offensive approach owed as much to track layout as to strategic principle. Existing commercial lines were ill-suited to counter invasion: no enemy would be obliging enough to direct his advance against Prussia's major railroad junctions.

Moltke's planning blended neatly with the views of Otto von Bismarck, who became Prussia's prime minister in 1862. Historians have frequently and legitimately described Bismarck as Europe's last cabinet warrior. However willing to use the solvents of liberalism and nationalism, however extreme his rhetoric, Prussia's minister–president recognized that wars end with negotiation. He insisted on keeping that option always open. Less familiar, and less generally accepted, is Moltke's adherence to a similar principle. Moltke insisted that military considerations must determine the conduct of war, and clashed frequently and bitterly with Bismarck in 1866 and 1870–71. But he also held the firm belief that after victory, the soldier must yield to the statesman.[36]

Institutionalizing Prussia's RMA also involved matching soldiers to weapons and tactics. In 1858, before his appointment as war minister, Roon had presented a memorandum calling for a New Model Prussian Army that combined the traditional Prussian virtues: low cost and high fighting power. This apparent squaring of the circle involved converting most existing *Landwehr* formations into active army units and filling their ranks by increasing the numbers conscripted. The annual call-up would rise from 40,000 conscripts to somewhat over 60,000. This was still fewer than half the men theoretically available, but increasing the conscription rate from 26 to 40 percent would make the draft something less than the random process perceived by those subject to it. Roon set the term of service at three years in the active army beginning at age twenty, with four more as a reservist assigned to bring the line units to field strength upon mobilization. Only after completing those seven years would the troops, by then in their late twenties, pass into a *Landwehr* whose primary mission was to provide occupation and garrison units.

In 1859 the new soldier-king, Wilhelm I, gave Roon the chance to implement his recommendations. Supporters said that relieving the *Landwehr* of first-line operational missions it clearly could no longer perform did no more than place the burdens of war where they rightfully belonged: on those who were youngest, fittest, and least encumbered by civilian responsibilities. The army described the third year of active service as necessary to polish the marksmanship, fire discipline, and prompt response to changing conditions that were the essence of the modern soldier – particularly one carrying a breech-loading rifle and expected to fight in small formations and dispersed skirmish lines. Critics shrank from the cost, and also argued that the purpose of the third year of service was merely to indoctrinate the young with militarist and conservative principles. Advocates of the addi-

---

[36] See Dennis E. Showalter, "German Grand Strategy: A Contradiction in Terms?," *Militärgeschichtliche Mitteilungen* 48 (1990), pp. 65–102, and "The Retaming of Bellona: Prussia and the Institutionalization of the Napoleonic Legacy," *Military Affairs* 44 (1980), pp. 57–63; Michael Salewski, "Krieg und Frieden im Denken Bismarcks und Moltkes," in Foerster, ed., *Generalfeldmarschall von Moltke*, pp. 67–88. The standard general works remain Eberhard Kessel, *Moltke* (Stuttgart, 1957) and Rudolf Stadelmann, *Moltke und der Staat* (Krefeld, 1950). For Bismarck's approach to foreign policy in the 1860s, see above all Otto Pflanze, *Bismarck and the Development of Germany*, 3 vols. (Princeton, NJ, 1990), vol. 1. Eberhard Kolb, *Der Weg aus dem Krieg: Bismarcks Politik im Krieg und die Friedensahnbahnung 1870/71* (Munich, 1990) offers an excellent case study.

tional year agreed that two years were more than enough to inculcate the fundamentals of drill – Moltke himself said that task required less than two months. But for the army two years was a second-best solution, acceptable only as a final price for ending the struggle with parliament. Reduced training time would cost blood when the cannon next sounded, and Prussia's soldiers were not mercenaries. They were the sons of the state, and their lives were precious.[37]

Contemporaries and historians so universally dismissed that position as window-dressing for the underlying goal of inculcating "corpse-obedience" (*Kadavergehorsam*) in conscripts that it is worth emphasizing the relative absence of such an argument from the professional literature on Roon's proposed reforms. Negative evidence is always questionable, but it is reasonable to speculate on whether the possible social implications of the longer term of active service represented a kind of afterthought, a secondary consideration intended to appeal to conservative circles by no means universally pleased with reforms that included among their consequences an officer corps that would have to expand beyond the limits of the aristocracy's capacity to provide lieutenants – and to a king whose intransigence on the three-year issue had increased with time.[38]

As for the officer corps, the reformers argued that amateurs could no longer command on the modern battlefield. Particularly at company level, where most *Landwehr* officers were concentrated, skill in minor tactics, an eye for terrain, and the ability to act on one's own initiative were required complements to courage and enthusiasm. With the best will in the world, no one could acquire those qualities on weekends. They demanded full-time commitment and what later generations came to call professionalism.[39]

The intense debate over the proposal triggered the lengthy constitutional crisis that brought Bismarck to power, and has tended to obscure the fact that the Prussian parliament scarcely challenged the reforms themselves. The Jacobin notion of a necessary link between citizenship and military service influenced the Liberals of varying stripes who dominated the Prussian lower house. They also shared in a German nationalism that

---

[37] One of the more remarkable gaps in the historiography of modern Germany is a study of the Roon reforms from an institutional, rather than a political or ideological perspective. The best existing overviews are Messerschmidt, "Die politische Geschichte der preussisch-deutschen Armee," and Edgar Graf von Matuschka and Wolfgang Petter, "Organizationsgeschichte der Streitkräfte," in *Handbuch der deutschen Militärgeschichte*, vol. 4, part 2, pp. 177–83 and 319–22.

[38] See for example his statement of 7 January 1860 in *Militärische Schriften Kaiser Wilhelms des Grossen Majestät*, 2 vols. in 1 (Berlin, 1897), pp. 320–1.

[39] On this issue see generally Michael Geyer, "The Past as Future: The German Officer Corps as a Profession," in Geoffrey Cocks and Konrad H. Jarausch, eds., *German Professions, 1800–1950* (New York, 1990), pp. 183–212, and Steven E. Clemente, *For King and Kaiser: The Making of the German Officer Corps, 1860–1914* (Westport, CT, 1992).

had long singled out Prussia to play the decisive role in the unification of Germany, a mission for which it required a powerful army. The status of the *Landwehr* and the three-year term of active service, which dominated political debate and the newspapers, were mere stalking-horses. The ultimate issue was who was to be master: whether crown or parliament would control the force emerging from the reorganization that began in 1860 and continued even after parliament refused funding. The Liberals, confident that they would prevail, were correspondingly willing to give the soldiers room to knot the noose for their own eventual hanging.[40]

Roon's reforms neither triggered revolution in Prussia nor upset Europe's balance of power. The army's peacetime establishment increased by over 65,000 officers and men to a total of 211,000. Its war strength, however, grew more modestly, from 335,000 to 368,000 – hardly enough to trip alarms elsewhere on the continent. In fact the expansion initially seemed likely to make an unsatisfactory situation worse. In the maneuvers of 1861, for example, senior officers continued to employ mass formations in frontal attacks while conspicuously ignoring terrain features and maneuver tactics. Despite a "rocket" from no less a personage than the Crown Prince, the same officers were making the same mistakes two years later.[41]

But at regimental level the army was beginning to learn how to use its rifles and respond to enemy firepower. The expeditionary force sent to Schleswig-Holstein in 1864 departed in a cloud of rhetoric about bayonet charges and hand-to-hand combat. In practice, Prussian officers from commanding general Prince Frederick Charles downward observed the employment of shock tactics by their Austrian allies and concluded that they were a recipe for disaster – or at least for unacceptable casualties. The Prussians preferred to give the Danes a chance to come to them. And time and again the needle-gun, even in the hands of confused or disorganized troops, turned Danish charges into target practice.[42]

Tactical weaknesses remained. The combination of company columns and skirmish lines was difficult to control in the attack – so difficult that some officers continued to advocate battalion-sized close-order formations. The thrust of opinion within the army, however, accepted the argument that training and discipline could compensate for the dispersal that rifled weapons made necessary. The army had in fact little choice. Prussia's

---

40 Despite their limited focus, Rolf Helfert, *Der preussische Liberalismus und die Heeresreform von 1860* (Bonn, 1989) and "Die Taktik preussischer Liberaler von 1858 bis 1862," *Militärgeschichtliche Mitteilungen* 53 (1994), pp. 33–48, are the best recent analyses of these issues.

41 See "Die preussische Infanterie," *Allgemeine Militär-Zeitung* (1861), No. 46, and Friedrich Wilhelm III, *Tagebücher*, ed. H. O. Meissner (Leipzig, 1929), pp. 109–10, 214–15.

42 Showalter, *Railroads and Rifles*, pp. 113–16.

Liberals had by no means given up the struggle for control of the state. Instead they were waiting for Bismarck, Roon and Moltke to create the kind of disaster that would force the government to abandon its authoritarian stand or risk destruction. Prussia's military professionals had staked their position in Prussian society and their state's international position on their ability to develop a conscript army able to win a modern war without bleeding Prussia white.

The year 1866 was both test and turning point for the Second Era of Reform. Against an Austrian army committed to massed bayonet charges in close order, senior officers such as Frederick Charles suggested that officers dismount and troops lie down, meet the Austrians with five or six well-aimed volleys, then counterattack anything still standing.[43] From the first days of the decisive campaign in Bohemia these apparently simple suggestions paved the way to victory. At Podol on 26 June a single Prussian company fired 5,700 rounds, an average of twenty-two per man, in thirty-three minutes during an encounter battle that cost the Austrians 1,000 of the 3,000 men they sent into action. Prussian casualties amounted to 130. The next day at Nachod the Prussian V Corps engaged the Austrian VI Corps in another contest of "target against marksman." For a loss of less than 1,200 V Corps inflicted over 5,600 casualties, including many who surrendered rather than risk trying to withdraw under the Prussian rifles. On 28 June another Austrian corps lost 5,500 men in futile attacks against inferior Prussian forces around the village of Skalitz. And when Prussian infantry attacked or counterattacked, the poorly trained Austrians consistently fired too high or too slowly to stop the skirmish lines and company columns that came forward like clouds of hornets.

Ludwig von Benedek, commanding the Austrian Northern Army, was so shocked by casualties as high as 50 percent in some regiments that he issued an order forbidding infantry attacks without artillery preparation. Prussian riflery repeatedly turned back the vaunted Austrian columns with ease. Prussian troops took hundreds of prisoners shocked into incoherence by the hail of bullets from the needle-gun. Tales of victory spread from regiment to regiment. Morale soared.

The battle of Königgrätz on 3 July was the needle-gun's apogee. In the center a series of Austrian attacks into Prussian-occupied woods created a smoke-shrouded inferno with no flanks or rear, a contest of ramrods and bayonets against rifle bolts. Prussian units dissolved into groups of men commanded by anyone who set an example. But the conscripts, both active soldiers and reservists, trusted their officers and their rifles. From first to last, the Austrians committed forty-nine battalions to the fight in this sector.

---

43 "Einige Winke für die unter meine Befehle ins Feld rückenden Truppen," in Graf Gottlieb von Haeseler, *Zehn Jahre im Stabe des Prinzen Friedrich Karl: Erinnerungen*, 3 vols. (Berlin, 1910–15), III, pp. 22–32.

The needle-gun, in the hands of desperate men, destroyed or disorganized twenty-eight of them. Austrian officers managed to rally thirteen more, but the survivors were so badly shaken that they were virtually useless. A single Prussian division, twelve battalions strong, had done most of the damage.

The Austrians had focused their attention so firmly on their center that they failed to detect an even greater threat from the north until far too late. About 2:30 P.M. elements of the Prussian Second Army struck the Habsburg flank with an impetus little if at all inferior to that of Stonewall Jackson's corps at Chancellorsville. But mass was less important than surprise; Prussian companies took advantage of standing grain, broken ground, and smoke-thickened mist to mow the Austrians down in windrows. Prussian rifle fire rendered Austrian artillery positions untenable within minutes. Prussian companies did not bother to form square before opening fire to smash Austrian cavalry charges. The Austrians once more mounted counterattack after desperate counterattack. But the Prussians held their ground and worked their rifle bolts until the surviving Austrians finally abandoned the field.[44]

CULMINATION AND RESPONSE: 1870–71 AND BEYOND

In the immediate aftermath of Königgrätz, journalists and observers on both sides proclaimed the needle-gun as the key to Prussian victory. Ironically the Prussian army was quick to disagree – at least for public consumption. The victorious army of 1866 was at once a major symbol of Prussia's military virtues and a major integrating element of the new North German Confederation. A good way to reconcile to Prussian methods and discipline the territories annexed to Prussia after the war and the states of the new North German Confederation was to stress the worth of their populations as soldiers. The government's presentation of the victorious army of 1866 as the rightful heir to the "people's uprising" of 1813-15 against Napoleon, recruited from citizens in uniform doing their patriotic duty, eased the Prussian parliament's acceptance of Bismarck's offer to end the constitutional crisis.[45]

Prussia's men rather than their weapons thus received the credit for victory. Military considerations also influenced a post-1866 shift in focus away from hardware. Moltke's emphasis on concentrating in the face of the

---

[44] Showalter, *Railroads and Rifles*, pp. 125–39, and Wawro, *Austro-Prussian War*, pp. 124–273, are the most detailed modern accounts with a tactical focus. Quotation: Alfred von Schlieffen, "Cannae," *Gesammelten Schriften*, vol. 1 (Berlin, 1913), p. 101.

[45] Karl Georg Faber, "Realpolitik als Ideologie: Die Bedeutung des Jahres 1866 für das politische Denken in Deutschland," *Historische Zeitschrift* 203 (1966), pp. 1–45, remains a useful overview of the political and moral dilemmas confronting the Prussian Liberals in 1866.

enemy – "march divided, fight united" – required an army consisting of units that were essentially equal in quality. It was impossible to be certain beforehand which troops would face the greatest strain or play the decisive role; even Napoleon had not always used his Guard to best advantage. Moreover, the army of the post-1866 North German Confederation possessed a first-line war strength of over 550,000, plus another 400,000 garrison troops, reservists and *Landwehr*. Instead of the nine corps of the Prussian army of 1866, it had thirteen plus an independent division. That expansion was far larger than the original increase of 1860, and demanded a corresponding emphasis on common doctrine and training methods at all levels from general staff to rifle company.[46]

Above all, the window created by Prussia's most obvious technical advantage was beginning to close. Dreyse's rifle was twenty-five years old, its basic design a decade older. New developments on both sides of the Atlantic eclipsed it. French arsenals were beginning to produce the Chassepot, a paper-cartridge breech-loader more reliable and longer-ranged than its Prussian counterpart, and the American Civil War had given metallic cartridges an extended field test. Prussia had reaped the advantages of being first in the field. Now it suffered the inevitable consequence: obsolescence.[47] The needle-gun's decisive contribution to victory in 1866 was irrelevant to the future challenges facing the Prussian army; resting on past laurels had proved fatal in 1806. Prussia's next opponent would obviously hardly be as willing as the Austrians to present mass formations as targets for the breech-loader or to pit bayonet charges against rapid fire.

The campaign of 1866 had also clearly demonstrated the problem of maintaining control of skirmish lines and company columns. Prussian officers were fully aware of the high levels of straggling and shirking that accompanied their looser formations; only Austrian weaknesses in skirmishing and marksmanship had prevented them from taking full advantage. What would be the result against an enemy that regarded the rifle as something more than an inferior pike and was skilled in open-order combat – as were the French?

Between 1866 and 1870 both drill regulations and maneuver practice assumed the use of close-order formations in the attack. At the same time regimental officers put greater emphasis than ever on fire discipline, on controlling skirmish lines, and on indoctrinating men to push forward independently should they lose contact with their units. Terrain exercises absorbed more and more training time at the expense of close-order drill.

46 See the "Instructions for Large Unit Commanders," and Klaus-Dieter Kaiser, "Die Eingliederung der ehemals selbständigen norddeutschen Truppenkörper in die preussische armee in der Jahren nach 1866," Dissertation, University of Berlin, 1972.
47 See most recently Ortenberg, *Waffen und Waffengebrauch*, p. 61.

But proponents of columns and skirmishers, close formations and open order alike believed that morale, training, and discipline were more important than weapons. Prussian fighting spirit and Prussian tactical skill would carry the day even against breech-loaders. In Moltke's words, "superiority is no longer to be sought in the weapon, but in the hand that wields it."[48]

These tendencies reflected a fact indicated by the strength figures given earlier and often overlooked in accounts stressing Prussia's mid-century development of a mass army. Roon and Moltke were primarily concerned with quality, not numbers. Superior strength fell into the "nice to have" category. But in contrast to their successors in 1914, they had no intention of creating large numbers of second-line formations for field use. The North German Confederation expected to wage and win its wars with its active units.

The events of 1870–71 justified that assumption. The French army took the field with a tactical doctrine that almost exactly replicated Prussia's in 1866: meeting attacks with massed rapid fire, then counterattacking. Time and again in the war's early weeks Prussian commanders obliged, sending their men forward in head-down frontal assaults. At Wörth a single charge cost more men than the entire army had lost at Königgrätz. At St. Privat the Prussian Guard suffered 30 percent casualties in an advance in columns up an open hillside – the longest mile in the Guard's history. But Prussian officers learned swiftly. Mass and élan gave way to flexible formations supported with concentrated artillery fire. Prussian casualties dropped significantly. Soon one French field army had surrendered, another was hopelessly besieged, and Napoleon III's empire yielded to revolution – a dire portent for the loser of any future war, and the culmination of an RMA that had began over a third of a century earlier with an experimental musket cartridge.[49]

The Prussian revolution in military affairs proved short-lived. By the mid-1870s "railroads and rifles" were the heart of every major continental army. Prussia's rivals likewise imitated – without quite replicating – the general staff system. Universal short-term conscription became the dominant form of military service. That process was not mere imitation. It reflected the existence of a common European *Mentalität*, a common mindset generating similar approaches to common problems: in this case the challenge of maximizing military effectiveness under the new rules that Prussia had established. In the decades that stretched toward 1914, Europe's armies became increasingly symmetrical – recruited alike, trained alike, commanded alike. Innovations, whether in armament, doctrine, or

---

[48] Moltke, "Instructions for Large Unit Commanders," pp. 201–07.
[49] Kraft Karl zu Hohenlohe-Ingelfingen, *Letters on Infantry*, trans. N. L. Walford (London, 1889), and *Letters on Artillery*, trans. N. L. Walford (London, 1888), present the war's tactical aspects from a Prussian perspective.

organization, were incremental rather than fundamental. That pattern persisted through the First World War and into the 1930s. Not until May 1940 did asymmetrical forces again contend for the mastery of Europe. But for a brief period in the 1860s, Prussia changed the face of European war and the balance of power of a continent.

7

The battlefleet revolution, 1885–1914

HOLGER H. HERWIG

Midshipman John Arbuthnot Fisher first went to sea in 1863 on the ironclad HMS *Warrior*. The ship represented the highest state of the naval architect's art, had cost £265,000 (about 5 million gold marks), was 151 meters long, displaced 9,180 tons, and mounted forty 68-pounder guns. Its Penn trunk power plant developed 5,270 horsepower for a top speed of 14 knots. A 11.5-centimeter midsection armor belt protected 45 centimeters of teak hull. Two years later, across the North Sea, Midshipman Alfred Tirpitz began his career aboard the Prussian navy's first propeller-driven vessel, the protected frigate SMS *Arcona*. The *Arcona* had a 1,365-horsepower steam power plant, displaced 2,361 tons, was 71.8 meters long, and had a best speed of 14 knots. It mounted six 68-pounder and twenty 36-pounder guns; maximum firing range was 5,000 meters. The *Arcona*'s hull was made of sturdy oak, and the ship had cost 2.2 million gold marks.

In 1914–15, in his second term as First Sea Lord, Fisher supervised the entry into service of HMS *Queen Elizabeth*, laid down in 1912. It was 195 meters long, displaced 27,500 tons, and was the world's first oil-fired turbine-driven battleship. Belt armor had increased to a maximum of 33 centimeters; the 75,000-horsepower power plant provided a top speed of 24 knots; the main armament of eight 15-inch (38.1-centimeter) guns fired a broadside of 7,000 kilograms up to 25 kilometers; and the ship had cost £2.6 million (about 50 million gold marks) to build and arm. Across the North Sea, Tirpitz, in his capacity as State Secretary of the Reich Naval Office, had also begun construction in 1912 of a new class of battleship. The *Bayern* and its three successors displaced 28,061 tons, were 180 meters long, and cost 49 million gold marks each. SMS *Bayern*'s triple Parsons steam turbines produced 48,000 horsepower for a top speed of 22 knots, and its main armament of eight 38-centimeter

(15-inch) guns fired a broadside of 6,000 kilograms to a maximum range of 20.4 kilometers.[1] Both Fisher and Tirpitz thus experienced massive changes in naval technology during the course of their careers.

Those developments, when embodied in the mighty battle fleets that faced each other across the North Sea in 1914–18, constituted a genuine revolution in military affairs, an exponential increase in naval striking power that prefigured the RMA of three-dimensional naval combat with aircraft and submarines twenty years later. Yet the technological improvements that culminated in the first decade of the twentieth century in the Dreadnought battleship and battlecruiser were in their origins and initial conception not revolutionary at all: they were the product of a long process of gradual evolutionary change.

BUREAUCRACY AND CHANGE

Revolutionary change maximizes uncertainty and risk. Success is never guaranteed. New weapons demand new habits, new thinking, and new training. Enemy unpredictability, weather, friction, and the uncertainties inherent in battle are quite daunting enough without inviting further confusion through novelties of uncertain value. Military leaders therefore normally rely on precedent and experience. And bureaucracies by their nature and dynamics, which revolve around the creation and maintenance of routines, shun innovation even when their backs are to the wall.[2] Bureaucrats rarely get ahead by urging innovation on their superiors; they instead create committees to give new ideas decent burial. And flag officers do not like surprises.

It is therefore striking that naval innovation from the mid-nineteenth century onward largely emanated from within the seemingly hidebound bureaucracies of the Royal Navy, the Imperial German Navy, and the U.S. Navy. Britain emerged from the Napoleonic Wars supreme at sea. Timber and pitch, dockyards for shipbuilding and foundries for casting cannon, stores of sail and rope, and experienced manpower had long been abundant within Britain or its formal or informal empire. The technology of British sea power had changed little for over a century: the number of guns aboard warships roughly doubled from 1700 to 1815, but the basic formula – tiers of muzzle-loaders firing broadsides of solid shot, bar-shot, grape-shot, or canister – had not changed. Tactics had correspondingly changed little, although Nelson's supreme confidence in the

[1] Battleship data: Siegfried Breyer, *Schlachtschiffe und Schlachtkreuzer 1905–1970* (Munich, 1970), pp. 126, 161, 167, 277, 300.
[2] See William H. McNeill, "The Structure of Military–Technical Transformation," The Harmon Memorial Lectures in Military History Nr. 37 (United States Air Force Academy, 1994).

superiority of British ship-handling and speed of fire had introduced greater flexibility and scope for initiative than had once been customary. British success impelled the Lords of the Admiralty in 1828 "to discourage to the utmost of their ability the employment of steam vessels"; any such technological innovation was "calculated to strike a fatal blow at the naval supremacy of the Empire."[3]

Yet even their lordships were powerless to arrest the advent of steam, the first in a series of waves of innovation sometimes described as the first Industrial Revolution, that of textiles, steam, and iron.[4] Indeed the Royal Navy found such vessels ever more useful in carrying the flag – as well as round-shot and shrapnel – upriver to recalcitrant Asian empires from Rangoon to Shanghai and Beijing.[5] Steam came into its own at sea by the 1840s; the paddle-wheel SS *Sirius* made the first Atlantic crossing under sustained steam power in 1837. Paddle-wheels soon yielded to propellers, and oak or teak to iron hulls. By the 1850s 1,600-horsepower power plants such as that of the SS *Great Eastern* dwarfed the 320 horsepower of the *Sirius*. And by 1840, France and Britain had equipped their ships of the line with large-caliber guns firing explosive shells.

But this was no revolution. Even the great French warship of the 1860s, *La Gloire*, with its 11.5-centimeter iron armor, still carried sail and mounted its muzzle-loaders in tiers. No strategic, operational, or tactical innovations accompanied its introduction. Nor did the French follow their prototype with a battle fleet of *Gloire*-class warships. Britain, with far superior industrial plant and greater financial capacity, soon caught up with the French fleet technologically and surpassed it numerically.[6] For three decades, an ungainly assortment of sail–steam hybrids armed with muzzle-loaders polluted the sea lanes of the world, each ship or class incrementally faster, better-armed, more heavily armored, and longer in range than the last. Steam, iron hulls, and explosive shell produced only gradual change.

A second wave of innovation, corresponding to the second great nineteenth-century wave of industrial technologies – cheap steel, electricity, chemicals, and the internal combustion engine – arrived from the late 1880s onward. The resulting technological breakthroughs included but were not restricted to the replacement of compound by triple-expansion engines, of cylindrical by water-tube boilers, of compound by nickel–steel

3 Michael Lewis, *The History of the British Navy* (Baltimore, MD, 1957), p. 224.
4 For the concept of waves or clusters of innovations, and their timing in the nineteenth century, see especially David S. Landes' still unsurpassed *The Unbound Prometheus: Technological Change and Industrial Development in Western Europe from 1750 to the Present* (Cambridge, 1969).
5 See Daniel R. Headrick, *The Tools of Empire: Technology and European Imperialism in the Nineteenth Century* (New York, 1981), Chapters 1–2.
6 William H. McNeill, *The Pursuit of Power: Technology, Armed Force, and Society since A.D. 1000* (Chicago, 1982), p. 227.

armor, of black and brown powder by nitrated propellants and explosives, and of iron muzzle-loaders by steel breech-loading artillery. But the technology was not self-generating: its application to naval warfare depended on the coming to power in Britain and Germany of a group of technically-minded naval officers uncharacteristically willing to foment and hasten technological change. Men such as Fisher and Tirpitz appreciated that the giant steel, chemical, and electrical firms of the new industrial economy stood at their beck and call, ready to join with government to develop what William H. McNeill has termed a "command technology."

The new generation of naval leaders understood that their societies were ready to embrace new military technology, that large segments of the press saw the oceangoing iron monsters as symbols of national power, and that sailors and statesmen alike were only too willing to pour the national treasure into these undertakings. The first global "military–industrial complexes" – Krupp in Germany, Armstrong and Vickers in England, Schneider-Creusot and Canet in France, Bethlehem Steel and the New York Shipbuilding Company in the United States, and Putilov in Russia – soon rivaled the government arsenals on which navies had until then primarily relied. Rather than wait for industry to develop new technology, the world's navies began to design – and demand – the guns, power plants, optics, hydraulics, and electrical control systems they needed. And both Fisher and Tirpitz proved masters at priming journalists with disinformation and at mounting massive public campaigns to promote their respective fleets.

The great naval powers were nevertheless content to play a game of modest evolution, of technological tit for tat. A glance at any edition of *Jane's Fighting Ships* or Brassey's *The Naval Annual* up to 1914 reveals the basic escalatory pattern:[7] in warship displacement from the 10,500 tons for HMS *Centurion* in the 1880s to the 27,500 of the HMS *Queen Elizabeth* in 1912–13; in costs from the £620,000 for HMS *Centurion* to the £2.6 million for HMS *Queen Elizabeth*; and in firepower from four 12-inch guns to eight 15-inch guns. Top speeds likewise increased by seven or eight knots; power plants and ship length more than doubled; crew sizes almost doubled. And British expenditure on battleship construction increased by more than 1,000 percent, from £624,000 in 1888–89 to £7.2 million in 1912–13.

Yet throughout, change was incremental. Displacement crept up by no more than 2,000 tons for each successive generation of ships. In part, that slow pace resulted from the limits that existing docks, locks, and (in the German case) the depth of the Kaiser-Wilhelm Canal linking the Baltic to the North Sea imposed on displacement. The development of main arma-

---

[7] See for example *The Naval Annual 1913* (Portsmouth, 1913), pp. 216–20.

ment mirrored this same pattern: from 11-inch/28-centimeter and 12-inch/ 30.5-centimeter guns from the 1890s onward, to 13.5-inch/33-centimeter in 1910, to 15-inch/38-centimeter in 1913.

Rigid constraints dominated the designers who drove warship displacement, armor, gun caliber, speed, and range ever upward. Diminishing returns in all four areas ultimately limited further development. The modern battleship was a delicately balanced machine. Power plant, guns, armor, displacement, and bunkering capacity were intimately interrelated; major improvement in one characteristic immediately demanded sacrifice in one of the others. And the balance between the variables of performance and fighting power shifted from one warship type to another. In destroyers speed, maneuverability, and offensive power took precedence over protection and endurance; battleships reversed that relationship.

In the cycle of innovation that developed from the late 1880s onward, ever more powerful and ever-larger and heavier steam plants demanded ever-greater displacement. The increasing caliber of the guns of potential enemies necessitated ever-thicker belt armor, which prompted further increases in main armament caliber. The resulting guns were soon too ponderous to mount in tiers along the sides of warships. When mounted amidships, they needed a clear field of fire, which meant that masts and sails had to go. The arrival of the explosive shell forced navies to protect their great guns with armored turrets. These in turn had to be capable of revolving so as to bring them on target quickly, which required heavy hydraulic equipment and thus more steam power. To increase rates of fire, navies abandoned laying and firing guns individually in favor of broadside firing – which required electric ignition and Krupp and Armstrong breech-loading steel guns. And no sooner had naval engineers and treasuries accomplished these Herculean feats in a single prototype than likely adversaries began the process all over again with larger ships, thicker belt armor, bigger guns, heavier explosive shells of greater penetrating power, and greater speed.

Yet no tactical innovations accompanied these improvements. The Nelsonian notion of laying ships close to the enemy and smothering him with a "hail of fire" was still in vogue in 1900. Navies tested their bigger guns at six and even at ten kilometers, but tactical doctrine still assumed ranges no greater than 2,000 to 3,000 meters. Standard practice ranges in the Royal Navy remained at 1,500 meters or less. Roll, pitch, and yaw wreaked as much havoc with accuracy as in Nelson's day. Gigantic mêlées in which ships of the line fired ponderous eighty-ton muzzle-loaders at close range, even if no longer yardarm to yardarm, at relatively stationary adversaries remained the ideal. Nor had navies yet thought of creating new academies or recasting existing ones to train or retrain executive and engineer officers in the developing technologies.

By the last decade of the century fertile minds – which the great naval historian and theorist Sir Julian Corbett once maliciously termed the "unused organs of Naval officers" – were nevertheless hard at work.[8] Their aim was to revise radically the way fleets fought on the high seas. Fisher, then a swiftly rising captain, fired the opening broadside in 1884 by inspiring the journalist W. T. Stead to publish alarmist pieces in the *Pall Mall Gazette*. Fisher hoped the articles would arouse the nation from what both men saw as a complacent torpor that endangered British supremacy. The result was a period of unprecedented expansion and development. Government and Admiralty almost immediately raised naval appropriations by 50 percent, or £5.5 million. In May 1889 Lord George Hamilton, the First Lord, gained passage through the House of Commons of a Naval Defence Act that brought a further 400 percent (£21.5 million) increase. The Act commissioned some seventy ships, half to be built in private yards. And through it the nation for the first time defined its security in terms of a yardstick derived from the navies of its potential enemies, at that point France and Russia: the "two-power standard" of a fleet of battleships "equal to the naval strength of any two other countries." The First Lord also suggested that this massive increase in Royal Navy fighting power would discourage rivals from attempting to match Britain. Deterrence theory had arrived.

In 1893 Lord Spencer further refined the Act to achieve the production of squadrons of homogeneous types.[9] The Admiralty had been aware of the benefits of standardization since the 1870s, but in the 1890s it still restricted this to squadron rather than to fleet formations. Battleships constructed under the Act increased 10 percent in displacement and 20 percent in cost. In 1894 the First Lord was also instrumental in organizing popular enthusiasm, private arms makers and shipbuilding firms, and the steel industry to form a powerful extra-parliamentary lobby, the Navy League. British naval enthusiasts ungrudgingly accepted the assistance of a U.S. Navy officer, Captain Alfred Thayer Mahan, whose wildly popular if tedious *The Influence of Sea Power upon History* defined from 1890 onward the dogma of the battle fleet.

The subsequent upheaval that naval historians have come to call the "Dreadnought revolution" is most closely associated with "Jackie" Fisher, appointed in 1904 to the newly created post of First Sea Lord. Fisher was as renowned for his intelligence, wit, determination, and industry as he was for his deviousness, ruthlessness, and vengefulness. Above all,

---

[8] Donald M. Schurman, *Julian S. Corbett, 1854–1922: Historian of British Maritime Policy from Drake to Jellicoe* (London, 1981), p. 44.
[9] See Jon Tetsuro Sumida, *In Defence of Naval Supremacy: Finance, Technology, and British Naval Policy, 1889–1914* (Boston, MA, 1989), pp. 13ff.

he was a man of action; the revolution in naval affairs between 1904 and 1909 was the "Fisher revolution."

That upheaval was not, as often supposed, limited to the single technological triumph of the construction of HMS *Dreadnought* in 1905–06. Its revolutionary character lay in its overall systemic impact. It involved the radical reform of existing training institutions, officer recruitment, tactical doctrines, fleet dispositions, and strategic thinking, as well as the creation of new types of fighting ships. And Fisher supported it through a powerful self-sustaining feedback loop whereby economic interest groups favoring increased public expenditure facilitated the passage of ever-larger naval appropriations bills, which in turn permitted and demanded new technologies in steel metallurgy, electrical systems, optics, hydraulic machinery, turbines, fire control calculators, and industrial chemistry. Fisher's RMA shook the Royal Navy to its core and recast it in the form in which it fought and won the First World War.

Fisher's most spectacular "revolutionary activity" was indeed the HMS *Dreadnought*. Its keel plates were laid in October 1905, and it was launched in February 1906 after only 130 days on the slips. Sea trials took place in October, commissioning ceremonies in December 1906. Fisher combined numerous existing technologies in the *Dreadnought*. Charles Parsons' reaction steam turbines allowed a best speed of 21 knots – two better than any battleship building or afloat. Ten 12-inch guns arranged in five twin turrets – one fore, two aft, one each port and starboard – revolutionized gunnery, for they gave the *Dreadnought* the firepower of two pre-Dreadnoughts in broadside firing, and three when firing forward. And that fire was deadly at a distance. Whereas effective range in the age of sail was at best 650 meters, and remained through the 1890s normally limited to 1,500 meters, Japanese warships in the Tsushima Straits in 1905 had pounded their Russian counterparts with devastating fire at ranges of up to 12,000 meters. HMS *Dreadnought* could fire a broadside of almost 3,100 kilograms at an effective range of 4,600 to 6,500 meters, and at a maximum range of 19,000 meters, beyond the effective range of the Royal Navy's rangefinders. Fisher dubbed his creation an "Old Testament" weapon.[10]

The First Sea Lord quickly followed HMS *Dreadnought* with a "New Testament" all-big-gun cruiser, HMS *Invincible*. At 17,200 tons displacement, this armored cruiser – a type classified after 1912 as a battlecruiser – had a best speed of 25 knots and a main armament of eight 12-inch guns. It was designed to act as a fast wing reinforcing the battle fleet's van or rear, and to be capable of hunting down Germany's fastest armed merchant raiders. Recent scholarship has unearthed evidence that suggests that

10   Gun data: Breyer, *Schlachtschiffe*, p. 126.

Fisher actually saw the *Invincible* rather than the *Dreadnought* as the "capital ship" of the future – in other words, that he sought to engineer a battlecruiser rather than a battleship revolution.[11]

The revolution in armament meant the abandonment of both the hallowed Nelsonian "hail of fire" and also the more recent "horizontal fire" of the 1890s. Even before the *Dreadnought*, Captain Percy Scott had abolished the traditional open sights in favor of a telescopic sight that greatly reduced angular error in aiming. Scott's system of "continuous aim" enhanced the fleet's average percentage of hits in its annual Gunlayer's Test and Battle Practice from less than 50 percent to almost 80 percent by 1907. The system of "salvo firing" under centralized control – which in time gave rise to the term "fire control" – allowed much better monitoring of shell splashes and hence far greater accuracy. In the same 1907 battle practice, HMS *Dreadnought* scored twenty-five hits in forty rounds at a range of 7,400 meters. Even more dramatically, she threw 9,660 kilograms of shell in eight minutes – 75 percent more than any other battleship. Tactically, Fisher organized the new Dreadnoughts into squadrons of four ships of almost uniform characteristics that were designed to fight as subunits within the main battle fleet.

Nevertheless, the absence of a means of measuring the course and speed of hostile warships bedeviled naval gunners for some years to come. Arthur Pollen, a civilian, showed mathematically that range would change by nearly 830 meters during the sixty-second interval that it took a 6-inch projectile, aimed to hit its target at the starting range, to travel 9,200 meters. Pollen then experimented successfully with a mechanized system of fire control featuring a gyroscopically stabilized range-finder, an automatic true-course plotter, a calculator to compute ranges and bearings, and a system of automatic sight-setting.[12] But bureaucratic infighting within the navy, clique rivalries, and the parsimony of the Admiralty's accountants combined to delay adoption of Pollen's fire-control system until midway through the Great War. The Grand Fleet paid a heavy price for these errors at the Battle of Jutland in 1916.

At the strategic level, Fisher realized that the days of the "two-power standard" were over. Britain's rivals were Imperial Germany and the United States, not France and Russia. In consequence he adopted a policy "Napoleonic in its audacity and Cromwellian in its thoroughness,"[13] and

11 This argument was first and most stridently put forth by Sumida, *In Defence of Naval Supremacy*; for a recent restatement, see Nicholas A. Lambert, "Admiral Sir John Fisher and the Concept of Flotilla Defence, 1904–1909," *Journal of Military History* 59 (1995), pp. 639–60.
12 Sumida, *In Defence of Naval Supremacy*, pp. 46ff.
13 Arthur J. Marder, *From the Dreadnought to Scapa Flow: The Royal Navy in the Fisher Era, 1904–1919*, 5 vols. (London, 1961–70), vol. 1, p. 40.

in 1904–05 scrapped no fewer than 154 warships of which seventeen were battleships. But the First Sea Lord was not content merely to trim the Royal Navy's motley sampler of vessels, many of which existed merely to chauffeur diplomats to exotic overseas ports. He also revamped the fleet's geographical distribution and command structure, consolidating the independent squadrons in the Pacific, south Atlantic, north America, and West Indies into an Eastern Fleet based on Singapore and a 4th Cruiser Squadron serving as a strategic reserve. The Home Fleet, renamed Channel Fleet, increased from eight battleships to twelve and was based on Dover; five battleships withdrawn from China augmented it in 1905. Fisher renamed the Channel Fleet the Atlantic Fleet, and stationed it at Gibraltar, within four days' steaming of England, with a force of eight battleships of the latest class. It stood ready either to support the Channel Fleet or to bolster the Mediterranean Fleet stationed at Malta. Fisher established that the principal fleets would carry out combined exercises twice a year; a squadron of battlecruisers reinforced each.

As Fisher put it with his usual verve and eye for the central idea, "*We cannot have everything or be strong everywhere. It is futile to be strong in the subsidiary theatre of war and not overwhelmingly supreme in the decisive theatre.*" By 1905 he had concentrated three-quarters of the navy's battleship strength against Germany. Britain's fleets would now exercise where they were most likely to fight: in the words of Fisher's hero, Nelson, "*The battle ground should be the drill ground.*"[14] In 1912 Winston S. Churchill, as First Lord of the Admiralty, carried Fisher's fleet redeployment to its logical conclusion. He transferred the battleships based on Malta to Gibraltar, and shifted the Atlantic Fleet to the Home Fleet, where it became 3rd Battle Squadron; a subsequent understanding with the French helped safeguard Britain's Mediterranean interests.

Recent scholarship has added new dimensions to Fisher's strategic revolution. Nicholas A. Lambert has argued that Fisher sought to recast British naval force structure and strategy further by deemphasizing the traditional battle fleet in favor of two separate entities: a main fighting fleet of battlecruisers to protect Britain's imperial interests, and a "flotilla defence" centered on torpedo-boats and submarines to deter invasion by attacking enemy troop transports and their escorts in home waters.[15] But service traditions and ingrained orthodoxy, as will emerge, militated against the immediate implementation of any such radical departures from the Royal Navy's time-honored reliance on capital ships.

"Jackie" Fisher was sufficiently astute to appreciate that radical change demanded equally radical reforms of education and training: naval policy

---

14   Ibid., pp. 40–3 (emphasis in original).
15   Lambert, "Admiral Sir John Fisher and the Concept of Flotilla Defence."

was more than simply "ordnance on target." To an age in which budget cuts invariably strike hardest at education and training rather than hardware, Fisher's personnel reforms between 1903 and 1905 are instructive. The so-called "Selborne Scheme," named after the then First Lord of the Admiralty, William, second Earl of Selborne, was no less radical than Fisher's technical, tactical, and strategic reforms. Fisher decreed that all executive officers, engineer officers, and Royal Marine officers be educated and trained together. And at a time when cadet training costs of £1,000 restricted naval officer candidacy to the affluent, he lectured the nation that "we are drawing our Nelsons from too narrow a class."[16] At the suggestion of Sir Julian Corbett, Fisher agreed to build a new common training facility, the Britannia Royal Naval College, Dartmouth, and to provide cadets with a four-year general education equivalent to that provided in a public school. Instruction centered on mathematics, mechanics, heat, and electricity; the science and practice of engineering; French and English composition and literature; general and naval history; and geography, navigation, seamanship, and religious knowledge.

Fisher's most radical reform of the officer corps was his decree that engineers would no longer form a distinct and less prestigious officer career, but rather constitute a specialization alongside gunnery, torpedoes, and navigation. The admiral had followed closely the U.S. Navy reform of 1899 that had ended the division between "line" and engineer officers.[17] And he was painfully aware of mounting public pressure from professional journals and associations to grant due recognition to engineering occupations. Fisher was doubtless also concerned about a developing shortage of talent: as of 1900 the Royal Navy had only 961 of its authorized establishment of 1,497 engineer officers. He therefore moved with his customary zeal to erase the image of the engineer as a "lesser breed" in the eyes of the "sacred priesthood of Executive Naval Officers," and to accord engineers equivalent status as "military officers." But it was difficult overnight to erase decades of viewing engineers as "greasers" or "chauffeur admirals." According to one estimate, one midshipmen in twenty leaving Dartmouth volunteered for engineering.

The Imperial German Navy faced a similar shortage of engineers, but rejected any reform modeled on the U.S. Navy or Fisher–Selborne precedents. Engineer officers in Germany trained in an Engineer Officer School entirely distinct from the Navy School for executive officer candidates. They wore neither the officer's sash, nor the imperial crown on their sleeves, nor sleeve stripes, nor gala uniforms. They could aspire only to "irregular" membership of the officers' club (*Kasino*), and could neither visit nor

[16] Marder, *From the Dreadnought to Scapa Flow*, vol. 1, pp. 30–1.
[17] Ibid., p. 49.

exchange visiting cards with executive officers on land. They did not answer to military honor courts, for in theory they lacked honor commensurate with that of the executive officers. Their spouses were addressed as "women," those of executive officers as "ladies." Their shipboard mess was separate from that of the executive officers. And the most senior engineer officer was theoretically subordinate even to the lowest second lieutenant.

Admiral von Tirpitz as well as his contemporaries and successors viewed the engineer as a mere "technical adviser" who could at best aspire to control machinery. The executive officer, by contrast, was a "combatant" who commanded men and ships in the name of His Imperial Majesty. Tirpitz did his utmost to discourage engineers from attending Germany's superb Technical Universities, fearing that advanced formal education might lead to demands for social and even military equality. His lack of enthusiasm for what he described as a "hodge-podge" of officers on the American model endured beyond 1917, when Admiral Reinhard Scheer again ruled against "the complete merger of the two corps." Scheer remained adamant that *The power to command is the concern of the executive officer.* The logic of technology was powerless against the inherited mentality of the Prusso-German naval officer corps.[18]

Fisher made his revolution from four principal ingredients: the adaptation of existing technologies to produce a new class of battleship and battlecruiser; the reorganization of fleet stations and commands in the service of a new strategy; the reduction of antiquated warships and representative yachts; and the recasting of officer education and training at Dartmouth. His rational and appropriate use of existing technology and his reorganization of time-honored structures made this the first true naval revolution since the arrival of the line-of-battle ship in the seventeenth century.

The "Fisher revolution" also brought about the world's first classic arms race and highlighted the attendant costs. As Lambert has argued, governmental pressure on the Admiralty to produce substantial savings in the soaring naval estimates provided much of the impetus for the First Sea Lord's naval reforms.[19] The escalating pace of technological change meant that new capital ships became obsolete more quickly and thus demanded ever-greater financial outlay on research and development for new prototypes. The naval estimates placed the Treasury under severe pressure, given that the new Liberal government was also determined to push through a costly social reform program; the result in 1909 and after was a clash over taxation with a fiercely recalcitrant House of Lords.

18 Holger H. Herwig, *"Luxury" Fleet: The Imperial German Navy 1888–1918* (London, 1987), pp. 123–30 (emphasis in original).
19 Nicholas A. Lambert, "British Naval Policy, 1913–1914: Financial Limitation and Strategic Revolution," *Journal of Modern History* 67 (1995), pp. 595–626.

Germany felt the financial pressure even more than Britain. Tirpitz had to follow Fisher's *Dreadnought* leap. Army planners, the government, the Reichstag, and the federal states challenged the resulting massive increases in naval outlays at every turn. Tirpitz's first Dreadnoughts, the *Nassau* class, entailed increases in unit cost of fifteen to twenty million gold marks over the previous *Deutschland*-class battleships. The greatly increased size of these new monsters in turn dictated further expenditure to expand docks, locks, and canals; between 1907 and 1918 the Reich spent in this way some 244 million gold marks, including 115 million on the Kaiser-Wilhelm Canal alone. An attempt to cover part of the resulting deficits through a modest inheritance tax triggered a full-scale Conservative revolt against the government and the "ugly fleet" that helped provoke the replacement of Chancellor Prince Bernhard von Bülow by Theobald von Bethmann-Hollweg in 1909; Kaiser Wilhelm II bemoaned what he termed the "ghastly" financial "screw without end."[20] No fewer than three state secretaries of the Treasury (Hermann von Stengel, Reinhold Sydow, and Adolf Wermuth) resigned rather than accept responsibility for Germany's mounting debts.

REVOLUTION OR EVOLUTION?

Even this revolutionary activity, however impressive, should not lull us into believing that Fisher's "revolution" came overnight, that it was complete, or – above all – that it gave Britain a lasting unilateral advantage. As suggested earlier, a deeply entrenched orthodoxy within the Royal Navy sought to obstruct Fisher's program. A "Syndicate of Discontent" – in the First Sea Lord's acid description – under the leadership of Admiral Lord Charles Beresford, commander-in-chief of the Channel Fleet (1907–09), railed against what Beresford termed the "dangerous lunatic" Fisher. The Syndicate charged that the First Sea Lord's reforms – from the Selborne Scheme to the scrapping policy, from the fleet relocation to the revolutionary new battleship and battlecruiser designs – were retrograde and dangerous.[21] Beresford and Rear Admiral John Jellicoe, who later commanded the Grand Fleet at Jutland in 1916, rejected Fisher's claims that a "flotilla defence" could guard the nation against invasion. Submarines remained an untried weapon, and the torpedo-boat flotillas, if denied the protection of heavy armored ships, would be at the mercy of an invasion armada. Above all, they argued, at some future point the British battle fleet would have no choice but to venture out into the North

20 Herwig, *"Luxury" Fleet*, p. 89.
21 See Richard Hough, *Admiral of the Fleet: The Life of John Fisher* (London, 1969), p. 212.

Sea and to bring to action its most likely adversary, the German High Seas Fleet.[22]

Perhaps most significantly, Fisher had failed to alter radically the Royal Navy's institutional culture or planning machinery. As late as 1910 his successor as First Sea Lord, Admiral Sir Arthur Wilson, rejected armor-piercing shells in favor of traditional high-explosive shells, decreed that naval engagements take place only at moderate ranges of around 4,600 meters, and asserted that the seizure of Helgoland Island was the necessary prerequisite for close blockade of Germany's North Sea ports. Wilson also lacked any conception of squadron or flotilla tactics, opposed the creation of a naval staff, and soon revealed himself to be utterly divorced from strategic reality as well as unsympathetic to the British Army's pressing need for sea transport to France.[23] Finally, like the members of the "Syndicate," he disdained research into submarine technology: underwater craft were suitable only for coastal defense, and "under-hand, unfair, and damned unEnglish."[24] Technological change had obviously failed to cause any corresponding revolution in His Lordship's thinking.

From a wider perspective, the period before 1914 – despite the swiftness of technological change – was unlikely to produce asymmetrical RMAs that conferred enduring advantages. Technology leaked swiftly across borders; this was an era mercifully free of the obsessive military and industrial secrecy that accompanied and followed the Great War, and by 1900 many European and extra-European states had acquired the industrial capacity and expertise needed to construct modern weapons. It was indeed often most convenient and cheapest to make use of another country's research and development. Britain purchased Krupp patents for armor plate and fuses and the Holland patents of the American Electric Boat Company for its submarines. Germany used British-designed Schultz-Thornycroft boilers and Parsons turbines.[25] With the exception of Germany, which strove for utmost secrecy in naval design – in large measure because Tirpitz was usually intent on circumventing Reichstag supervision – industrial and technological secrecy was highly unusual. In 1913, to give but one example, the Admiralty forced Armstrong to hand over gun mounting drawings to Coventry Ordnance Works – which the latter promptly used in equipping warships under construction for foreign powers. Nor was Admiral Fisher beneath giving copies of Alfred Yarrow's tube-boiler designs to rival shipbuilders.

---

22 Lambert, "Admiral Sir John Fisher and the Concept of Flotilla Defence," pp. 658–9.
23 James Goldrick's evaluation in J. R. Hill, ed., *The Oxford Illustrated History of the Royal Navy* (Oxford and New York, 1995), pp. 290–1.
24 Cited in Marder, *Dreadnought to Scapa Flow*, vol. 1, p. 332.
25 See Hugh Lyon, "The Relations Between the Admiralty and Private Industry in the Development of Warships," in Bryan Ranft, ed., *Technical Change and British Naval Policy 1860–1939* (London, 1977), pp. 52–7.

Another factor that helped to inhibit revolutionary technological break-throughs was the central importance of mechanical reliability. Radical experiments or inventions inevitably generate uncertainty. If the price was potential unreliability, naval establishments were more than willing to forgo the extra knot of speed from the turbines or additional thousand yards in gun range that enthusiasts such as Fisher or Scott demanded. British power plant designers, for example, adopted safety margins that notably increased unit weight over the designs of their German counter-parts – in an age in which naval architects strove to reduce weight by all available means in order to increase speed. Yet as the naval historian Hugh Lyon has suggested, British conservatism had its rewards – most dramati-cally in April 1918, when a gear wheel disintegrated in the engine rooms of the German battlecruiser SMS *Moltke*, causing the warship to lose virtually all power.[26]

Finally, the inherent limits of the human imagination converged with mechanical constraints to inhibit revolutionary breakthroughs before 1914, as evidenced most strikingly in the difficult career of the submarine. Scholars investigating Germany's unrestricted submarine campaign during the First World War have suggested that the absolute priority that Tirpitz had given to the battle fleet served the Reich poorly. Had the Germans shown greater foresight, a host of "gray sharks" might ostensibly have starved Britain out – as Sir Arthur Conan Doyle had suggested eighteen months before the start of the war.[27] But in reality the submarine was not an effective weapons system before 1914; not coincidentally, Germany was the last major naval power to adopt it.

In 1906 Tirpitz authorized Krupp to build the first prototype, a kerosene-powered *Karp*-class boat designated *U-1*; fourteen further kerosene boats followed between 1908 and 1910 despite their many disadvantages. Dense white exhaust signaled the boat's whereabouts on the surface; its sub-merged range with charged batteries was a bare fifty nautical miles at five knots. The boats had no radio communications when surfaced, much less submerged. German U-boats began to acquire diesel engines and the gyro-compasses necessary for submerged navigation only in 1910; British "D" and "E" boats did not receive gyrocompasses until 1914. Tirpitz under-standably husbanded available funds for his battleships; he refused to create what he termed "a museum of experiments."[28]

Understandably in view of its limitations, no doctrinal rethinking accom-panied the submarine's early development. Prevailing German doctrine dic-tated deployment of the boats as short-legged floating batteries for North

26 Ibid., p. 59.
27 See Michael L. Hadley, *Count Not the Dead: The Popular Image of the German Submarine* (Montreal and Kingston, 1995), p. 14.
28 Herwig, *"Luxury" Fleet*, pp. 86–7.

Sea coastal defense along the line Jade Estuary–Helgoland–Lister Tief. An obscure lieutenant of the Submarine Inspectorate at Kiel, Ulrich-Eberhard Blum, was responsible – in May 1914 – for the only pre-war study foreshadowing the U-boats' future role as a *guerre de course* weapon against British merchant shipping. Blum's estimate that it would take 222 submarines to blockade the British Isles effectively was not wholly unrealistic.[29] But it held little appeal for Tirpitz, who had no sympathy for commerce raiding in any of its potential guises; in any case Germany had a mere two dozen operational submarines, of which most were obsolescent kerosene boats. Both the German navy and its rivals had to bridge an enormous chasm in both technology and tactics before the unreliable submersible torpedo-boats of 1914 could realize their potential. To have wagered the Imperial Navy's future on the U-boat would have been akin to replacing the army's artillery and infantry with canvas-covered Rumpler Taube and Fokker biplanes.

RESULTS

By August 1914, Fisher and his successors had created the world's mightiest fleet. What Churchill described as the "crown jewels" consisted of twenty-one Dreadnought battleships and four Dreadnought battlecruisers. They were the culmination of four technologies: high-velocity heavy ordnance; telescopic gyroscope-stabilized gunsights; face-hardened alloy steel armor; and steam-turbine propulsion. These capital ships, with their centralized fire control systems that permitted effective fighting ranges of nearly twenty miles, ruled the waves from 1914 to 1918. No other weapons system threatened to displace them: neither torpedo-boat destroyers on the surface nor U-boats and mines beneath. The fleet itself employed destroyers as an offensive–defensive screen, and submarines sank not a single first-line capital ship in the entire course of the war.

Fisher's RMA thus defined naval combat in 1914–18 – but the consequences were hardly so revolutionary that an observer from the days of Nelson would not have understood the war's culminating surface struggle, the Battle of Jutland in May–June 1916. The size of ships and shells, and the firing of opening salvoes at ten or twelve kilometers might initially have seemed novel. Nor would the extreme caution of both combatants, a consequence of the enormous cost of the ships and the magnitude of the strategic stakes, have aroused Nelson's admiration. But the basic plot – powerful battle fleets shelling each other until one turned and fled –

---

[29] See Philip K. Lundeberg, "The German Naval Critique of the U-Boat Campaign, 1915–1918," *Military Affairs* 27 (1963), pp. 106–07, and Karl Lautenschläger, "The Submarine in Naval Warfare, 1901–2001," *International Security* 11 (1986–87), pp. 246–7, 254.

was thoroughly traditional. Jutland took place within a 200- by 200-kilo-meter box, and in only two dimensions. Aircraft and submarines played only ancillary roles, and most often failed in their reconnaissance or attack missions due to foul weather, poor visibility, mechanical breakdown, or confusion compounded by rudimentary communications systems.

These new playthings nevertheless once again attracted Admiral Fisher's ever-fertile mind. In 1915 he had been content to demand still-larger surface warships (or super battlecruisers): a new *Incomparable* that would be 360 meters long, displace 40,000 tons, steam at 35 knots, and mount six 20-inch guns. But by the end of the war, the old warrior had recognized that the great surface capital ships were obsolescent. The modern aircraft carrier arrived in the summer of 1917 in the guise of the former battlecruiser HMS *Furious*, converted through the addition of an 86- by 21-meter forward flight deck, arrester cables, and up to ten Sopwith Pups stored below decks. Two further carriers, the *Argus* and *Eagle*, received completely flush decks with offset island superstructures, the form of the modern carrier.

In June 1918 HMS *Furious* conducted the first carrier-launched strike against a land target, the German airship base at Tondern. Carriers joined the Grand Fleet that summer, and but for the sudden end to the war, the first combined air–surface fleet assault might have occurred in 1918 or early 1919. Fisher was ecstatic: "All you want is the present side of the Air Force – that's the future navy."[30] But few Royal Navy officers understood the possibilities inherent in integrating the carrier with another existing technology – the torpedo aircraft. As late as 1919, the head of the Technical Branch of the Royal Navy's Air Arm complained bitterly: "The potential value of the weapon is universally recognized; the development, however, is almost universally neglected."[31] Not until Taranto in 1940 and Pearl Harbor in 1941 did carrier-based torpedo aircraft attain maturity as a weapons system.

Fisher, as revolutionary as ever in his thinking, was more and more enthralled with the possibility of taking naval warfare into a third dimen-sion – beneath the waves. Before resigning in 1915 from his second term as First Sea Lord over the Dardanelles fiasco, Fisher had ordered a new class of high-speed, steam-propelled submarines armed with a single 12-inch gun. And by the end of the war, he was seriously studying the plans of a young submarine enthusiast for a "submarine battlecruiser" that was to displace 30,000 tons, steam at 30 knots, and mount eight 18-inch or 20-inch guns. Submarines, in Fisher's eyes, *"are the coming Dreadnoughts."*[32] The pro-

---

30 Cited in Sumida, *In Defence of Naval Supremacy*, p. 211.
31 Cited in Christina J. M. Goulter, *A Forgotten Offensive: Royal Air Force Coastal Command's Anti-Shipping Campaign, 1940–1945* (London, 1995), p. 20.
32 Sumida, *In Defence of Naval Supremacy*, pp. 263, 318 (emphasis in original).

ject proved technically and tactically impractical; the lethal independence of
the submarine awaited the advent of nuclear power. And the concept of
combined combat in the air, on the surface, and beneath the surface
awaited a later day – and constituted a second twentieth-century naval
RMA. But the overall shape of future developments had not escaped
Fisher, now in his seventy-seventh year as the Great War ended.

CONCLUSIONS

Fisher's RMA suggests that the nightmare of the military planner – that a
radical technological breakthrough might give an adversary a sudden decisive edge in war – is less threatening than often supposed.[33] From the 1860s
to the 1920s, from HMS *Warrior* to HMS *Queen Elizabeth*, the external
appearance, propulsion plants, protection, armament, and fire control systems of warships changed dramatically. Throughout the period, new technologies produced fundamental changes in capabilities, if not always in
tactics, every decade or so. But no single spectacular technological breakthrough dominated a particular stage or radically altered warfare at sea.

Fisher's RMA came toward the end of the period – and did not result
from the sudden introduction of wholly new technology. The steam power
plants, breech-loading guns, steel-alloy armor, turbines, cordite, and mon-
strous long-barreled 15-inch guns that could loft a shell up to thirty-two
kilometers were evolutionary developments stretching back over two decades or more. What Fisher accomplished was to integrate or synthesize
these existing technologies with the radical changes in naval strategy, tactics, education, and training required to exploit them at last to the fullest.
The result was something wholly new. It was the *combination* of reforms
and technologies that produced Fisher's RMA – a fundamental change in
mission capabilities and strategy. In the process, Fisher and his allies in the
"Fish Pond" – as they had intended – forced all existing battle fleets to
follow the Royal Navy or lose all combat effectiveness.

Technology permitted this outcome but did not drive it: that was the task
of politics and strategy. The development of new technologies by industrial
combines and naval authorities in the 1880s and 1890s was not an independent cause of the revolution that produced the great Dreadnought fleets
of 1914. It was the naval pioneers such as Fisher and Tirpitz who first
defined the mission – the maintenance or the destruction of British naval
supremacy – that they wished to pursue, then identified the technologies
essential for its accomplishment, and only then commanded private or

---

33 I am indebted for much of this analysis to Karl Lautenschläger, "Technology and the
    Evolution of Naval Warfare," in Steven E. Miller and Stephen Van Evera, eds., *Naval
    Strategy and National Security* (Princeton, NJ, 1988), esp. pp. 173–4, 218–20.

government yards to implement their visions by evolving or adapting technologies to the task. No one foresaw the full potential of these changes in advance, and mechanical constraints and human attitudes often militated against the full and immediate exploitation of brilliant innovations such as Arthur Pollen's centralized firing system. But in the end the professional ambition and competitive élan of Fisher, Tirpitz, and their planners welded existing technologies into an instrument of startling mobility and lethality.

8

The First World War and the birth of modern warfare[1]

JONATHAN B. A. BAILEY

The military revolution of the Great War fused industrial warfare and ideology into a relentless and merciless whole that ultimately – in the war's second round in 1939–45 – clasped fighting fronts and civilian populations within a single circle of fire and terror. The technological side of that revolution, "the rational and appropriate application of technical means to both attack and defense" – as one of its German authors described it – culminated in 1917–18 in perhaps the most significant conceptual development in all the long history of war.[2]

That development was the birth of "modern style of warfare": the advent of *three-dimensional* conflict through artillery indirect fire as the foundation of planning at the tactical, operational, and strategic levels of war.[3] Three-dimensional conflict was so revolutionary that the tumultuous development of armor and air power in 1939–45 and the advent of the information age in the decades that followed amount to no more than complementary and incremental improvements upon the conceptual model laid down in 1917–18.

---

[1] For a longer version of this paper that develops in detail the post-1918 and contemporary implications of the developments described, see Jonathan Bailey, *The First World War and the Birth of the Modern Style of Warfare*, Strategic and Combat Studies Institute Occasional Paper No. 22, British Army Staff College Camberley, 1996.

[2] Steven Metz and James Kievit (*Strategy and the Revolution in Military Affairs: From Theory to Policy*, Strategic Studies Institute, U.S. Army War College [Carlisle Barracks, PA, 1995], p. v) define an RMA as a "discontinuous increase in military capability and effectiveness arising from simultaneous and mutually supportive change in technology, systems, operational methods and military organizations"; the authors also cite Andrew Krepinevich as adding that an RMA "fundamentally alters the character and conduct of conflict" (p. 3). Quotation: Colonel Max Bauer, *Der Grosse Krieg in Feld und Heimat: Erinnerungen und Betrachtungen* (Tübingen, 1921), p. 70.

[3] For the emergence over the twentieth century of artillery and firepower as the dominant factors in warfare, see Jonathan Bailey, *Field Artillery and Firepower* (Oxford, 1989).

Many technological and tactical components of this revolution antedated the First World War, but the shock of war acted as a catalyst for its indispensable conceptual ingredients. From the solution to pressing tactical problems after 1914 emerged the unforeseen possibility that new techniques of deep attack might create a wholly new style of operations. And as the means of prosecuting deep battle subsequently became ever more sophisticated and powerful, the logic of the modern style of warfare has encroached upon – and now dominates – the strategic level.

WAR IN THREE DIMENSIONS

The modern style of warfare as described here means large-scale high-intensity conflict – for while the style is relevant throughout conventional warfare, it is *la grande guerre* that reveals its true form most clearly. The style has the following ideal-type characteristics:

a. It covers extended theaters and is fully three-dimensional.
b. Time is of critical importance, in the sense of tempo – relative rate of activity – and simultaneity. Speed and combination of arms in time and space outpace and overload the decision-making capacity of the opponent.
c. Intelligence is the key to targeting and maneuver.
d. Available hardware can engage high-value targets accurately throughout the enemy's space, either separate from or synchronized with ground contact.
e. Commanders can calibrate the application of firepower to achieve specific types of effect.[4]
f. Command, control, and communications (C3) systems and styles of command that fuse the characteristics above can break the enemy's cohesion and will with catastrophic consequences.

Translated to battlefield planning, a simplified offensive battle might look like this:

a. Staffs gather information about enemy dispositions by aerial, electronic, acoustic, and optical means.
b. They transform this information into intelligence about enemy intentions and potential targets throughout the depth of the enemy's positions.

---

[4] The precise lethal or nonlethal effect required determines the level of firepower employed. Precision munitions can create effects similar to those of more numerous but less precise ones; massed fire may however create shock effects that precise fire cannot achieve.

c. Commanders and staff make a plan to achieve a rapid penetration or breakthrough by maneuver forces that will neutralize or destroy the enemy in their path and throughout the depth of the enemy battle-space.

d. Fire is synchronized with air operations and the maneuver scheme to achieve maximum synergies of effect. The fireplan creates shock and dislocation, presenting the enemy with so many problems at once that his C3 system is paralyzed. Targets struck include enemy headquarters, communications systems, artillery, logistics, bridges, and depots. Fire blinds enemy observers and destroys strongpoints and field defenses. It attacks enemy positions in depth, striking especially at enemy reserves before they can join the ground contact battle. It seals off the battlefield. It decimates those who flee. And it simultaneously provides close support to the advancing maneuver force.

e. Commanders can adjust weight of fire discriminatingly to neutralize or destroy as required, and can calibrate duration and intensity, using appropriate types of weapon, ammunition, and rates of fire, according to whether they desire shock effect or a steady erosion of enemy morale.

f. Ruses and deceptions, including if necessary a complete dummy fire-plan, accompany these measures.

g. High-level centralized planning characterizes these operations, but commanders seek to make planning responsive to the unexpected.

This generic model would be familiar to those versed in the Cold War-era doctrine of the NATO and Warsaw Pact armies. It resembles the Egyptian crossing of the Suez Canal in 1973 and was more recently evident in alliance Gulf War planning. It was also the blueprint for battle tested by the British Army at Cambrai in November 1917, and emerged in more complete form both in the German offensives of spring 1918 – the "*Kaiserschlacht*" – and in the Allied counteroffensives that summer and autumn.[5]

Many of the characteristics of the modern style of warfare listed above are not in themselves modern: commanders have always understood the importance of time, knowledge of the enemy, superior firepower, and the role of decisive maneuver. The tactic of penetration to induce shock and disintegration is as old as warfare. It was used by Alexander at Gaugamela in 331 B.C., Marlborough at Blenheim in 1704, and Napoleon at Austerlitz in 1805. But not until 1917–18 did technology permit and tactics demand that these characteristics be brought together in a novel three-dimensional

[5] The failure of operations such as those at Cambrai and the Suez Canal crossing to meet their authors' aspirations in the exploitation phase does not invalidate the model.

"modern" concept that was truly revolutionary. The key innovation was the creation of a new approach to combat founded on indirect fire. A variety of technological developments combined with startling tactical originality driven by strategic necessity made that outcome possible.

The model of 1917–18 seems scarcely dated eighty years later. But in 1914, a mere three years earlier, it would have been entirely unfamiliar. Warfare in 1914 was a linear affair, with prevailing doctrines emphasizing flank attack, envelopment, and annihilation. It centered on the contact battle of physical encounter: masses of infantry and cavalry maneuvering, supported by artillery firing directly, generally at short range, with guns deployed in the open. The few available aircraft could carry out reconnaissance, but artillery lacked any means of locating targets in depth, and only the relatively few howitzers in service were capable of engaging targets in dead ground. Adjustment of fire was primitive and generally estimated on the gun position itself. Communication between observers and guns relied on semaphore, megaphone, and small numbers of telephones. In the British field army, all artillery ammunition was shrapnel, ineffective against well-dug-in troops. Means of supplying large quantities of artillery ammunition to maneuver forces in the field were lacking; partly in recognition of that fact, the army had little ammunition in stock. Finally, artillery planning at the operational level, except in siege warfare, did not exist – nor did the British Expeditionary Force (BEF) sent to France have artillery above divisional level. Operations were so straightforward that artillery planning staffs had remained small; given the purely tactical role envisaged for artillery, centralized high-level command would have been ineffective and unresponsive to the needs of the moment.

1914: THE TOOLS AT HAND

Many of the components of the indirect-fire revolution were far from new. The importance of being able to engage unseen targets was clear even in antiquity. The purpose of the trebuchet was to lob projectiles at defenders hiding behind walls; its successor was the mortar. Indirect fire had thus been common for centuries in siege warfare, but observers had generally not been able to adjust the fall of shot, and precision had been relatively unimportant.

The earliest battlefield use of indirect fire was probably at Paltsig in July 1759: the Russian artillery fired over the tops of trees.[6] By 1840 the British had given the howitzer the task of firing from cover at enemy artillery, but aiming was literally a matter of hit or miss, without calculation. Primitive

---

[6] Quoted by Christopher Bellamy, *Red God of War: Soviet Artillery and Rocket Forces* (London, 1986), p. 16.

indirect-fire systems relied upon a line of markers from the gun to a point
from which the target could be observed; that made them relatively immobile and therefore largely useless in any tactically fluid situation.

The Germans drew from the Franco-Prussian War the lesson that the use
of indirect fire could protect gunners from machine guns. Then a Russian,
Karl Guk, published in 1882 a seminal work on "Indirect Fire for Field
Artillery" that described all the essentials of aiming points, crest clearance,
and corrections to fire by an observer. The Germans took note of these
developments, and produced a device to facilitate indirect fire called the
Richtfläche. By 1904 Russian artillery was equipped with an indirect-fire
sight, and used it on a large scale at Liao-Yang in August. Thereafter
indirect fire became the norm in that war.[7] The U.S. Army immediately
noted this development and embodied it in its artillery "Drill Regulation"
of 1907.[8]

The British had experimented with indirect fire during the Boer War and
concluded that it was impractical in mobile warfare. It therefore remained a
neglected art, and the Royal Field Artillery lacked an effective indirect-fire
sight until 1913. In siege warfare, and with garrison and coastal artillery,
the problems of accurate survey were less severe; it was these branches, far
removed from the battlefield, that made most progress.

Yet despite the existence of many of the components that ultimately
merged to create the indirect-fire revolution, armies failed – or chose
not – to realize their potential. No apparent tactical necessity existed. All
armies in 1914 planned to conduct swift-moving operations that might
leave the artillery behind. The French army, with its admirable "75,"
emphasized the need for guns to deploy rapidly and swiftly deliver a high
volume of fire in support of the maneuver arms. But its doctrine of high
tempo and élan accepted that infantry might have to attack before the
artillery had deployed.

Nor did any apparent operational necessity for indirect fire exist – the very
concept of employing field artillery at the operational level to break through
enemy lines lay in the future. The sole exception to that generalization was
the attack on fortifications, such as those at Liège, that stood in the way of
maneuver. Their reduction in August 1914 required a complicated and highly
secret deployment of super-heavy German and Austrian siege guns.

In general, the armies of Europe failed to field appropriate guns and
ammunition. Because direct fire was the norm, their guns had relatively

---

7 Even so it was a primitive business. For example, at Cairn Hill the Russians could only
   send corrections to fire by written message passed from hand to hand down a chain of
   men lying flat on the ground (Denis and Peggy Warner, *The Tide at Sunrise: A History
   of the Russo-Japanese War, 1904–1905* [London, 1975], p. 363).
8 Boyd L. Dastrup, *Kings of Battle. A Branch History of the U.S. Army's Field Artillery*,
   Office of the Command Historian, U.S. Army Training and Doctrine Command, Fort
   Monroe, VA, 1993, pp. 149–50.

short ranges and were not designed to implement an indirect-fire concept. Longer-range guns would have been heavier, even less mobile, and thus still less appropriate to the prevailing direct-fire concept. That concept was notably persistent: in 1917, despite the evidence of three years of war, the U.S. Army still believed in light guns for mobile operations, and fielded one 3-inch gun for every piece of a heavier caliber.[9]

Because the primary role of artillery was not counterbattery fire and because artillerymen envisaged most counterbattery fire as a direct fire mission, howitzers were relatively few in number. Armies, particularly the German, did field indirect-firing pieces in 1914, but in relatively small numbers, and their purpose was to fire at high angles from cover at concealed enemy guns. Ironically, the Russian artillery, which had done so much to pioneer indirect fire, deployed mainly short-range direct-firing guns while the Germans deployed more heavy howitzers on the Eastern Front.

In addition, the combatants had in general designed their artillery ammunition for use against troops in the open. In the case of the British, the field army had neither high-explosive shells to destroy field defenses, shelters, and obstacles, nor gas shells – first employed by the Germans in 1915 – to neutralize positions. The point-detonating fuse, a major factor in the efficacy of high explosive, was not yet available, nor did ammunition stocks permit implementation of the sort of fireplan so familiar three years later. Pre-war doctrine had not envisaged the shortages that soon occurred. The British war establishment of 1913 allotted 1,000 rounds to each 18-pounder, with 300 in the UK and a further 500 to be provided from factories within six months. The batteries held only 176 of the 1,000 rounds – enough to sustain firing for a mere forty-four minutes at Rate 4.[10] Six such periods would consume the BEF's entire ammunition supply, although seventy-five minutes' worth remained in the UK and another sixty minutes' worth would theoretically become available within six months.[11] By comparison, by 1918 commanders on both sides expected to fire about 600 rounds per day from each light gun at the outset of an offensive.

While many of the means of applying indirect fire existed in some form, armies in 1914 regarded the technique as a method of tactical protection rather than as an improved form of attack, and accuracy remained problematic. Means of locating targets in depth and of predicting fire were equally lacking, given existing deficiencies in reconnaissance, mapping, survey, calibration,[12] ballistic calculation, and corrections to fire, as well as the neces-

---

[9] Dastrup, *Kings of Battle*, p. 164.
[10] Four rounds per minute.
[11] French guns had similar quantities of ammunition available and German guns rather less.
[12] The measurement of barrel wear to permit the adjustment of firing data to compensate for reduced muzzle velocity.

sary communications. But the issue was not merely technical. The primary reason for failure to exploit indirect fire, given that so many of the means were available or within reach, was lack of imagination, doctrinal laziness, and sheer miscalculation. As early as 1890 Moltke had expressed concern at the likelihood of a long war. In 1900 the Polish financier Jan Bloch had foreseen that the overwhelming lethality of defensive firepower would slaughter attacking infantry. Lord Kitchener had predicted that the Great War would last for years. But those steeped in the conservative military cultures of the day simply dismissed their views because the conclusions and consequences that flowed from them were unacceptable.[13]

The Russian army held its artillery – the pioneers of indirect fire – in the highest social and professional esteem. But even the Russian service harbored a deep suspicion of technical ability, and Russian officers consequently often failed to make the most of their assets. During the Russo-Japanese War a Russian general, upon seeing a battery take up position behind cover, ordered it out into the open because he refused to believe that it could engage an enemy that it could not see. And some Japanese officers believed that concealing guns in dead ground amounted to cowardice.

In the British Army, the élan of horse artillery summed up the ethos of the gunner; survey, calculation, and static operations were the unspeakable diet of garrison and coastal artillery. The use of maps by artillery officers to fix targets was considered to be ungentlemanly, for it devalued the time-honored skill of estimating range by eye. The service apparently resisted the introduction of high-explosive ammunition partly because of rumors that it gave off noxious fumes – which would not have been a proper way to wage war. The logistical complications that would result and the lack of perceived need for high explosive was probably decisive. In May 1914, Captain Hill of the Royal Garrison Artillery addressed the Royal Artillery Institute on the subject of indirect fire. His audience greeted with hoots of laughter his assertion that within two months of the outbreak of war, field artillery would be making corrections for meteorological variations.

The French, Germans, and Americans were no better. Artillery did not enjoy wide esteem in the German army: the most influential German originator of the modern style of warfare, Georg Bruchmüller, was on temporary active duty throughout. He ultimately received the *Pour le Mérite* for his contributions to a series of striking German successes, but never received promotion above colonel and retired on a lieutenant colonel's pay. Despite the emphasis on indirect fire in the U.S. Army's 1907 manual,

---

13 Colin McInnes has explained that it was the clear understanding by military establishments that a long war would cause massive social upheaval that made them reject the possibility of such a war (McInnes, *Men, Machines and the Emergence of Modern Warfare 1914–1945*, Strategic and Combat Studies Institute Occasional Paper No. 2, British Army Staff College Camberley, 1992, pp. 3–5).

Lieutenant Colonel E. McGlachin noted as late as 1916 that some of the most experienced graduates of the army's School of Fire could not conduct indirect-fire missions.[14] The U.S. Army had the equipment and theory to apply indirect fire, but lacked the qualified personnel and presumably therefore also the will.

1914: THE PROBLEM ASSESSED

In the battles of summer 1914, artillery normally deployed in the open, rapidly expended its ammunition, and perished. At Le Cateau, the artillery of 5th Division deployed within 500 meters of the infantry it supported; enemy fire swept it away. The same fate befell the Germans in numerous battles such as that at Bertrix. Machine guns and rapid rifle fire spoke for the defense, and brought maneuver to a grinding halt. Artillery firepower was as yet inadequate to open the road for the offensive. It soon became clear that the problem required an entirely new approach that would attack the problem from first principles. The solution, albeit initially an imperfect one, took four years to evolve – and in essence is still with us today.

The tactical problem was clear. The attacker needed to breach or flatten obstacles, destroy or neutralize as many as possible of the troops that manned them, conduct counterbattery fire to protect his own attacking infantry, and fire at unseen targets in the enemy depth in order to protect troops exploiting success before their accompanying artillery could come forward. In 1914–15 artillery could do none of these adequately, and in most cases could not do them at all; gunners merely sought to survive. As early as 30 October 1914, British artillery received instructions to use reverse slopes against the threat from observers for the German 5.9-inch howitzer – but implementing that order was frequently impossible. Only the 60-pounder could outrange the "5.9," but the former's trajectory was so flat that it was often unable to hit back.

In the battles of 1915 – Neuve Chapelle, Festubert, and Loos – British planners came to understand the new fundamentals of firepower and battlefield geometry by trial and error. At Neuve Chapelle, 10–12 March 1915, the British Army deployed 354 pieces against 60 German on a sector 1,200 meters wide, a density not matched until 1917. Yet they could only fire 200–400 rounds per gun, and targeting was defective although aerial photography was available for the first time. At Festubert on 15 May 1915, a fireplan lasting forty-eight hours rather than the thirty-five minutes of Neuve Chapelle preceded the attack. But the destructive effect was still inadequate and the length of the bombardment precluded surprise. At Loos – 15 September 1915 – the attack sector was eight times wider and

---

[14] Dastrup, *Kings of Battle*, pp. 154, 160.

the density of guns only one-fifth that at Neuve Chapelle. To achieve the weight of fire required, the guns had to fire for a longer period, once again compromising surprise.

The principal issues remained unresolved. Was it necessary to physically destroy enemy obstacles and trenches, or rather to neutralize the men defending them? How much fire for how long would achieve the desired results? Did some universal mathematical formula govern the amount of fire required? And if so, was this formula best expressed in terms of guns per yard of front, or of rounds delivered on a given front over a given period? Of what caliber should those guns be? Was the potential rate of fire of the appropriate calibers the key, or was it rather the availability of ammunition per day? If the artillery could achieve an adequately high rate of fire over the critical period, did it matter that it could not sustain that rate? How long should fire be applied before the maneuver phase began? How long should a battle last – five days or five months?

These perplexities were not merely tactical. Battlefield success without an operational dimension produced mere attrition. The operational conundrum for both sides was how to achieve both break-in *and* break-out. The Germans rendered vain Allied tactical successes, such as they were, by constructing and withdrawing to ever-deeper and more formidable fortified zones within which their defense was ever more "elastic" – culminating in the Hindenburg Line. They sited their main lines of resistance in such depth – and often on reverse slopes – that the enemy infantry reached them after leaving its largely static artillery support behind, and faced decimation by massive defensive fire and counterattack. A "rule of thumb" developed that reserves should be held nine kilometers to the rear and be capable of counterattacking within two hours from the start of an attack. The range of artillery thus determined the shape of the battlefield.[15] Locating and engaging targets in depth and moving the guns accompanying the infantry rapidly forward became of central operational importance.

THE BIRTH OF MODERN WARFARE, 1916–18

Brutal necessity thus forced armies to address the tactical and operational problems of 1914. The solution emerged through a series of landmark battles: the Brusilov Offensive of 1916, the British Army's battles on the Somme that same year, the Cambrai attack of November 1917, the German offensives of spring 1918, and the British offensives that followed.

15   Foch summed up French doctrine: "Battle consists of a repetition of operations in which, first, one attacks a position with all the necessary artillery, then one throws enough infantry forward to take that position while the artillery progresses to the following position" (quoted in Hubert C. Johnson, *Breakthrough! Tactics, Technology and the Search for Victory on the Western Front in World War I* [Novato, CA, 1994]).

The German offensive at Gorlice-Tarnow in 1915 and the Russian attack devised by Brusilov in summer 1916 already included modern elements. In both cases the commanders placed great emphasis on coordinating artillery fire with the movement of other arms and on concentrating fire on carefully selected and reconnoitered targets. The artillery commander of Russian 9th Army was Lieutenant Colonel V. F. Kirey, whose books on the subject the Red Army republished in 1926 and 1936 as standard works. He stressed that planning should begin with and be based on the number of guns and shells available. The frontage and selection of a narrow breakthrough sector followed. In the case of Russian 9th Army, the front extended over fourteen kilometers and the breakthrough sector was 3.5 kilometers wide. Kirey's principal concern was not so much achieving breakthrough as maintaining the momentum of the attack through deep penetration and continuing fire support. Kirey achieved this by sheltering heavy guns in bunkers close to the front to provide "reach" later in the battle, and by providing light mountain guns to accompany the assaulting troops – a task carried out by self-propelled guns in the Second World War and thereafter. Kirey also kept the preliminary bombardment short in order to preserve surprise and reduce the time available to the enemy to deploy reserves. Ammunition shortages and the worn condition of the Russian guns also dictated brevity.

Indirect fire played a major part. In 1916, the Russians conducted their first registration point shoot: the adjustment of fire onto one target to identify inaccuracy, then switching to another while applying the known correction to achieve accuracy and surprise. They remained weak, however, at taking indirect fire a crucial stage further to achieve accurate prediction, for although they had good maps they seemed to lack the means to calculate data from them or to use aerial photography. As a result, their predicted fire was inaccurate and they could not engage targets effectively without observation and adjustment of fire. Kirey and his units nevertheless located and surveyed targets and divided the artillery into groups with specific tasks such as the suppression of strong points and the breaching of obstacles. Observation officers were placed in the front line in order to correct fire.

The number of guns deployed in the battle and their density was low by Western Front standards, but the Russian artillery was remarkably effective. The concentration of an inferior number of guns against him caused the Austrian commander, Karl von Pflanzer-Baltin, to observe incorrectly that "the enemy's great superiority in long-range artillery is . . . of unprecedented effectiveness." Kirey also wrote on anti-tank tactics even though he had never seen a tank, and suggested – a war ahead of his time – engaging tanks with anti-aircraft guns.

The Brusilov Offensive was a conceptual breakthrough in the application of indirect fire, but its formulae would have failed against the more formidable obstacles and opposition on the Western Front. To defeat these required an immense weight of fire. Indirect fire was still inaccurate because the ability to locate targets precisely was as yet imperfect, and existing systems of ballistic calculation contained inconsistencies. Destroying targets consistently therefore required a heavy weight of fire delivered in the target's general vicinity, and thus prolonged the length of the fireplan. In addition, guaranteeing accurate fire onto trenches and obstacles in front of assaulting troops required advance registration. But marshalling guns, ammunition, and men, registering the guns, and applying fire over weeks and even months compromised surprise, allowing the enemy to strengthen his positions and position his reserves. Expanded defensive preparations in turn further increased the weight of fire that the attacker required.

The entire enterprise began to buckle under its own weight. Fireplans became so extensive and complex that only centralized high-level planning could create them, but no means existed to adjust them as events unfolded. Coordination with the infantry was poor; when an attack succeeded, the infantry often drew ahead of the rigid phase lines laid down in the plan. When resistance or obstacles held the infantry up, the fireplan tended to move on, leaving them exposed to enemy fire and counterattack.

British planners on the Somme used artillery as a giant sledgehammer to crush everything in its path. They sacrificed coordination and flexibility to the destructive effect they confidently expected but which in general failed to erase German resistance. The Somme nevertheless represented a further advance in the development of indirect fire. It established the principle of high-level targeting, planning, and command, and it was a success for the new artillery logistical organization. Artillery commanders had applied procedures, however imperfect as yet, to make indirect fire more accurate. Registration became the norm although it brought with it the lethal penalty of forfeiting operational surprise.

The missing ingredient was the ability to fire accurately without registration: predicted fire. That capability not only made surprise possible; it also allowed the engagement of targets in depth without the use of a forward observer if the gunners could determine target locations with precision. Experiments with prediction on the Somme were disappointing, but the experts persisted over the course of the following year.

On 20 November 1917 the army launched an offensive at Cambrai that possessed a twofold decisive importance. It was the first occasion on which any army used massed tanks – the attackers fielded a total of 476. Even more significantly, it was the first successful application of a large-scale predicted fireplan, the inspiration of Brigadier General H. H. Tudor, who pioneered armor and artillery cooperation. The attack ultimately collapsed due to British failure to anticipate the swiftness and ferocity of the German counterthrust. But the initial fireplan was highly successful. The decision to use tanks to cut the German wire released artillery resources from that task, shortened the fireplan, and thus increased surprise. Accurate aerial reconnaissance and improved mapping and ballistic calculations allowed the guns to engage their predicted targets effectively. On a front of ten kilometers 1,003 pieces participated in fires orchestrated through highly detailed centralized planning. The 150 batteries that reinforced the sector before the attack remained silent and camouflaged until the actual bombardment. Newly arriving guns had to calibrate elsewhere before deploying, and fired without registration. The fireplan came in three parts: a moving barrage to support the infantry and tanks; simultaneous attack by heavy guns on strong points, communications and reserves; and a counterbattery program using tear gas and then high explosive. A number of batteries also received the task of following up to repel counterattacks. Later analysis revealed that the British guns using predicted fire had successfully engaged 90 percent of the enemy batteries. The only shortcoming was the failure of artillery communications in the follow-up phase, an indication that years of static war had taken its toll on maneuver skills. A further notable success was the coordination of the fireplan with air power; 289 aircraft took part as reconnaissance aircraft, artillery spotters, ground attack aircraft, and bombers.

The Germans immediately replied in kind. On 30 November 1917 their XXIII Reserve Corps fired a preparatory bombardment at Cambrai against the outgunned British VII Corps. The bombardment was similar to one that Bruchmüller had devised and fired at Riga in September 1917. It was also the first appearance of Bruchmüller himself on the Western Front; Ludendorff had attached him to XXIII Corps as an adviser. Bruchmüller's aim was to convert the army in the West to the techniques pioneered on the Eastern Front. On 28 February, the *Oberste Heeresleitung* issued a new set of tactical instructions that incorporated many of Bruchmüller's ideas, although it still clung to registration and opposed the new predicted fire techniques that Captain Pulkowski had proposed.[16] The authors of the instructions recognized the need to organize artillery according to task and to reinforce the counterbattery group during the critical preparatory bombardment. They also aimed to position all guns as far forward as possible and to synchronize a nonpersistent gas bombardment with close support for the infantry assault. Finally, they accepted the need for abbreviated registration.

Bruchmüller's tactical system had six principal components: neutralization, task organization, preparation of the battlefield, combined-arms coor-

---

[16] The fireplan at Riga did not use prediction, but rather an abbreviated registration that dispensed with establishing exact ranges. The Pulkowski method included allowance for barrel wear, meteorological variation, and ammunition by manufacturing lot.

dination, security and surprise, and fire planning.[17] The fire support for Ludendorff's spring 1918 operational knock-out blow against the British using infiltration and decentralized command techniques rested on Bruchmüller's methods.[18] The German high command promulgated the new approach in *The Attack in Positional Warfare*, published in January 1918; the aim was tactical infiltration leading to operational breakthrough.[19]

On 21 March 1918, the Germans attacked between Arras and La Fère with 6,608 guns of which approximately 2,598 were heavy or super-heavy, achieving a 2.5:1 superiority in artillery over the British facing them. On the first day of the offensive, the German guns fired 3.2 million rounds of which a third were gas. The preparatory fireplan was not the fully evolved model of later months but comprised seven phases with some subphases. In later offensives the planners reduced the phases to three, followed by a rolling barrage in front of the attacking infantry. In the seven weeks before the offensive, the German army had retrained 6,000 officers in the new techniques, and all newly arrived batteries recalibrated their guns on ranges well in the rear. By the time Ludendorff broke off the offensive on 5 April, the Germans had seized more ground than the total of all Allied gains during the entire war.

But Ludendorff's tactical success was an operational and strategic failure. In part this was due to the disappointing performance of 17th Army, one of the three involved. Its artillery chief, Lieutenant General von Berendt, had been a lieutenant with Bruchmüller and now resented his advice. Despite clear orders to the contrary, von Berendt compromised surprise by firing a registration; most of his guns also ceased firing at one point for half an hour. Ludendorff was blunt: "The vitalizing energy that emanated from Colonel Bruchmüller was lacking. This is another instance of the decisive influence of a personality on the course of events in war, as in life generally."[20] On 26 March the Kaiser personally decorated Bruchmüller at the front with oak leaves for his *Pour le Mérite*.

17   For Bruchmüller's methods, see David T. Zabecki, *Steel Wind. Colonel Georg Bruchmüller and the Birth of Modern Artillery* (Westport, CT, 1994), Chapters 3–6 (a work of excellent investigative scholarship that demonstrates how Bruchmüller came to have a profound effect on twentieth-century concepts of warfare).

18   Concepts of infiltration had also become common currency in the British Army by the summer of 1918. Thus "Hints on Training" issued by XVIII Corps in August 1918 urged, "When in doubt go ahead. When uncertain, do that which will kill most Germans. Do not fear an exposed flank": Paddy Griffith, *Battle Tactics of the Western Front: The British Army's Art of Attack, 1916–18* (London, 1994), p. 98; see also p. 99 for a XXII Corps order of 18 July 1918 that described the efficacy of engaging strongpoints in the enemy depth while simultaneously attacking his front.

19   Jürgen Förster, "Evolution and Development of German Doctrine," British Army Conference, "The Origins of Contemporary Military Doctrine," Larkhill, 28 March 1996.

20   Erich Ludendorff, *My War Memories, 1914–1918* (London, 1919), vol. 2, p. 606.

On 9 April, The Germans again attacked the British on the Lys with an artillery ratio of 3.3:1 and a density of 100 guns per kilometer, their highest of the war. The high command attached Bruchmüller and his entire staff to 6th Army for the operation, which also gained tactical success but lost momentum for want of reserves to exploit early gains. The further offensives followed this same pattern. At Chemin des Dames on 27 May, Bruchmüller was chief of artillery for the entire army group and achieved total surprise; preparatory fire was more accurate and of shorter duration than ever before.[21] At Noyon and Champagne-Marne in June and July, the formula was less successful, largely because the Allies now understood the new tactics and had begun to adopt them in defense.

The *"Kaiserschlacht"* had proved that novel techniques could break into British defenses and achieve astonishing results, but it was a failure in operational and strategic terms. Ludendorff's hammer-blows failed to achieve break-out to the Channel coast or to Paris. Worse still, in each case the German commanders had lost control of the battle after five or six days. As the storm troopers moved on, a mass of ill-trained infantry followed in old-fashioned tight formations at the mercy of British and French firepower. Nor could the German army support logistically the advances it had made.

Ludendorff's victories bled the German army white: almost a million casualties between March and July 1918 led to a vicious spiral of collapse thereafter.[22] Worse still, the army's best units suffered the most losses. By June, Ludendorff had completely wrecked twenty-seven of the thirty-six elite "attack" divisions. Their destruction left a relatively unsophisticated mass of infantry to fight on. The mounting losses forced the Germans to rely increasingly upon artillery to hold their crumbling positions.[23] Between July and the Armistice they lost about 760,000 more men on the battlefield, while an estimated million deserted or refused to serve. On 1 August 1918 the Germans still had ninety-eight combat-ready divisions on the Western Front; on 11 November only four remained.[24]

On 4 July 1918 the British launched an offensive at Hamel. The operation, although modest both in size and success, established a

---

[21] It also provided formidable evidence of the extent to which artillery practice had progressed in four years. On 27 May 1918, the second 9-inch round fired from a railroad gun at 23,000 yards hit the British heavy artillery headquarters at Guyencourt (Timothy Travers, *How the War was Won: Command and Technology in the British Army on the Western Front 1917–1918* (London, 1992), p. 103).

[22] Ibid., p. 108.

[23] Ibid., p. 157. The unravelling of German fortunes on the Eastern Front in the Second World War showed a similar pattern: the relatively few elite armored formations soon eroded, leaving doomed infantry armies to fight a primitive attritional battle. In 1940 the elite advance guard achieved operational success; in 1918 and 1941–45 that proved impossible.

[24] Ibid., p. 154.

more sophisticated model of mechanized land/air warfare than that pioneered at Cambrai the previous autumn. The planners made their preparations in the utmost secrecy, and once again did without a
preliminary bombardment. Tanks advanced behind a creeping barrage
with infantry following. The tanks moved freely, seeking opportunity
targets while artillery sealed off the flanks and concentrated on counterbattery fire, especially against German anti-tank guns. The most impressive improvement was in the liaison between aircraft and artillery, both in
the observation role and in the planning of deep bombardment. Hamel
proved that artillery and tanks could work together, and cast the infantry in a subsidiary role.

It also became clear that under the peculiar conditions of the Western
Front, artillery could win battles almost alone, thereby reducing infantry
casualties. Successes such as that of 9th Division at Meteren on 19 July
1918, which repeated the success at Messines a year earlier, were due
almost entirely to crushing artillery dominance. But the army again
employed the "Hamel" model on a huge scale on 8 August in the Battle
of Amiens, the high point of tanks and aircraft in a predominantly infantry–
artillery war. The battle was not so much a breakthrough as a three-dimensional envelopment across the whole front; it was also the last 1918 battle
in which tanks played so large a role. From September through October
1918 the British Army lost 62 percent of its tanks; artillery had to fill the
resulting gap. Reliance on artillery increased right up to the Armistice, if
only to save manpower. The highest British expenditure of shells in the
entire war occurred on 28–29 September 1918: the gunners fired 945,052
rounds to breach the Hindenburg Line.[25]

Debate continues over whether improvements in strategy, tactics,
weapons, technology, leadership, staff efficiency, or merely greater
mass led to the British successes of summer 1918. Travers has articulated
the army's two contrasting approaches as the artillery-based offensive on
the one hand and the reliance on mechanized operations on the other.
The role of artillery was nevertheless critical to both. A German officer,
speaking on 21 August 1918, expressed the view that a BEF attack
conducted with tanks, infantry, and artillery in combination would
always break through. With infantry and artillery alone, the attackers
would break through three times out of four. And attacks conducted
with infantry and tanks alone would succeed only one time in four.[26]
In the final analysis the artillery-based method won the battles of 1918;
artillery firepower restored to the battlefield the maneuver that infantry
firepower had destroyed in 1914.

[25] Ibid., p. 180.
[26] Ibid., p. 140.

TOOLS AND LESSONS OF THE INDIRECT-FIRE
REVOLUTION

The vast attritional experiments at Verdun and on the Somme established that an appropriate concentration of fire made it possible to advance two to three kilometers virtually anywhere. But that method bought tactical success by sacrificing any prospect of surprise or operational success. In an astonishingly short time, hitherto conservative military establishments identified the technical obstacles and devised a series of techniques to make operational success possible once more. The heroes of this story were artillery generals such as Major General Sir Herbert Uniacke and Brigadier General H. H. Tudor, who sought to ensure that the army learned lessons from every battle and did not repeat its errors. They had their counterparts on both sides of the line. The techniques they developed have stood the test of time and remain the basis of modern gunnery.

From 1915 air observation and photography permitted precise targeting throughout the theater, and up-to-date mapping of the ever-changing trenches. After its first use at Neuve Chapelle in 1915, photography became standard practice by 1916, although not until 1917 did the combatants overcome image distortion and achieve adequate precision. Advances in military survey enabled guns to fix their own positions exactly, an achievement that the static nature of the war made easier. Yet inaccuracies occur even when exact locations of gun and target are known; artillerymen on both sides devised means to minimize those errors, gathering meteorological data and making calculations to compensate while allowing for the wear on each gun barrel (calibration), the displacement of each gun from the point of survey, the effects of temperature on the propellant charge, and the variations in ammunition manufacture by batch. By 1918 the 18-pounder had achieved a nominal accuracy of eighty meters over a range of four kilometers, a standard similar to that expected of a field gun today.

Communications to adjust the fall of shot remained problematic; shellfire cut telephone lines and radios remained primitive. Aerial observers developed elaborate if precarious signaling systems for direct communication with their guns. By 1918 the French army had 50,000 telephone engineers, with 200 signallers per artillery regiment – and the demands of war had stripped houses all over France of their telephone wires. The combatants also developed the first electronic warfare techniques: the interception of wireless and telephone communications.

The artilleryman's basic tools changed almost beyond recognition: heavy guns and howitzers became the rule. In 1914 the British Army possessed only six heavy batteries compared to seventy-two field batteries. By November 1918 it had 440 heavy batteries compared to 568 field batteries, a transformation typical of the other major combatants. The ordnance these guns delivered included by 1918 a wide variety of high-explosive and gas shells and fuses, the most important of which were the instant and delay fuses. The instant fuse gave high-explosive effects similar to those of shrapnel, but did not require the same skill to fire. In its way it was as significant as the radar proximity fuse of 1944.

From 1917 onward air power, as well as providing reconnaissance and artillery observation, played an increasing role in deep attack and coordinated ground–air operations. The British practiced low-level strafing of troops by aircraft on the Somme; on 31 July 1917 German aircraft received the mission of bombarding British troops attacking Pilkem Ridge in one of the first close air support bombing missions of the war. The Germans massed 730 aircraft for the "*Kaiserschlacht*," and created *Schlachtstaffeln* for employment at the decisive point of an attack on the orders of the ground commander, flying at low altitude in close formation to shatter enemy morale. On 18 March 1918 *Oberleutnant* Ritter von Greim flew the first successful anti-tank mission over the Somme. The French also created a dedicated air formation, the *Division Aérienne*, to support the ground battle.

The British, largely through the vision of Lieutenant Colonel J. F. C. Fuller, gave aircraft a major role in the Battle of Cambrai. For the Amiens offensive of August 1918 the British command tasked aircraft to fly ahead of the tanks, identifying and destroying anti-tank guns. Interdiction against railroad lines bringing up reserves became common. On 4 June 1918, 120 French Breguet XIV bombers dropped 700 bombs on a large body of German reserves sheltering from artillery in a steep-sided ravine. Air power could also supply units from the air, as demonstrated in July 1918, when air-drops sustained a cut-off French battalion at Château Vandières until its relief two days later. Colonel William ("Billy") Mitchell's suggestion that American infantry parachute onto Metz from converted Handley Page bombers was yet another precursor of modern three-dimensional operations, creating shock in the enemy's depth. As the role of air power increased, so the importance of counter-air operations grew, matching the analogous growth of artillery counterbattery operations.

Correspondingly, artillery and command underwent an institutional revolution: new command, intelligence, and planning organizations arose at both tactical and operational levels. In the British Army, the corps artillery commander commanded by 1916 all divisional artillery within his corps. He set the timing within fireplans and allocated observers to batteries throughout the formation. By 1918, artillery planning had become an army-level function, decentralized to divisions once an attack had been launched, and half the divisional artillery advanced with assaulting troops ninety minutes after zero hour. It was also accepted by spring 1918 that infantry could not count on artillery SOS fire whenever they deemed it necessary.[27] Instead, artillery commanders made the decision to commit resources at a higher level based on broader intelligence perspectives.

The Germans did not have a corps artillery until February 1916, and it functioned initially as a mere reserve pool of ordnance. Coordination between divisional and corps artillery did not exist, and the former could not call for the support of the latter. But by spring 1918 the Germans had task-organized their artillery into seven functional groups divided into sub-groups – a revolutionary departure from traditional command hierarchies.[28] The Germans had by then fully recognized the distinction between the close and deep battles, and the need to coordinate the two. By 1918, German artillery received times, tasks, and areas of fire from the army-level command, but group and subgroup selected targets. Training and planning emphasized all-arms coordination and fireplanning flexible enough to match the new infantry tactics.[29]

The combatants created enormous new logistical organizations to service the unprecedented demands of artillery. The armies of 1914 were already armies of the Industrial Revolution, but they were nevertheless mere shadows of what the Great Artillery War brought forth. The Royal Artillery became larger than the Royal Navy, and by 1917 the ratio of gunners to infantrymen in many battles had risen to 8:10. In the British and German cases, the ratio of gunners to infantrymen doubled between 1914–18 and in the French case it tripled. Similarly, the U.S. Army's nine field artillery regiments in April 1917 had risen to 234 by the Armistice.[30] In 1914 the Russian army had 797 heavy artillery pieces; by 1917 it had 2,550.[31] To support the voracious appetite of their guns, the combatants created gigantic new arms and munitions industries with immense social consequences.

THE FIRST WORLD WAR: INDIRECT FIRE AND MILITARY REVOLUTION

The First World War changed the face of twentieth-century warfare in many ways. It brought the tank and anti-tank duel, air-to-air combat, strategic bombing, aerial reconnaissance, and air defense, and the alluring

---

27 SOS Fire was a routine action whereby defensive fire could be summoned at immediate notice by the infantry from its affiliated artillery.
28 Zabecki, *Steel Wind*, pp. 36–42.
29 For the German army's new methods, see Bruce Gudmundsson, *Stormtroop Tactics: Innovation in the German Army 1914–1918* (New York, 1989) and Timothy T. Lupfer, "The Dynamics of Doctrine: The Changes in German Tactical Doctrine During the First World War," *Leavenworth Papers* 4 (1981).
30 Dastrup, *Kings of Battle*, p. 163.
31 Richard Simpkin, *Deep Battle: The Brainchild of Marshal Tukhachevskii* (London, 1987), p. 109.

prospect also arose that aircraft might act as "flying artillery" in support of armored operations. Logistics came to rely upon the internal combustion engine and operational and tactical command to depend upon electronic battlefield communications. The horrors of chemical warfare became a matter of routine. Political and ethnic fanaticism, aggression, and self-defense galvanized industrial societies to mobilize their manpower totally and to transform themselves into gigantic armament factories.[32] At the technological level, artillery came to dominate warfare, and indirect fire to dominate artillery.[33] That revolution generated an immense demand for battlefield intelligence and command, control, and communications systems to manage both that intelligence and the fireplanning that it served. The need for ever-greater accuracy and range and ever less collateral damage – for reasons of military expediency – became characteristic of the technical advances that followed that revolution.

The indirect-fire revolution required radical reorganization of the contending armies: the virtual demise of cavalry and the creation or expansion of new corps and branches for machine guns, tanks, air defense, chemical warfare, signals, mechanical engineering, and air combat. In due course separate air services emerged. Organizational flexibility, so alien to the spirit of pre-1914 armies, was a vital component of the revolution.

The Schlieffen Plan and the German offensive of 1914 that derived from it had epitomized a style of warfare – two-dimensional linearity – as old as war itself. Frontal breakthrough was part of the commander's repertoire, but annihilation through envelopment guaranteed total victory. The enemy flanks were the decisive point; the center could give ground to accentuate the movement of the flank or flanks.[34] The Germans played this maneuver scheme out on a grand scale in August–September 1914. They failed – and soon no flanks existed, as mass armies sustained by railroads and industrial

---

32 Guy Hartcup's *The War of Invention* (London, 1988) describes scientific developments in 1914–1918.

33 The casualty figures demonstrate the dominance of artillery after 1914. Artillery inflicted 58 percent of British casualties on the Western Front in the First World War; the figure rose to 75 percent in the North African theater in the Second World War. German artillery accounted for 51 percent of Russian casualties; in 1945 that figure rose to 61 percent, although the German army traditionally neglected its artillery. Conversely, artillery inflicted an estimated 70 percent of German materiel and personnel losses in the Second World War and accounted for 60 percent of American dead in the Korean War. The Soviet army calculated in the 1980s that its rocket forces and artillery comprised 80 percent of its fighting power. Air power has become ever more significant, but has served above all to complement surface-to-surface fire. The challenge is to optimize the division of labor between the various sources of firepower acting in conjunction with the maneuver arms.

34 For this comparison, Guenter Roth, "Operational Thinking in Schlieffen and Manstein," in Militärgeschichtliches Forschungsamt, *Development, Planning and Realization of Operational Conceptions in World Wars I and II* (Herford, 1989).

economies filled the entire battlespace from the Channel to the Swiss border. That outcome was a millennial watershed in war.

The muddle, misery, and bloodshed of the following four years were in effect a search by trial and error, assisted by tactical and technical brilliance, to replace a system that had prevailed for thousands of years. The new style employed three dimensions and a psychological aspect. The object was not to flank, envelope, and annihilate, but rather to break through from the front while simultaneously devastating the full depth of the enemy rear. Paralyzing breakthrough, not envelopment, became the object, and indirect firepower was its key. Yet severe constraints still limited the effectiveness of the new model; the armies of the Great War lacked the transport to move troops, guns, and supplies over rough terrain in the offensive, and communications to maintain decentralized control over the fireplan once the offensive had begun. Mechanized transport, close air support, and wireless communications eventually resolved in great part these difficulties, but the crippling deficiencies under which they still labored in 1918 had not prevented the birth of the modern style of warfare. They were subsequent technical fixes, not conceptual revolutions.[35]

What historical factors gave rise to such profound changes in the methods of applying organized violence? What was the foundation of the revolution of 1917–18? How to distinguish between underlying principles and physical trappings, techniques, and tactics? The key to the indirect-fire revolution was the synthesis of long-standing ideas about warfare and the dawning comprehension, under duress, of the potential of existing gunnery technology to create a novel approach. Before the war, military ideas and structures rested on entirely different conceptions; a catalyst for revolution was required. That catalyst was the brutal shock of the battles of 1914, which invalidated all existing doctrine. The revolution occurred because the military establishments of the day had failed to yield to the multiple pressures for change that they were free to ignore in peacetime – but not in war. Some observers of the Russo-Japanese War had felt the warning tremors of the earthquake to come; staffs and high commands had dismissed or ignored them. The tectonic plates of firepower and maneuver were shifting; neither social and technical conservatism, nor the misperceived lessons of previous wars, nor convenient general staff theories could restrain them.

---

[35] Earl H. Tilford (*The Revolution in Military Affairs: Prospects and Cautions*, Strategic Studies Institute, U.S. Army War College [Carlisle Barracks, PA, 1995]) has asserted that the First World War was a military–technical revolution which was not translated into an RMA until after it had ended; that view neglects the already-established conceptual basis of the RMA that came to fruition in 1918, and overemphasizes the importance of the technical enhancements that followed.

Armies had planned to deploy ever-larger masses of infantry, whose tactical mobility was essentially unchanged since the Paleolithic era, in the face of similar forces also armed with increasingly lethal, faster-firing, longer-range weapons. Armies had failed to anticipate the consequences of a preponderance of infantry firepower over infantry tactical mobility, and in the summer of 1914 the plates buckled. The secondary shock from this military earthquake occurred in the following autumn and winter when the newly developed trench lines further magnified the power of the defensive, and made immobility inescapable. The result was bloody stalemate, and the gestation of a new concept that at last harnessed industrial firepower to the offensive and made maneuver possible once more.

The revolution of 1917–18 was not one in which a single combatant gained an asymmetrical advantage over all other contenders. By 1918 both sides had come to understand the geometry and dynamics of the modern style of warfare through a bloody process of mutual education. Both were competent in operating within its framework; the balance of economic power and the astonishing strategic misjudgments of the Germans ultimately determined the outcome. But within the new model two approaches nevertheless emerged.[36] Both rested on the three-dimensional firepower of artillery and air power, but the first, as seen at Cambrai and in more developed form in the Battle of Amiens the following August, incorporated greater use of machines on the battlefield itself. The second approach, as employed in the *"Kaiserschlacht,"* the British attack at Meteren in July 1918, and the British attack on the Hindenburg Line, depended even more totally upon artillery. The Germans adopted the second approach because they lacked a mechanized alternative, as did the American army at St. Mihiel in September 1918.[37] The British concluded that the second method was less costly, and from September 1918 a shortage of tanks precluded further development of the first in any event.[38] In that dualism within the overall framework of the modern

36 See Travers, *How the War was Won.*
37 As Jehuda L. Wallach (*The Dogma of the Battle of Annihilation* [Westport, CT, 1986], p. 19) has pointed out, Ludendorff must carry some of the blame for Germany's failure to field tanks; also Rod Paschall, *The Defeat of Imperial Germany, 1917–1918* (Chapel Hill, NC, 1989), p. 173.
38 The two approaches developed in 1918 remain valid today despite the intervening swift technological changes. For example, British commanders saw massive use of artillery as a means of reducing casualties in the assault on the Hindenburg Line. The Gulf War Coalition likewise opted for the second approach, based predominantly on firepower supported by maneuver. Deep fires demolished fixed defensive positions and their strategic foundations at long range with minimal loss, and ground troops moved forward to occupy the terrain; Foch would have heartily approved. But in other circumstances, especially when parity in firepower prevails, the first approach may yield greater leverage. In both cases three-dimensional firepower remains indispensable, as it has since 1918.

style of warfare lay the origins of the tactical and operational debates that shaped the outcome of the Second World War and remain of central importance in the twenty-first century. The interaction between the strategic setting and available technology still governs the fundamental choice – discerned in 1918 – at the operational and tactical levels of war: between maneuver supported by firepower and firepower supported by maneuver.

9

May 1940: Contingency and fragility of the German RMA

WILLIAMSON MURRAY

The Second World War resumed, after twenty years' unquiet truce, the military revolution of 1914–18. The greatest war in history was not a mere sequel: it was the *continuation* after brief respite and under new management of the bid for world mastery that Imperial Germany had launched in 1914. It was the culmination of the Great War's fusing of French and Industrial Revolutions into an unholy trinity of mass fanaticism, science and technology, and the matchless organizational and productive-destructive capacities of the industrial state.

But despite the clarity with which the modern style of warfare described in the preceding chapter emerges in retrospect, the tactical, operational, and technological meaning of the Great War was far from clear to those who surveyed the wreckage after 1918. The unparalleled profusion of RMAs that sprang up in the interwar period on the basis of the insights acquired and technologies introduced in 1914–18 gestated amid ambiguities both multiple and profound.[1] Those who contributed to the development of new techniques remained uncertain of their potential until the grim audit of war in 1939–45. The adaptation of combined-arms tactics and operations to the pace of the internal combustion engine by *Reichswehr* and *Wehrmacht* offers perhaps the most striking example of the extent of those uncertainties and ambiguities.

By late May 1940 the results of the combined-arms armored warfare RMA appeared clear at last in the devastating victory of the German armies over the Allied forces in northern France. A French observer, flying high over the advancing Germans, described the outcome:

---

[1] The most obvious interwar RMAs were combined-arms maneuver warfare, strategic bombing, carrier warfare, amphibious warfare, and air defense: see especially Williamson Murray and Allan R. Millett, eds., *Military Innovation in the Interwar Period* (Cambridge, 1996).

The [German] tank detachments that move easily across the countryside because no French tanks oppose them produce irreparable damage even though the actual destruction they cause is apparently superficial – the capture of local command staffs, severed telephone lines, burning villages. [The tanks] play the role of those chemical agents that destroy not the organism as a whole, but its nervous system. Throughout the landscape across which the Germans have swept like lightning, the [French] army, even if it appears almost intact, has ceased to be an army. It has been transformed into separated clots. Where an organism existed, there remains only a collection of disconnected organs. Between the clots – however combative the men may be! – the enemy moves as he wishes. An army that is nothing more than the numerical sum of its soldiers ceases to be effective.[2]

The German breakthrough on the Meuse and its explosive exploitation conquered France, eliminated British influence on the continent, and established German hegemony in western Europe. In less than three weeks, German ground forces led by armored spearheads defeated the French army – a task in which the Germans, despite four years of massive bloodshed, had failed in 1914–18. The victory of 1940 was so crushing, so convincing, that it has served as the shining exemplar of *the* revolution in military affairs of the mid-twentieth century.

And yet a closer look at the manner in which the Germans innovated in the 1920s and 1930s and at their planning and conduct of operations in 1940 suggests that even the most seemingly clear-cut revolutions in military affairs are far less clear-cut from the point of view of those who determined the course of events. For French and British officers in summer 1940, the Germans had clearly developed a revolutionary style of war.[3] But to some German officers the secret of German success was the careful evolutionary development of concepts that had their origins in the battles of the First World War. And as sophisticated a general staff officer as General Erich Marcks, soon to be called upon by the army's chief of staff to draw up the initial plan for BARBAROSSA, explained the roots of German success in terms far removed from skillful and innovative tactics and operations. To Marcks, the startling extent of the *Wehrmacht*'s triumph was at least as bound up with the ideological commitment of German troops:

---

[2] Antoine de Saint Exupéry, *Pilote de guerre* (New York, 1942), pp. 94–5.

[3] The French – like the Germans themselves – appear to have drawn the lesson that morale and ideological inspiration were major factors in German victory: see Robert O. Paxton, *Parades and Politics at Vichy: The French Officer Corps under Marshal Pétain* (Princeton, NJ, 1966). J. F. C. Fuller, whose interwar theories of armored warfare the British Army had seemingly spurned, strongly influenced the conclusions that the British drew from 1940; his "all-tank" emphasis unfortunately precluded understanding of the combined-arms roots of German success.

... the change in men weighs more heavily than that in technology. The French we met in battle were no longer those of 14/18. The relationship was like that between the revolutionary armies of 1796 and those of the [First] Coalition – only this time *we* are the revolutionaries and Sans-Culottes.[4]

This chapter seeks to trace the complexities of this seemingly least problematic of revolutions in military affairs. That purpose involves analyzing three principal sets of issues and evidence. The first is the origins and nature of the processes of innovation and adaptation that gave the Germans the forces that fought in spring 1940. The second is the character of the planning processes through which the Germans and their opponents prepared for battle. And finally, the battlefield events themselves offer a rich vein of evidence regarding the ambiguities and uncertainties that the participants faced. The battle of France may well have represented the culmination of a revolution in military affairs. But the nature of that revolution was very different from those described or dogmatically predicted by the naive technological determinists whose views have shaped the debates at the turn of the twenty-first century.

ADAPTATION AND INNOVATION FROM *REICHSWEHR* TO *WEHRMACHT*: 1920–40

Historians have the bad habit of beginning the examination of crucial historical events at the event itself, and then working backward to discern the decisions and turning-points that seemingly led to that event through an imaginary straight-line sequence of cause and effect. The historical process works very differently. Individuals and organizations confront disparate choices with no means of discerning a clear path forward.[5] The decisions they eventually take reflect personal idiosyncrasies and organizational cultures; historians frequently ignore internal debates and overlook roads not taken. Historical actors often take correct decisions for reasons that appear bizarre in retrospect. And commanders and military organizations are rarely wholly honest – whether in the aftermath of victory or that of defeat – about what actually happened.

Historians also tend to see connections between events and developments that in the end play roles in the precipitating moment – but

---

4   *Generalmajor* Erich Marcks, 19 June 1940 (emphasis in original), quoted in Knox, "The 'Prussian Idea of Freedom'"; see also Knox, "1 October 1942: Adolf Hitler, *Wehrmacht* Officer Policy, and Social Revolution," *The Historical Journal* 43:3 (2000), pp. 801–25.
5   As Wolfe suggested before his conquest of Quebec: "War is an option of difficulties," a statement that also applies in full measure to military innovation.

which in fact may have no connection.[6] A number of historians have for instance ascribed significance to the appointment in 1926 of a career signals officer – Heinz Guderian – to lead the *Reichswehr*'s tank development program, given the role that radio later played in the tactical and operational control of panzer units. But it is far more likely that the army selected Guderian simply because he was available, while those on the fast track for promotion saw a job in tanks – prohibited to the *Reichswehr* for the foreseeable future – as distinctly uninviting.

How then can analysts of revolutions of military affairs make sense of the past? A starting point is the recognition that the past is not linear – clear paths to the future are the stuff of fiction – and that past events can only suggest questions and possibilities. History, to paraphrase Clausewitz, can sharpen our judgment about the nature of war and about the sort of organizational behavior that can encourage effective innovation.[7] But it cannot suggest clear and unambiguous roads to future revolutions in military affairs.

The German case nevertheless offers a general lesson about the uses of the past. Commentators often claim that military organizations habitually focus myopically on the last war and thus render themselves incapable of fighting the next; the traditional picture of the origins of Blitzkrieg correspondingly features a revolutionary German army leaping intrepidly into the technological future while the stolid British and French remain mired in the 1914–18 mud. But nothing could be further from the truth. The French proved incapable of deriving lessons from 1914–18 other than those that served preconceived and ultimately ahistorical notions, and the British Army did not seek to distill the lessons of the Great War until 1932, then heavily censored the resulting report because its authors had dared to criticize British performance.[8]

---

6 Burton Klein and others have assumed a connection between Germany's less than impressive economic performance in the early 1940s and its development of Blitzkrieg tactics before the war. They suggested that the Germans had developed a "Blitzkrieg strategy" as a means of avoiding having to mobilize the German economy and disturb Germany's civilians; the road to final victory lay through a series of short wars using a new and revolutionary system. In actuality, the Germans had no such intention: they developed their combined-arms system of war entirely independently of strategic considerations (see Burton Klein, *Germany's Economic Preparations for War* [Cambridge, MA, 1959], and Alan Milward, *The German Economy at War* [London, 1965]; for a refutation of this thesis, Williamson Murray, *The Change in the European Balance of Power, 1938–1939: The Path to Ruin* [Princeton, NJ, 1984], pp. 3–52, and "Force Structure, Blitzkrieg Strategy, and Economic Difficulties: Nazi Grand Strategy in the 1930s," *Journal of the Royal United Services Institute*, April 1983).

7 Carl von Clausewitz, *On War*, eds. and trans. Michael Howard and Peter Paret (Princeton, NJ, 1975), p. 141.

8 For the culture of the interwar British Army, see particularly Brian Bond, *British Military Policy Between the Two World Wars* (Oxford, 1980).

It was rather the Germans who studied the last war with the utmost care.
Almost immediately after its end, the *Reichswehr*'s first chief of staff and
second commander, General Hans von Seeckt, organized no fewer than
fifty-seven committees to study what had really happened in 1914–18,
"while the impressions won on the battlefield are still fresh and a major
proportion of the experienced officers are still in leading positions." He
charged those committees, with his habitual decisiveness, to produce:

> short, concise studies of the newly gained experiences of the war and consider
> the following points: What situations arose in the war that had not been
> considered before? How effective were our prewar views in dealing with the
> above situations? What new guidelines have been developed from the use of
> new weaponry in the war? Which new problems put forward by the war have
> not yet found a solution?[9]

The crucial issue, as Seeckt's last question emphasized, was that the
Germans used a thorough review of recent battlefield *experience* as a
point of departure for thinking about future war. The creation of revolutionary military capabilities in peacetime thus depends to a considerable
extent on thorough analysis of the past.

But the spirit in which armed forces undertake such analysis – a spirit
that in turn derives from their military culture – is as vital as the fact of
the analysis itself. The German interest in experience was accompanied by
an insistence on the unvarnished truth; Ludendorff well expressed this
aspect of his army's ethos in describing in his memoirs his visits to the
Western Front in 1916: "[Staffs] knew I wanted to hear their real views
and have a clear idea of the true situation, not a favorable report made to
order."[10]

Correspondingly, German interwar doctrine, as crystallized in 1921 in
Leadership and Combat of Combined-Arms Forces and reworked by
Generals Werner von Fritsch and Ludwig Beck in 1932 into
Truppenführung, the manual that guided the Prusso-German army in the
preparation and fighting of its last and greatest war, reflected the actual
battlefield that had existed in 1918.[11] As significant as what Fritsch and
Beck wrote was their status; they were not inmates of some think-tank on
Berlin's outskirts to which the German army had delegated the task of
doctrinal speculation, but rather the army's future commander-in-chief
and chief of staff.

---

[9] James S. Corum, *The Roots of Blitzkrieg: Hans von Seeckt and German Military
      Reform* (Lawrence, KS, 1992), p. 37.
[10] Erich Ludendorff, *Ludendorff's Own Story, August 1914–November 1918*, vol. 1 (New
      York, 1919), p. 24.
[11] *Führung und Gefecht der verbundenen Waffen* (Berlin, 1921); Germany,
      Oberkommando des Heeres, H.Dv. 300/1, *Truppenführung* (Berlin, 1936) (published
      1933).

The Germans thus built on their war experience in a coherent, careful, evolutionary fashion. Not surprisingly, they were open to technological changes that might reduce their post-1918 inferiority. *Truppenführung* made clear that tanks, for instance, would play a crucial role – although the German army did not yet possess a single such machine. The manual underlined the new weapon's vital importance in exploiting breakthroughs: "As a rule tanks are committed to the attack where a decision is sought."[12] And in addition to their own internal studies and debates, the Germans also followed carefully and analyzed exhaustively the British experiments with tank units on Salisbury Plain.[13] Yet in the end German armored tactics were simply the conscious adaptation to the internal combustion engine and radio of the conceptual framework, developed in 1917–18, of the combined-arms battle resting on fire and maneuver, decentralized decision-making, and relentless exploitation. That was the link between the battlefields of March 1918 and those of May 1940.

One central point requires further emphasis: the doctrinal framework and command and control system that the Germans – in sharp contrast to their opponents – derived from experience. The new approach rested on a genuine understanding of the nature of warfare as a domain of constant transformation that was not subject to accurate prediction. *Truppenführung* made the point with the greatest clarity in its two opening paragraphs:

1. The conduct of war is an art, a free creative activity that rests on scientific foundations. It makes the most extreme demands on the individual.
2. The conduct of war is based on continuous ongoing development. New tools of war give armed conflict an ever-changing shape.[14]

In other words the German army saw military innovation not as a step or series of steps that led to a static outcome, but rather as a continuous ceaseless process of change and adaptation impelled not merely by technology, but also by the nature of the battlefield and of the enemy.

The absolute domination of industrial firepower had created circumstances never before seen. *Truppenführung* summarized eloquently the resulting harsh necessities: "The emptiness of the battlefield demands fighters [*Kämpfer*] who think and act on their own and can analyze any situa-

[12] *Truppenführung*, particularly paragraph 339.
[13] Among other important documents along these lines see Reichswehrministerium, Berlin, 10 November 1926, "Darstellung neuzeitlicher Kampfwagen," National Archives and Records Administration (henceforth NARA), microcopy T-79/62/000789; Reichswehrministerium, "England: Die Manöver mit motorisierten Truppen," September 1929, NARA T-79/30/000983; and Der Chef des Truppenamts, December 1934, "England: Manöver des Panzerverbandes, 18. bis 21.9.34," NARA T-79/16/000790.
[14] *Truppenführung*, p. 1.

tion and exploit it decisively and boldly."[15] Unlike their opponents, the Germans understood that war offered fleeting opportunities that disappeared like the morning mist if leaders – from general to rifleman – failed to grasp them. To German analysts, the decentralized command and control system that they had received from Prussian tradition – from Scharnhorst through Moltke the Elder – and had further expanded and extended in the lost war was the only conceivable solution. The system even demanded that when necessary, artillery, infantry, and other supporting branches should coordinate and act together even *without* direction from above.[16] The result was a command style that forced commanders to focus their attention downward and outward onto the battlefield. The limited flow of information up the chain of command compelled them to see for themselves: that was why Guderian, Rommel, Model, and innumerable others led from the front.

That all other European armies had for centuries followed an entirely different and highly centralized model – control from the top downward, from army to battalion, company, and platoon level – did not trouble the Germans. As they presumably knew when they scoffed at French and British "schematism," commanders at every level in centralized systems inevitably focus not on what is happening on the battlefield but rather on providing information to those above them in the chain of command.[17] In May 1940 French company commanders for the most part remained in their bunkers, attached to the field telephones that linked them to their superiors. German generals were on the banks of the Meuse.

The military culture that supported the Prusso-German approach to war had taken over a century to evolve; decrees from above cannot magically decentralize warfare. German commanders had had to *learn* to devolve creative freedom and authority upon their juniors – an unprecedented and largely counterintuitive step. And those juniors – who included a highly professional corps of non-commissioned officers – required relentless schooling, training, and encouragement in preparing to use that freedom wisely. The uncompromising goal, as Hans von Seeckt had set it forth in 1921, was to make "of each individual member of the army a soldier who, in character, capability, and knowledge, is self-reliant, self-confident,

---

15 Ibid., paragraph 10.
16 For the Prussian army's cult of individual initiative, see especially Knox, "The 'Prussian Idea of Freedom'"; Dieter Ose, "Der 'Auftrag': eine deutsche militärische Tradition," *Europäische Wehrkunde* 31:6 (1982), pp. 264–5; Bruce I. Gudmundsson, *Stormtroop Tactics: Innovation in the German Army, 1914–1918* (Westport, CT, 1989); and Martin Samuels, *Command or Control? Command, Training and Tactics in the British and German Armies, 1888–1918* (London, 1995).
17 I am much indebted for this point to Colonel Karl Lowe, USA (Ret.), currently at the Institute of Defense Analyses, Alexandria, Virginia.

dedicated, and joyful in taking responsibility [*verantwortungsfreudig*] as a man and as a military leader."[18]

Armor and motorization fit seamlessly into this culture and into the combined-arms deep-battle approach that the Germans had come close to perfecting in 1917–18.[19] The German doctrinal framework already emphasized decentralized tactics and rapid exploitation; tanks and motorized infantry, artillery, and supply echelons were thus an evolutionary improvement – incorporating speed, decisiveness, and sustainability – within existing concepts, not a revolutionary capability destined to replace existing branches, as with the all-tank theories that crippled both interwar innovation and Second World War operations and tactics in the British Army.

Before the *Reichswehr* possessed a single tank, *Truppenführung* had established exploitation as the role of armored units. But throughout the 1930s German commanders and staff officers harbored substantial doubts as to whether panzer units, even constituted (as they were) as combined-arms teams with their own integral motorized infantry and artillery, could actually fight independently of infantry formations. After one field exercise in the mid-1930s, the senior general (and future senior field marshal) Gerd von Rundstedt turned to Guderian and commented: "*Alles Unsinn, Alles Unsinn, mein lieber Guderian* [all nonsense, all nonsense, my dear Guderian]."[20] But a continuing and often rugged series of exercises allowed the Germans to test the new instrument. In 1935 the outcome of the army's fall maneuvers persuaded the commander-in-chief, General Werner Baron von Fritsch, to establish the first three panzer divisions.[21] Yet that spring, even before Fritsch's decision, his chief of staff, Ludwig Beck, had organized a staff study of the potential operational role of a panzer corps. A year later, as the first panzer divisions were establishing themselves in their garrison areas, Beck's staff had already begun to study the potential of panzer armies.[22]

The key to German success was a willingness to learn from combat and from realistic experiment. From the development of defense-in-depth tactics in 1917 to the exercises and deployments of the late 1930s, *Reichswehr* and *Wehrmacht* evaluated *experience* more thoroughly and perceptively than

[18] Seeckt's famous order of the day of 1 January 1921, in Manfred Messerschmidt and Ursula von Gersdorff, eds., *Offiziere im Bild von Dokumenten aus drei Jahrhunderten* (Stuttgart, 1964), pp. 224–6.

[19] See especially Murray, "Armored Warfare," in Murray and Millett, eds., *Military Innovation in the Interwar Period.*

[20] M. Plettenberg, *Guderian: Hintergründe des deutschen Schicksals, 1918–1945* (Düsseldorf, 1950), p. 14.

[21] Robert O'Neill, "Doctrine and Training in the German Army," in Michael Howard, ed., *The Theory and Practice of War* (New York, 1966), p. 157.

[22] Erich von Manstein, *Aus einem Soldatenleben, 1887–1939* (Bonn, 1958), pp. 241–2.

their potential opponents. The occupation of Austria in 1938, for instance, triggered an extensive series of after-action reports that revealed systemic problems in mobilization, deployment, and training. Guderian claimed after the war that the panzer forces had experienced relatively few difficulties in their drive on Vienna. The general was – as was his custom – being economical with the truth: numerous breakdowns immobilized tanks and other vehicles, and poor convoy discipline led to a large number of accidents.[23]

Once the general staff had analyzed these after-action reports, carefully planned and focused exercises and training programs ensured that combat units addressed the problems identified. The result was a process of steady incremental improvement and innovation that amounted over the long term to systemic change, but without the risk of following false paths due to the misplaced enthusiasms of reformers or the troglodytic opposition of conservatives. The new panzer units went through the same process as the rest of the army, and the after-action reports were just as harsh on their weaknesses as on those of the infantry divisions.

Panzer units participated in the *Anschluss* as divisions and as independent regiments within infantry corps. Planning for the invasion of Czechoslovakia that summer likewise involved armored divisions as parts of infantry corps.[24] But for the invasion of Poland, German innovation at the operational level had advanced a further step: panzer and motorized infantry divisions now operated together as independent corps.[25] The speed and mobility of these new large formations played an essential role in converting tactical advantages in the breakthrough battle into far-ranging and devastating exploitation at the operational level.

Indeed so impressive was the success of German armor in Poland that the German army high command (the *Oberkommando des Heeres*, or OKH) converted four of the light motorized divisions (which had not proven themselves) into panzer divisions. It also now concentrated two of the four panzer corps, including Guderian's XIX Panzer Corps, into a panzer group – the equivalent of a full-scale army – under General Ewald von Kleist. Guderian suggested later that the purpose was to rein in his move-

---

23 Heinz Guderian, *Panzer Leader* (New York, 1957), pp. 34–6. See however the overall army-level after-action report, Heeresgruppenkommando 3., Ia Nr. 400/38, 18 July 1938, "Der Einsatz der 8. Armee im März 1938 zur Wiedervereinigung Österreichs mit dem deutschen Reich," NARA T-79/14/447 (see particularly pp. 11–12 and 26–7); also Generalkommando XIII A.K., Ib Nr. 1500/38, "Erfahrungsbericht über den Einsatz Österreich, März/April 1938," NARA T-314/525/000319.
24 See Murray, *The Change in the European Balance of Power*, pp. 225–31.
25 For the German campaign against Poland, see Robert M. Kennedy, *The German Campaign in Poland, 1939* (Washington, DC, 1956), and Klaus A. Maier et al., *Germany and the Second World War*, vol. 2, *Germany's Initial Conquests in Europe* (Oxford, 1991), part 3.

ments during the exploitation phase of the battle. But the more likely explanation is the obvious one: OKH aimed at increasing the operational effect of armor by concentrating much of it in a single large armored *Schwerpunkt*. The performance of Kleist's Panzer Group over the first three weeks of the French campaign so satisfied the OKH that it created another panzer group under Guderian himself to destroy the remainder of the French armies in June 1940. That step understandably did not lead to retrospective complaint from Guderian.

One of the pervasive myths of Second World War historiography is that of the "tank-*Stuka* team" that supposedly combined close air support with armored mobility.[26] The actual evolution of German air–ground cooperation was more prosaic, and reflects how innovation actually proceeds in an effective military force. Experience in the Spanish Civil War had caused the Germans to reinvent the tactics and procedures of close air support to help infantry in the breakthrough battle. But the mission nevertheless remained at the bottom of Luftwaffe priorities, although in contrast to the Royal Air Force (RAF) and the U.S. Army Air Corps, the German air force at least took the army's need for close support seriously.

The Luftwaffe in consequence provided noteworthy support to ground forces in the frontier breakthrough battles in Poland. But close air support for armored columns remained a primitive affair that depended on display panels, smoke grenades, and large Nazi flags draped over the tops of *Wehrmacht* vehicles. Not surprisingly, Luftwaffe aircraft regularly bombed German mechanized forces throughout the campaign. For the most part, German panzer units suggested in their after-action reports that the Luftwaffe had bombed the enemy more often than friendly units; most army commentators were satisfied.[27] But the tank–*Stuka* team was clearly still a figment of Dr. Goebbels's ever-active imagination. In April 1940, 2nd Panzer Division and the Luftwaffe carried out promising experiments, using Luftwaffe pilots as forward air controllers with lead panzer elements. But in the end the two services felt that the coming campaign in the West was too imminent to change procedures. Not until the attack on the Soviet Union did the German army possess a responsive system of close air support for its mobile formations.

---

[26] See Richard Muller, "Close Air Support: The German, British, and American Experiences, 1918–1941," in *Military Innovation in the Interwar Period*, Chapter 4, and Williamson Murray, *German Military Effectiveness* (Baltimore, MD, 1992), Chapter 2.

[27] Luftwaffe aircraft had however attacked a lead battalion of 10th Panzer Division for several hours, killing a number of soldiers; the division was not so charitable (10. Panzer Div., Abt. Ia Nr. 26/39, "Erfahrungsbericht," 3 October 1939, NARA T-314/614/632); see also Williamson Murray, "The Luftwaffe Experience," in Benjamin Franklin Cooling, ed., *Case Studies in the Development of Close Air Support* (Washington, DC, 1990).

1940: PLANNING AND PREPARATION

The actual planning and conduct of the French campaign offers a unique view of what a revolution in military affairs looks like through the eyes of those who conducted it – or suffered under it. The outcome reflected French as well as German actions. Had the French high command not made egregious mistakes at every stage in its preparations for the inevitable war with Germany, the battle on the banks of the Meuse might not now figure as the central event in a revolution in combined-arms armored warfare.

It is hard to see in retrospect how the French could have made greater errors in preparing for battle. Their interwar doctrine has rightly received considerable attention from historians – for it played a substantial role in the disaster.[28] From the beginning, France's military leaders already knew the answers they were looking for, and displayed little interest in evidence, either from the 1918 fighting or from British and German experimentation. What fit *la doctrine* received attention, what did not they discarded or actively suppressed. That top-down approach to doctrine also extended to command and control, and was deeply ingrained in the army's culture and personally congenial to figures such as Marshal Philippe Pétain and General Maurice Gamelin. It led to solutions diametrically opposed to those of the Germans: not further decentralization and greater mobility but a cautious style of warfare in which commanders obsessively controlled from above every step and action.[29] The leitmotiv of their approach was the well-worn motto, "the artillery destroys, the infantry occupies." Not surprisingly, the French also carefully scripted their own exercises and experiments to give the result they deemed correct. That approach was invariably successful – until the large-scale exercise that the Germans scripted for them in 1940.[30]

Yet ironically the German crossing of the Meuse on 13–14 May 1940 involved a straightforward infantry–artillery battle over ground and with forces that the French had prepared for a full six months. The fighting around Dinant, Monthermé, and Sedan was ideally suited to maximize the effectiveness of the French approach to war, and in fact French forces did rather better than historians have claimed or French preparations might have led observers to expect.

What doomed France and made the German RMA were two irretrievable errors – one tactical, one operational – by the French high command in the

---

[28] See especially Robert A. Doughty, *Seeds of Disaster: The Development of French Army Doctrine, 1919–1939* (Hamden, CT, 1985) and Eugenia C. Kiesling, *Arming Against Hitler: France and the Limits of Military Planning* (Lawrence, KS, 1996).

[29] German casualties in the spring 1918 offensives had been so high that French interwar military leaders, given their preoccupation with casualties, would not in any case have adopted the tactical system the Germans had developed.

[30] On French training and experiments, see Kiesling, *Arming Against Hitler*.

months immediately preceding the campaign. At the tactical level, the French shifted their infantry companies about as if they were interchangeable parts. Throughout the winter companies moved at intervals into and out of the line to construct field fortifications. These construction duties limited the training time available to infantry and artillery units, and constant rotation into new and unfamiliar sectors radically reduced the cohesion and experience level of the defense. Along the front at Sedan the French command had intermixed no fewer than fifteen companies from three different regiments – the map of company defensive positions, color-coded by regiment, looked as if the army suffered from a bad case of measles.[31] Battalion and regimental commanders inevitably lacked control over individual sectors and had no clear picture of what was happening. Moreover, the fact that French commanders remained immobile in their various headquarters exacerbated the difficulties of responding to the German attack.

But the greatest French mistake was operational. In early spring 1940, General Gamelin, in his capacity as commander-in-chief, ordered a major change in French dispositions. Up to that point 7th Army, which contained the most mobile and modern units in the French army, was deployed in the area around Rheims, a position that ironically placed it ideally to counter a major German thrust through the Ardennes. Admittedly, that was not why Gamelin had chosen the deployment area; he probably intended 7th Army as a swing force to counterattack should the Germans seek to break through the Maginot Line – which the French recognized as a possibility – or advance through Belgium and the Low Countries as they had in 1914.

Then German plans for a blow through northern Belgium fell into Allied hands, due to the crash-landing in Belgium of a careless Luftwaffe staff officer. The news encouraged Gamelin to change his deployment. He alone decided – no evidence exists that French political leaders influenced him – to move 7th Army in its entirety to his far left wing in order to link up with the Dutch.[32] Gamelin thus deprived himself of his last substantial reserve force on any front.[33] The thrust through the Ardennes, which ironically also entered German planning as a result of the compromising of the original plan in January, thus no longer faced a French reserve that might prevent breakthrough or exploitation.

---

[31] Karl Heinz Frieser, *Blitzkrieg-Legende: Der Westfeldzug 1940* (Munich, 1995), pp. 180–5.

[32] For the evolution of Gamelin's plans see Robert A. Doughty, *The Breaking Point: Sedan and the Fall of France, 1940* (Hamden, CT, 1990), pp. 14–16.

[33] At the emergency meeting of 16 May 1940 between the French and the new British prime minister, Winston Churchill, Churchill went straight to the point: "*Où est la masse de manoeuvre?*" Gamelin's reply, to the astonishment of the British, was "*Aucune*" (Churchill, *The Second World War*, vol. 2, *Their Finest Hour* [Boston, MA, 1949], p. 46).

OKH did not know its good fortune until after French defeat; German worries throughout the exploitation phase were entirely reasonable. But the weak French response to the German attack across the Meuse convinced the commanders at the front, especially the panzer corps and division commanders – masters of that intuition the Germans call *Fingerspitzengefühl* – that the French had no large reserves.

On the German side of the fence, Hitler began to demand an immediate attack on the Low Countries and northeastern France even before the *Wehrmacht* had finished mopping up the debris of the Polish armed forces and state. The OKH objected fiercely, because the September 1939 campaign had revealed substantial weaknesses in the tactical performance of both regular and reserve units.[34] Again the German system of combat analysis swung into action. By the second week of October the OKH had designed a thorough program of training to repair the deficiencies it had noted and bring the troops up to a common high standard of performance.[35] At the same time a fierce quarrel exploded between Hitler and the generals over the army's combat-readiness. The upshot was that due to weather conditions in late fall and early winter – among the worst recorded – and the leakage of the plans in January, the Germans in the end postponed the offensive until the following spring.[36] In the meantime, the army could and did spend seventeen hours a day and six to seven days a week implementing with precision and enthusiasm the OKH training syllabus. That ruthless and relentless training stands in stark contrast to the generally lackadaisical practice of most French units during the "Phoney War."[37]

The planning process for the coming offensive against the West – *Fall Gelb*, Contingency Yellow – began in early October and reveals a great deal about the German approach to war and the process through which German panzer forces turned a close tactical advantage into one of the greatest victories in military history. Franz Halder, the army's chief of staff, developed the initial plan in early October 1939. Halder aimed to drive across the Low Countries and northern France down to the Somme River in order to occupy territory and acquire air and naval bases from which to knock Britain out of the war.[38] Virtually no one was happy with

[34] See Williamson Murray, "The German Response to Victory in Poland: A Case Study in Professionalism," *Armed Forces and Society*, Winter 1981.
[35] See in particular, among much similar evidence, Heeresgruppe A, Ob, 31 October 1939, "An den ObdH," NARA T-311/236/000884 and Heeresgruppe A, Abschrift von Abschrift, "Besprechung am 11.11.39," NARA T-311/236/000853.
[36] Telford Taylor, *The March of Conquest: The German Victories in Western Europe, 1940* (New York, 1958), pp. 61–4, 170.
[37] French training during the Phoney War was not nearly as inadequate as during peacetime (see Doughty, *The Breaking Point*, pp. 105–06), but it never approached the intense pressure the Germans routinely put on their troops.
[38] The best account in English of German planning for *Fall Gelb* remains Taylor, *March of Conquest*, pp. 155–86.

the result, but that was hardly Halder's fault: he had simply followed the political guidance that the Führer and his military secretariat, the *Wehrmacht* High Command, had provided.[39]

In November 1939 the young and aggressive chief of staff of Army Group A, General Erich von Manstein, suggested the removal of several panzer divisions from the main drive into Belgium and their assignment to his own army group's push through the Ardennes. Hitler also found a possible attack through the Ardennes intriguing. By mid-month Guderian's XIX Panzer Corps, along with two panzer divisions and one motorized infantry division, had redeployed to Army Group A.[40] Manstein was happy in his memoirs to take credit for the eventual breakthrough to the Channel. But in reality his initial proposals were above all an attempt to assist the main drive in the north with a supporting attack on its flank. The pressure exerted by Manstein and the commander of Army Group A, General Gerd von Rundstedt, nevertheless provided the catalyst for the momentous planning changes of mid-winter.

Once much of the original plan fell into Allied hands at the end of January and Hitler consequently accepted a lengthy postponement, OKH could fundamentally recast its plan. The driving force behind shifting the center of gravity of the attack from the north to the center was Halder.[41] By February, the Germans were well along on the detailed planning needed to implement a very different conception of *Fall Gelb*: the concentration of most available panzer divisions for a drive through the Ardennes. But Halder nevertheless held a different view of the shape of the upcoming offensive than that of the more aggressive armor commanders.

War games and planning conferences that Halder conducted at OKH in February and March 1940 brought out these differences.[42] Halder and the army commander-in-chief, General Walther von Brauchitsch, believed that the armored divisions would fail to punch through; they were convinced that the main breakthrough would not come until the infantry divisions had closed on the Meuse on day ten or eleven. The armor commanders put forward an entirely different view: the panzer divisions would reach the Meuse by day three or four, and would use their organic infantry and artillery to break through on their own. The most remarkable thing about the German planning process was that the high command left to *decision by battle* these seemingly irreconcilable differences over a vital issue.

[39] See Murray, *The Change in the European Balance of Power*, pp. 330–8.
[40] Taylor, *March of Conquest*, pp. 167–8.
[41] On Halder's role, see Taylor, *March of Conquest*, especially pp. 172–3; for a different emphasis, see Christian Hartmann, *Halder, Generalstabschef Hitlers 1938–1942* (Paderborn, 1991), pp. 172–84.
[42] Taylor, *March of Conquest*, pp. 169–75.

Even the direction of the exploitation remained undetermined. A breakthrough on the third or fourth day would offer the possibility of exploitation toward the Channel coast and the envelopment of the Allied forces committed in Belgium. A delay in the breakthrough until day ten or eleven, by contrast, would allow substantial French reserves to move southward from the Allied left wing and northward from the Maginot Line toward the Meuse. From that point onward, exploitation toward Paris rather than the Channel would offer the greatest opportunities. Guderian hints at the debate in his memoirs: in a discussion over the possible exploitation of a successful breakthrough, the panzer commander ostensibly predicted a Meuse crossing on day 5, and replied to a Hitler question about his objective by indicating a strong preference – "unless [he] receive[d] orders to the contrary" – for the Channel over Paris.[43]

The Germans took a number of steps to deal with contingencies that might arise before the breakthrough battle itself. The OKH assigned four of the eight roads in XIX Panzer Corps' area of operations to Guderian for his movement through the Ardennes, and the remaining four to regular infantry divisions.[44] The rationale was probably that the infantry would counter any French attempt to move sizeable units into the Ardennes to delay the Germans. In that case the infantry divisions would do most of the fighting up to the Meuse – and keep the panzer divisions fresh for the break-out. The performance of two reserve companies of Belgian *Chasseurs Ardennais* at the little town of Bodange suggests what the French might have done had they been more aggressive: a few hundred combative Belgians held 1st Panzer Division for almost a full day.[45]

German planners also feared that the French might disrupt their advance by a move into the Ardennes from the south. They therefore air-landed by Fiesler Storch a small force of well-trained infantry from 34th Infantry Division to seize key bridges on the roads leading north into the Ardennes; motorcycle troops soon reinforced to provide a screening force.[46] Significantly, 10th Panzer Division, on the southern flank of the advance to the Meuse, received two roads for movement. That decision reflected a desire that it drive to the Meuse as swiftly as possible so that follow-on infantry could move in to cover the open flank. What the Germans sought to avoid above all was extensive fighting *in* the Ardennes. Considering the obstacles that relatively small groups of American infantry – most notably 101st Airborne Division at Bastogne –

43 Guderian, *Panzer Leader*, p. 92.
44 One of the major difficulties confronting the Germans was the sheer inadequacy of the Ardennes road network (Frieser, *Blitzkrieg-Legende*, p. 125).
45 Doughty, *The Breaking Point*, pp. 46–53.
46 Ibid., pp. 53–5.

threw in the path of a later German armored advance in 1944, the planners of 1940 were entirely right.

1940: THE CONDUCT OF OPERATIONS

The Germans confronted a number of daunting problems even before their forces reached the Meuse. The first was how to move panzer and motorized infantry divisions from their pre-attack deployment areas to the frontier. Panzer Group Kleist had nearly 40,000 trucks and motor vehicles (including 1,222 tanks) with a theoretical march length of 1,540 kilometers.[47] The cantonments of Guderian's panzer corps reached back to the Rhine at Koblenz, a distance of over 100 kilometers, while Reinhardt's XXXXI Panzer Corps had to settle on the right bank of the Rhine and travel over 150 kilometers to reach the Luxembourg frontier.[48] The limited road network of the Rhineland also had to carry – in addition to seven panzer and three motorized infantry divisions – the movement to the Luxembourg and Belgian borders of substantial numbers of regular infantry divisions. No army had ever attempted a motorized movement on this scale before.

Not surprisingly, the Germans ran into difficulties even before they reached the Meuse. On day three, 12 May, infantry divisions moving from the northeast directly crossed the path of Reinhardt's panzer corps and got themselves tangled up with the movement of Guderian's 2nd Panzer Division as well. The result was a monumental traffic jam that brought movement to a halt for much of the day.[49] Luckily for the Germans, the Allied powers had invested relatively little in air power and had focused much of the airpower available on what their senior leaders took to be the main threat – while RAF Bomber Command, in accordance with its doctrine, launched its aircraft to bomb trees and kill cows in the Ruhr instead of supporting the ground battle. But enough French aircraft got through to cause Guderian to complain bitterly to his superiors and his war diary about Allied air activity as his forces crossed the Semois. The difficulties the Germans encountered in the movement phase suggest the dangers they would have faced had the Allies been more aggressive, had they focused more knowledgeably on German weaknesses, and had they deployed larger numbers of aircraft.

On the evening of 12 May the three German panzer corps emerged safely from the Ardennes and closed on the Meuse from Dinant to Sedan. But the actual crossing operations were a "damn near-run thing."[50] In effect the

---

[47]   Frieser, *Blitzkrieg-Legende*, p. 125.
[48]   Ibid., pp. 128–31.
[49]   Ibid., pp. 132–6.
[50]   As the Duke of Wellington said of Waterloo.

Germans faced a straightforward infantry river-crossing operation in which infantry and artillery (with air support when available) assaulted well-dug-in and well-sited enemy positions. Infantry units had to cross the Meuse under heavy French artillery and machine-gun fire with support from the motorized artillery attached to the panzer divisions. They then had to seize a deep enough bridgehead to allow the combat engineers to construct bridges for the tanks and the rest of the division to cross. Until their bridges were laid, geography largely confined the panzer regiments to the role of spectators. River-crossing operations are never easy, nor was this one.

The French for the most part fought well, and in many places inflicted heavy casualties on attacking German units. From north to south, 5th and 7th Panzer Divisions from Hoth's Panzer Corps attacked just south of Dinant; 6th Panzer Division of Reinhardt's Panzer Corps attacked near Monthermé; and 2nd, 1st, and 10th Panzer Divisions of Guderian's XIX Panzer Corps attacked at Sedan. Some crossings received Luftwaffe support, but most did not.

In the north, 5th Panzer Division pushed a small group of infantry across a coffer-dam the French had failed to blow. But for the most part its efforts failed with heavy losses.[51] To its south, the crossing of 7th Panzer Division would have failed without the extraordinary efforts of a junior major general named Erwin Rommel.[52] The defenders shot his lead companies to pieces; only Rommel's inspiring leadership kept the crossing going in the face of tenacious resistance. In the afternoon, after his division had seized a tenuous foothold, Rommel personally wielded a light machine gun to fight off a French counterattack supported by tanks. That evening he jumped into the river to help his engineers complete their bridge.[53] Once most of his division was across on 14 May, Rommel broke free, while 5th Panzer Division absorbed a series of major French counterattacks. Without Rommel's leadership, 7th Panzer Division would probably not have made its crossing, and the French had sufficient strength in the area to contain the relatively small bridgehead that 5th Panzer Division had seized.

In the German center, Reinhardt's lead 6th Panzer Division closed on Monthermé on the evening of 12 May. On the following day its motorized infantry captured a small peninsula formed by a bend in the Meuse – but French defenders contained it for the next day and a half. Then on 15 May the French area commander ordered a retreat from the Meuse, as French forces crumbled in the north around Dinant and in the

---

51 Ibid., p. 285.
52 See in particular Rommel's account: Erwin Rommel, *The Rommel Papers*, ed. B. H. Liddell Hart (New York, 1953), pp. 8–11. Frieser, *Blitzkrieg-Legende*, p. 289, suggests that Rommel's performance in the crossing of the Meuse outshines even that of Guderian.
53 Frieser, *Blitzkrieg-Legende*, p. 289.

south around Sedan.[54] French forces at Montherme then collapsed completely as well, opening the way at last for a swift and deep advance by 6th Panzer Division in the center of an attack corridor that now stretched from Dinant to Sedan.

Guderian's attack across the Meuse at Sedan in mid-afternoon on 13 May was the crucial thrust that opened the road to rapid exploitation.[55] Unlike the other two panzer corps, XIX Panzer Corps received extensive support from the Luftwaffe, which attacked French positions along and behind the Meuse for three hours before the crossing began. On Guderian's right, 2nd Panzer Division's 2nd Rifle Regiment failed entirely; French defenders shot its assault boats out of the water and killed most of the German infantry before they could get to the river. On the left, 10th Panzer Division did no better: it lost forty-eight out of fifty assault boats. At best, a few badly shot-up and isolated platoons managed to cross the Meuse.

But the situation in the center was different. Here 1st Panzer Division possessed two rifle regiments, its own and the elite *Grossdeutschland* Regiment.[56] The armored division's infantry made the most successful crossing, but its lead companies, as elsewhere, suffered heavy casualties. Several factors aided 1st Panzer Division. A three-hour air bombardment drove the French artillerymen from their tubes, denying the French infantry much-needed supporting fires. And a single German combat engineer sergeant with his squad destroyed seven bunkers in a key sector of French defenses north of Wadelincourt, punching a hole in the French line that helped disorient the units holding neighboring positions.

Despite heavy losses, the surviving Germans pressed on. By midnight the heights overlooking Sedan were in their hands, but construction of pontoon bridges for the motorized portions of 1st Panzer Division had only just begun. Not until the 1st Rifle Regiment and *Grossdeutschland* had cleared the Meuse banks could 2nd and 10th Panzer Divisions begin to cross. Yet even while the engineers worked desperately to complete the bridges for the armor, German infantry continued to press southward. The top-down nature of French doctrine and the desire of French commanders to control everything insured a slow response. The two infantry regiments and two tank battalions that formed the reserve of French X Corps, the area command, received movement orders as early as 1600 on 13 May. All four units were within twenty kilometers (and one infantry regiment was within five kilometers) of the advancing Germans. But the French did not succeed in launching a counterattack – using only one of the infantry regiments –

---

54 Taylor, *March of Conquest*, pp. 227–8.
55 This account of the battle relies on Frieser, *Blitzkrieg-Legende*, pp. 190–260 and Doughty, *The Breaking Point*, pp. 131–265.
56 See the maps in Frieser, *Blitzkrieg-Legende*, pp. 198–9, 214, 227, 233, 241, and 261.

until 0900 on 14 May.[57] By that point the Germans had moved substantially heavier forces, including some tanks, across the river. The French counterattack swiftly collapsed.

That Guderian held his tanks back as a separate exploitation force, and allowed the infantry to carry the fight throughout most of 14 May, suggests the indeterminacy and flexibility of German doctrine.[58] By the following day he had become convinced of the utility of tank–infantry cooperation, and German armor was supporting the infantry in the fighting around Stonne. Nevertheless, 14 May was the day the French lost the battle. By then Guderian had already turned 1st and 2nd Panzer Divisions westward, while 10th Panzer Division and Infantry Regiment *Grossdeutschland* were still pushing south. Substantial French reserves were also arriving, in particular XXI Corps, with 3rd Armored Division and 3rd Motorized Infantry Division, neither of which had reached a high state of training. Their corps commander, General F. L. A. V. Flavigny, had been one of the French army's tank advocates before the war. But he allowed his division commanders to talk him out of launching a counterattack on 14 May; instead, he deployed the two divisions in a linear defense south of Stonne, and waited on events.[59]

Flavigny's immobility offered the German commanders on the scene the final convincing proof that the French were incapable of blocking either the German breakthrough or the exploitation that was getting underway. By 20 May, the lead division of Guderian's XIX Panzer Corps had reached the English Channel and the German army had severed the entire Allied left wing from the body of the Allied forces and from its logistical support. The battle of France was over.

CONCLUSION

The defeat of France within a few weeks in 1940 has remained one of the most astonishing and seemingly revolutionary events in twentieth-century military history. Not surprisingly, a whole host of explanations appeared in its aftermath: French national degeneracy, fifth columnists from the Right, Communist treason from the Left, an alleged unwillingness of the French to fight, and of course the revolutionary developments in German military doctrine. Sixty years later, events and their causes appear clearer. The

---

57 Frieser, *Blitzkrieg-Legende*, p. 227.
58 It is worth noting that Rommel used his tanks, as soon as he could get them across the Meuse, to support the infantry battle. As an infantryman who had recently taken command of a panzer division he displayed greater understanding of the function of tanks in combined-arms warfare than did Guderian.
59 Doughty, *The Breaking Point*, pp. 278–93 provides a particularly useful discussion of Flavigny's performance.

French did fight in 1940: in 1940 their armed forces lost 123,426 dead, 5,213 missing in action, and 200,000 wounded.[60] We can also dismiss the legends – either leftist or rightist – of national collapse as symptomatic of the ferocity of French politics rather than indicative of historical truth.

In the light of over sixty years of analysis, the defeat of 1940 appears a military event explicable by military causes, particularly actions by the French army and high command, and especially by Gamelin. The outcome also reflected many of the best qualities of German military culture and institutions. Nevertheless, a number of idiosyncratic factors enabled the Germans to maximize their advantages. The first was a willingness to take extraordinarily heavy casualties in the face of strong French opposition. Whatever the advantages of decentralized *Auftragstaktik*, the German breakthrough also owed much to the ideology that conditioned commanders and troops to drive forward no matter how small the chances of personal survival: racism and professionalism had fused to create in a quite literal sense the "loyalty unto death" of National Socialist rhetoric. But German victory was also precarious in the extreme; Guderian himself characterized the breakthrough on 13–14 May of the French defenses at Sedan by his XIX Panzer Corps as "almost a miracle."[61] Success hung from a few fragile threads: the suicidal combativeness of the German infantry, Rommel's brilliant personal leadership in forcing the crossing at Dinant, and a bridgehead secured by a single one of Guderian's three panzer divisions. The French would not have needed large forces to block the initial thrust across the Meuse, and change the entire course of the campaign.

But they neither assembled nor committed any such forces – and the result was the German revolution in military affairs. In the largest sense the Germans' considerable advantages in doctrine and training appear to have yielded relatively small advantages at the tactical level. But the *Wehrmacht* then leveraged tactical success into a shattering operational victory. In retrospect, German interwar efforts at innovation had aimed at incremental improvement; only in the long term and thanks to French inadequacies at the point of decision in 1940 did they produce a striking – and temporarily asymmetrical – operational revolution.

But incremental and evolutionary improvements in doctrine, training, and technology were only one source of German victory. As important was a military culture developed over more than a century, from the Prussian reforms of 1807–14 onward. That culture demanded effectiveness and "joy in responsibility" of every member of the army from rifleman to general, commanded constant training and practice, encouraged experiment and innovation, inculcated honesty and trust across ranks, units,

60   Kiesling, *Arming Against Hitler*, p. xii.
61   Guderian, *Panzer Leader*, p. 84.

and branches, nurtured its junior leaders, and punished failure only at its second or third occurrence. The slow, steady, systemic improvements of *Reichswehr* and *Wehrmacht* only became a revolution in military affairs on the banks of the Meuse. But in no sense and at no time had the German army pursued revolutionary technological change for its own sake. What it had done instead was to harness armor, firepower, radios, and the internal combustion engine to a conception of war grounded firmly in historical experience.

10

The future behind us

WILLIAMSON MURRAY AND MACGREGOR KNOX

The early Greek imagination envisaged the past and the present as in front of us – we can see them. The future, invisible, is behind us. . . . Paradoxical though it may sound to the modern ear, this image of our journey through time may be truer to reality than the medieval and modern feeling that we face the future as we make our way forward into it.[1]

The essays in this volume have focused on the transformations in the art of war that have marked the rise of the West. The purpose of this final chapter is entirely different. It is to draw general conclusions about the nature of military revolutions and of revolutions in military affairs, and to explore what that past might suggest about the potential for such revolutions in the future. In view of the claims of the enthusiasts that the United States is riding the crest of an American revolution in military affairs, these are intriguing questions indeed.[2]

The pace of technological and social change and the continuing antagonisms between states make it highly probable that war, military revolutions, and revolutions in military affairs will play a central role in the century that has just begun. Foresight is vital to the American armed forces, both in their efforts to adjust to the vast strategic changes consequent on the collapse of the Soviet Union and the rise of China, and in their attempts to conceptualize and address pressing issues that range from defects in their organizational cultures to the procurement of the weapons systems with which they will fight throughout the first third of the twenty-first century.

---

[1] Bernard Knox, *Backing Into the Future: The Classical Tradition and Its Renewal* (New York, 1994), pp. 11–12.
[2] For a recent example, see the improbable claims of Admiral William A. Owens, with Ed Offley, *Lifting the Fog of War* (New York, 2000).

175

Yet attempts to discern what the past might suggest about the future face enormous difficulties. As one of the editors has pointed out, with a nod to Georg Wilhelm Friedrich Hegel,

> The owl of history is an evening bird. The past as a whole is unknowable; only at the end of the day do some of its outlines dimly emerge. The future cannot be known at all, and the past suggests that change is often radical and unforeseeable rather than incremental and predictable. Yet despite its many ambiguities, historical experience remains the only available guide both to the present and to the range of alternatives inherent in the future.[3]

MILITARY REVOLUTIONS

In the introduction the editors posited the existence of two separate and distinct phenomena: military revolutions and revolutions in military affairs. The first has normally resulted from massive social and political changes that have restructured societies and states, and fundamentally altered the manner in which military organizations prepared for and conducted war. Such revolutions have been unpredictable and to a great extent *uncontrollable*. Revolutionary change of that kind is entirely possible – even likely – in the twenty-first century. But military organizations that face it will find themselves at best engaged in a desperate struggle to adapt to drastic changes in the very patterns of culture and society.

Military revolutions in the past have transformed with startling speed and force all aspects of war, from policy and strategy to tactics. The combination of an increasingly rapid pace of technological change, of the immense capacity of Western nation-states to mobilize their populations, and of the popular passions on which that mobilization depended created a nightmare world for the politicians and generals of the first half of the twentieth century. From its very beginning in the summer of 1914, the First World War unleashed enthusiasms and hatreds that no politician could control. Those passions and the scale of losses from the first battles onward meant there was no going back, no credible prospect of a negotiated settlement. The sanctity of the national cause and the weight of sacrifice it entailed made only two outcomes conceivable: total victory or total defeat. Simultaneously, technology transformed the terrifying conditions of the 1914–18 battlefield so swiftly and continuously that the opposing sides found it difficult to respond by framing appropriate tactical and operational doctrine. Technology did not simplify war, as contemporary superstition now claims: *it made it exponentially more complex*. Each new

---

[3] MacGregor Knox, "What History Can Tell Us About the 'New Strategic Environment,'" in Williamson Murray, ed., *Brassey's Mershon American Defense Annual, 1995–1996* (Washington, DC, 1996), pp. 1–25.

scientific development, each new *weapons system* (a notion born, if not fully exploited, in the war of 1914–18) demanded fresh thought and ever-greater tactical, technical, and logistical expertise.

The constantly changing tactical and technological equation and the willingness of the contending sides to pay virtually any price made decisive victory impossible for four long years.[4] The more tender-hearted among the war's political leaders and the millions of bereaved might wring their hands at the immense losses, but the "sausage machine" ground relentlessly on.[5] In the end, three factors brought deliverance: the exhaustion of the German people-in-arms and the crumbling of the German state; the commitment to the Allied side of United States economic power and of 2.1 million fresh troops to France by fall 1918; and the reinvention in 1917–18, at terrifying cost and within narrow technological limits, of battlefield movement.[6] The sequel – the far greater war of 1939–45 – killed three times as many people as the Great War through ideological furies that made those of 1914–18 seem tame and through the perfection of movement in three dimensions across oceans and continents. Then the advent of nuclear weapons both helped end that war and inaugurated a new era in which great powers, as one wit has put it, made war as porcupines make love: carefully.

The world may well confront yet another such revolution in the twenty-first century, and the swift changes in information technology currently underway appear the most likely candidate for the role of protagonist. But as the great military revolutions of the past have suggested, changes in society and politics – not in technology alone – are the most revolutionary forces of all. It is those social and cultural forces, perhaps unleashed or

---

4   As Paul Kennedy has suggested, tactics held the key to military effectiveness in the First World War; and particularly on the Western Front, tactical problems were subject to constant change, as each side reacted to the efforts of its adversary ("Military Effectiveness in the First World War," in Allan R. Millett and Williamson Murray, eds., *Military Effectiveness*, vol. 1, *The First World War* [London, 1988], p. 331).
5   Yet alternatives existed. By summer 1917 the British Expeditionary Force under Sir Douglas Haig was in a position to launch a series of deadly limited offensives against German positions in the West. Haig instead launched and sustained a single massive, protracted drive with the delusional objective of a breakthrough in an area – Flanders – in which the German defenses and the terrain were least favorable to an attacker. Yet Haig shared responsibility: the British prime minister, David Lloyd George, knew the level of casualties such an offensive would involve but failed to exercise his powers as leader of the British government to prevent Haig either from launching it or from continuing it after persistent rain had turned the Ypres salient into a swamp (see particularly the brilliant study by Robin Prior and Trevor Wilson, *Passchendaele, the Untold Story* [New Haven, CT, 1996]).
6   German casualties in Ludendorff's 1918 spring offensives were nearly one million men in the four months from mid-March to mid-July; the German victories achieved a casualty bill more than double those suffered by the attacking armies of 1916–17 in each of the four-month battles at Verdun, on the Somme, and at Passchendaele. British losses in the final "hundred days" advance through and beyond the Hindenburg Line were likewise heavy.

amplified as in earlier periods by new technologies, that will determine the nature of any coming military revolution and will decisively affect how military organizations prepare for and conduct war.

Yet even military revolutions have limits: they have not changed in the past – and cannot change in the future – war's underlying nature. Perhaps the most striking claim of contemporary Beltway pundits is that technological innovation, particularly in information technology, will purge the conduct of war of the uncertainties and ambiguities of the past. For those happy powers that set the technological pace, war will become an essentially frictionless engineering exercise. One of the most ardent proponents of this post-Clausewitzian world-view, Admiral William A. Owens – former vice-chairman of the U.S. Joint Chiefs of Staff – has put his case in glowing terms:

> The technology that is available to the U.S. military today and now in development can revolutionize the way we conduct military operations. That technology can give us the ability to see a battlefield as large as Iraq or Korea – an area 200 miles on a side – with unprecedented fidelity, comprehension, and timeliness; by night or by day, in any kind of weather, all the time.[7]

Cynics might suggest that Admiral Owens has set an ambitious objective indeed for a government and armed forces whose numerous intelligence agencies, equipped with a breath-taking range of high technology, were incapable of identifying correctly the Chinese embassy in Belgrade that U.S. forces partially destroyed during the spring 1999 Kosovo War.[8]

Such individual examples of the persistence of friction should not obscure the general systemic issue. Friction, uncertainty, and confusion in warfare are not superficial annoyances to be gradually eliminated by technological "progress." War is *inherently* nonlinear. It is a collision of two living wills. And as Clausewitz suggested, no other human activity is so "continuously or universally bound up with chance."[9] The technological utopians are free to reject Clausewitz – who saw more warfare at first hand than they are ever likely to – as an unworldly early nineteenth-century figure whose Kantian philosophical framework held no place for technological change.[10]

---

7 Owens, *Lifting the Fog of War*, p. 4.
8 The extravagant claims of the technological enthusiasts have misled European conspiracy-mongers into suggesting that the United States deliberately attacked the Chinese embassy. The *New York Times* (17 April 2000, p. A1) has however offered a carefully documented account that makes plain that the United States targeted and struck the embassy as the result of simple – and predictable – bureaucratic incompetence (Clausewitzian friction) within its intelligence services, particularly the Central Intelligence Agency.
9 Clausewitz, *On War*, p. 85; see also the outstanding article of Alan Beyerchen, "Clausewitz, Nonlinearity, and the Unpredictability of War," *International Security*, Winter 1992/1993.
10 See however the useful analysis of Michael Handel, "Clausewitz in the Age of Technology," in Handel, ed., *Clausewitz and Modern Strategy* (London, 1986), pp. 51–92.

But the scientific insights of the twentieth century suggest that the qualities Clausewitz discerned in war were nothing less than reflections of the nature of the universe. As a recent – and also combat-experienced – commentator has suggested, to overturn the role of friction in war,

> one would need to overthrow nonlinear dynamics, the second law of thermodynamics, the fundamental tenets of neo-Darwinian evolutionary biology, and all the limiting metatheorems of mathematical logic, including Kurt Gödel's famous incompleteness theorems and Gregory Chaitin's extension of Gödel's work to demonstrate the existence of randomness in arithmetic. No small task indeed![11]

The obsessions of the technological utopians derive equally from the deeply and quaintly American belief that all human problems have engineering solutions, and from the profoundly un-American (to those familiar with the United States' proud and violent history) post-Vietnam search for technological silver bullets that will permit U.S. forces to wage war without suffering – or perhaps even inflicting – casualties. The utopians' "face of battle" is a bank of computer displays, and in their fond imaginings war is nothing more than dealing out punishment in doses precision-calculated to send political signals or keep the natives under control.[12]

Clausewitz had utter contempt for those of his contemporaries who suffered from similar delusions:

> Kind-hearted people might of course think there was some ingenious way to disarm or defeat an enemy without too much bloodshed, and might imagine this is the true goal of the art of war. Pleasant as it sounds, it is a fallacy that must be exposed: war is a . . . dangerous business . . .

No technological marvels can alter war's unpredictable nature as a "paradoxical trinity" composed of "primordial violence," politics, and chance.[13]

REVOLUTIONS IN MILITARY AFFAIRS

If military revolutions are cataclysmic events that military institutions aspire merely to survive, revolutions in military affairs are periods of innovation in which armed forces develop novel concepts involving changes in doctrine, tactics, procedures, and technology. These concepts require time to work out. They involve extensive experimentation, which often results in

---

11 Barry D. Watts, *Clausewitzian Friction and Future War* (Washington, DC, 1996), p. 132.
12 For an anticipation of this approach in microcosm, see the still astonishing memorandum by John McNaughton, Assistant Secretary of Defense for International Security Affairs, "Proposed Course of Action RE Vietnam," 24 March 1965, *The Pentagon Papers: The Defense Department History of United States Decisionmaking on Vietnam* (Boston, MA, 1972), vol. 3, pp. 694–702.
13 Clausewitz, *On War*, pp. 75, 89.

failure. Their development also demands a culture that allows innovation and debate unfettered by dogma. Their driving force is rarely technology; the technological capabilities of forces that have realized revolutions in military affairs have often been inferior to those of their opponents. And revolutions in military affairs take place almost exclusively at the operational level of war. They rarely affect the strategic level, except insofar as operational success can determine the larger strategic equation – often a tenuous linkage.

Moreover revolutions in military affairs *always* occur within the context of politics and strategy – and that context is everything. New Zealand will not realize a revolution in military affairs in the foreseeable future: its strategic environment is too benign to inspire one. And in the broader context of war between industrialized powers, the strategic level of war is the decisive one. Flawed strategy will bring the most expert and battle-hardened forces down: "Mistakes in operations and tactics can be corrected, but political and strategic mistakes live forever."[14] That is indeed the principal and overriding lesson of America's misadventure in Vietnam.[15] Harry Summers's famous anecdote puts the issue clearly: in April 1973 two colonels involved in the implementation of the Paris peace accords, Summers and a North Vietnamese counterpart, fell into conversation about the war in which both had fought. Summers pointed out that North Vietnam had never defeated American forces on the battlefield. The North Vietnamese replied that such a claim might be true but was irrelevant. North Vietnam had won the war.[16]

Despite the bloody lessons taught in Vietnam, the nature and quality of United States strategic thought as the nation enters the twenty-first century suggest that coherence and appropriateness in future American strategic decision making are unlikely.[17] Ignorance of history – even the history of the United States – and of foreign cultures and languages is pervasive throughout both policy elites and general population. That is an astonishing

---

14 Allan R. Millett and Williamson Murray, "Lessons of War," *The National Interest*, Winter 1988/1989.
15 For the fundamental flaws in the basic strategic assumptions under which the U.S. government intervened in Vietnam, see Herbert R. McMaster, *Dereliction of Duty: Lyndon Johnson, Robert McNamara, The Joint Chiefs of Staff, and the Lies that Led to Vietnam* (New York, 1997).
16 Harry G. Summers, Jr., *On Strategy: The Vietnam War in Context* (New York, 1982), pp. 21, 29 note 1. The alleged failure of North Vietnamese forces to defeat U.S. units on the battlefield was one of the more threadbare myths of a war that generated more than its share of fantasy (for analysis of a significant – early – American defeat, see Lt. Gen. Harold G. Moore [Ret.] and Joseph L. Galloway, *We Were Soldiers Once . . . and Young* [New York, 1992]).
17 See Williamson Murray, "The Emerging Strategic Environment: A Historian's Thoughts," *Strategic Review*, Winter 1999, pp. 36–8.

weakness in the purported era of globalization, and a decisive impediment to the formulation of a coherent strategic vision.[18] Nor is improvement in prospect, given the intellectual bankruptcy of much of the U.S. educational system.

An underlying and unified national strategic concept should in principle determine the structuring, composition, and employment concept of the armed forces. In the contemporary United States, no such concept exists, and U.S. forces innovate not merely in a strategic vacuum but in an operational one as well. The cluster of innovations that purportedly herald the coming of an "American RMA" entirely lack coherence. Service advocates and enthusiasts for one or another of the bewildering variety of acronym-studded procurement programs rarely explain how the new technologies relate in an integrated way to the age-old problem of "compelling the enemy to do our will," always assuming that the United States has a will and strategic design sufficiently coherent to impose.

The absence as yet of a clear challenger to America's position has compounded the difficulties in systemic change and innovation caused by this intellectual and strategic–operational vacuum. Every major cluster of innovations during the interwar period that resulted in a revolution in military affairs – combined-arms ground warfare, carrier warfare, and amphibious warfare – depended on the existence of concrete adversaries against which to frame innovation. And those RMAs also derived from evolutionary problem-solving approaches and visions tempered by deliberate study of past experience, and were embedded in organizational cultures that fostered critical thought and open debate.[19]

The Germans, for example, needed real-world opponents such as the French, Polish, and Czech armies against which to develop the capabilities that eventually led to their impressive victories in 1939-40. Yet the operational framework within which the Blitzkrieg revolution developed proved less impressive when it came to coping with the Soviet Union. BARBAROSSA demanded logistical and intelligence capabilities that far surpassed those required in campaigns against Germany's immediate neighbors. The spaces of European Russia dwarfed anything the Prusso-German army had ever confronted, while Nazi racial ideology and professional arrogance impelled the Germans to underestimate Soviet capabilities by a wide margin not merely at the outset but throughout the war.[20]

---

18 One of the few hopeful signs in the muddled landscape of U.S. strategic thinking is the report of the United States Commission on National Security/21st Century, *New World Coming: American Security in the 21st Century* (Washington, DC, 1999).

19 See Williamson Murray, "Innovation: Past and Future," in Murray and Millett, *Military Innovation in the Interwar Period*, p. 311.

20 See Williamson Murray and Allan R. Millett, *A War To Be Won, Fighting the Second World War* (Cambridge, MA, 2000), Chapter 6.

In facing the strategic and operational challenges of a war against Japan, the U.S. Navy and Marine Corps did an even more impressive job of innovating than the Germans. Not only did the two services develop remarkable operational and tactical capabilities, but their war-gaming, experiments, and exercises explored the larger logistical and intelligence problems that a Pacific War was likely to raise. The two services could not necessarily solve most of those problems before the outbreak of war, especially in view of the funding constraints under which they suffered until 1940. But advance exploration of the issues speeded considerably the process of adaptation during the conflict itself.[21]

The marines in particular confronted a seemingly insurmountable obstacle. The British disaster at Gallipoli in 1915 had led military experts and professionals – including most in the United States – to write off amphibious warfare in general and opposed landings in particular as impractical. But as war-gaming at the Naval War College soon showed, the enormous logistical demands of a Pacific offensive required the capture of forward operating bases in the island chains that stretched toward Japan. The United States could not project its power across the immense distances of the central Pacific in any other way.

With their institutional survival at stake, the marines refused to accept the verdict of Gallipoli. They resolved instead to *learn* from British mistakes. That resolve and the overriding importance to the navy of developing the capability to land on heavily defended atolls led by the 1930s to a long series of fleet exercises and experiments aimed at identifying and solving practical problems.[22] The marines also succeeded in creating a culture in which honest examination of exercises and experiments could take place, and in which the results of experiments and fleet exercises fed directly into training and preparation for war.

Military organizations that innovated without a clear opponent in mind had a far more difficult time. At least through the mid-1930s the RAF and the U.S. Army Air Corps developed their doctrine and concepts against generic opponents. As a result, much of their thinking about the potential and techniques of strategic bombing was both mechanistic and unduly optimistic. The RAF refused to study the last war; its principal leaders

---

21   Admiral Chester Nimitz, the commander of U.S. naval forces from the aftermath of Pearl Harbor to Tokyo Bay, went so far as to "credit the Naval War College for such success [as] I achieved during the war" (W. B. Potter, *Nimitz* [Annapolis, MD, 1976], p. 136). Imponderables nevertheless remained, such as the type and duration of bombardment required to wreck Japanese beach defenses sufficiently so that attacking forces would not suffer prohibitive casualties. Tarawa provided necessary if costly lessons in that regard.

22   See Allan R. Millett, "Assault From the Sea: The Development of Amphibious Warfare Between the Wars – The British, American, and Japanese Experiences," in Murray and Millett, *Military Innovation in the Interwar Period*, Chapter 2.

shared a messianic belief that technology had rendered all previous experience obsolete, and they framed their force structures, doctrine, and employment concepts in the light of technological changes that had yet to occur. That approach had a disastrous impact on the British strategic bombing campaign during much of the Second World War.[23]

Perhaps the evidence of the Great War with respect to strategic bombing was ambiguous. But the 1914–18 conflict did offer two very clear air power lessons. First, all air operations required air superiority; without it, attacking forces suffered unsustainable losses. Second, finding and hitting targets under anything other than perfect daylight visibility posed intractable challenges. As a British naval aviator noted,

> Experience has shown that it is quite easy for five squadrons to set out to bomb a particular target and for only one of those five ever to reach the objective; while the other four, in the honest belief that they have done so, have bombed four different villages which bore little if any resemblance to the one they desired to attack.[24]

Yet such lessons disappeared almost entirely from the RAF's institutional consciousness after 1918. The result of this unwillingness to learn from the past was that the RAF entered the war of 1939–45 with a mystical faith in the survivability of bombers. RAF leaders and planners were also convinced that identifying, finding, and destroying targets posed no insuperable difficulties, despite much experience gained in exercises that demonstrated the exact opposite. The RAF's organizational culture was largely impervious to evidence, until an outside source – the Butt Report on bombing accuracy of August 1941 – forced upon the service's unwilling leadership the recognition that it had wasted an entire year and the lives of innumerable aircrew.

American airmen were no more open-minded. Billy Mitchell, despite the stridency of his arguments, at least recognized the underlying lesson of the 1914–18 air war: air superiority was the *sine qua non* of air power. But by the early 1930s the staff of the Air Corps Tactical School in Montgomery, Alabama had passed far beyond Mitchell's relative realism and were blithely proposing that great formations of self-defending bombers could fly deep into enemy airspace to attack vital economic targets without the protection of long-range escort fighters – and without suffering unacceptable casualties.

---

23 For an examination of how close the Germans came to failing, see Chapter 9 of this work and Robert A. Doughty, *The Breaking Point: Sedan and the Fall of France*, 1940 (Hamden, CT, 1990).

24 Quoted by Group Captain R. A. Mason, "The British Dimension," in Alfred F. Hurley and Robert C. Erhard, eds., *Air Power and Warfare* (Washington, DC, 1979), p. 32.

This proclivity to disregard the present as well as the past and to regard *evidence* with suspicion carried over into the Second World War in both the RAF and the U.S. Army Air Force. RAF belief that the bomber – in Stanley Baldwin's long-remembered but wholly misleading words – "would always get through" led to a dramatic failure to realize the full potential of strategic bombing until late in the war. Both British and American services ignored the powerful defensive lessons of the Battle of Britain in favor of their pre-war doctrinal fantasies.[25] Refusal to entertain notions that contradicted a cherished vision also led the chief of the air staff, Sir Charles Portal, to inform Churchill in 1941 that long-range escort fighters – the obvious means of achieving the air superiority required for effective strategic bombing – were technologically unfeasible. As the prime minister remarked, Portal's claim "closed many doors."[26]

Until the end of 1943 both air forces pursued operational and tactical approaches that led repeatedly to wholly avoidable disasters – Schweinfurt, Berlin, Nuremberg – and to loss rates that no military organization could sustain for long. Not until the unintended appearance of just such an escort fighter – the P-51 Mustang – could U.S. daylight operations destroy the Luftwaffe fighter force and open the road to systematic attack on German industry and transport by the RAF and the Eighth U.S. Air Force. In the end, the Combined Bomber Offensive played a vital role in winning the Second World War. But the infatuation of the British and U.S. air leadership with technological assumptions that contradicted both past experience and current operational–tactical realities raised immeasurably the cost of victory in aircraft and lives.[27]

The Luftwaffe unfortunately did rather better.[28] It developed its doctrine and combat concepts within a simple operational framework and strategic goal shared with the German army, and aimed at the defeat of Germany's opponents in central Europe. As a result, it was far better prepared to make immediate and direct contributions to the overall conduct of military operations than were the air forces of Britain and the

25 For the RAF's outright rejection of the lessons of past military experience see PRO AIR 20/40, Air Staff Memorandum No. 11A, March 1924.
26 Sir Charles Webster and Noble Frankland, *The Strategic Air Offensive Against Germany*, vol. 1, *Preparation* (London, 1962), p. 177. Air Marshal Sir Hugh Dowding had suggested to the Air Ministry in March 1940 that the RAF would soon need a long-range escort fighter, only to be brusquely put down.
27 Air Vice Marshal D. C. T. Bennett, commander of Bomber Command's Pathfinder Force, who flew regularly on active operations, commented after the war that were he in command in the next war, he would make all air vice marshals fly on operations; for every one killed, the RAF would save 200 crew lives (oral interview with D. C. T. Bennett, RAF Staff College, Bracknell).
28 See Murray, *Luftwaffe*, Chapter 1; idem, "Strategic Bombing," in *Military Innovation in the Interwar Period*, Chapter 3.

United States.[29] The past thus suggests that pure technological development without the direction provided by a clear strategic context can easily lead in dangerous directions: either toward ignoring potential enemy responses, or – even more dangerously – into the dead end, graphically illustrated by the floundering of U.S. forces in Vietnam, of a technological sophistication irrelevant to the war actually being fought.

As well as requiring real-world opponents, revolutions in military affairs despite their name in fact consist primarily of evolutionary peacetime changes through which military organizations alter their conceptual picture of future war in response to technological change. The resulting adaptation of concepts and doctrine results in gradual systemic alterations to how organizations fight. The full impact of evolutionary change over twenty years may not be readily apparent even within the organization. Only the audit of war, a war conducted against a significantly backward opponent, will demonstrate that an RMA has occurred. And the resulting revolution will usually be most obvious to the defeated.[30]

A further crucial element in successful interwar innovation lay in the nature of the visions that drove the innovators. The most successful organizations avoided wild leaps into the future; their innovations remained tied to past experience, derived from conceptually sophisticated and honestly assessed experiment, and depended on the ability to learn from both success and failure. The *Reichswehr*'s chief, General Hans von Seeckt, believed that movement was the essence of operations and saw the internal combustion engine as a potentially decisive means of restoring battlefield mobility. Yet he noted shortly after the army's first experiments with motorization that while he "fully approve[d] of the . . . exercise's conception and leadership, . . . there [was] still much that [was] not clear about the specific tactical use of motor vehicles." He therefore ordered that the exercise after-action report be made available to the army's major staffs and commands "as a topic for lectures and study."[31] Seeckt was not interested in laying down visions of distant future capabilities. His refusal to draw premature conclusions underlines the importance, in revolutions in military affairs, of the evolutionary solution of specific immediate problems.

---

29   In view of the claims of postwar historians that the Germans had no interest in strategic bombing, it is ironic that the Luftwaffe was in fact better prepared at the outset to perform strategic missions than the bomber forces of the RAF and USAAF. The Germans at least understood that any such campaign faced two central obstacles – bombing accuracy and the achievement of air superiority – and had taken steps to overcome them (Murray, "Strategic Bombing").

30   And often the most seemingly decisive victories will on closer examination also prove – in Wellington's famous phrase – "damn near-run things," as already suggested with regard to German success in 1940.

31   Reichswehrministerium, Chef der Heeresleitung, "Harzübung, 8.1.22," National Archives and Records Agency, microcopy T-79/95/000622.

William Moffett likewise possessed a vision: that naval aviation was capable of major contributions to the navy's combat power far surpassing its original roles of reconnaissance and artillery spotting for the battle fleet. But the process of carrier innovation in the U.S. Navy remained tightly connected to solving practical problems. War games at the Naval War College had indicated that pulses of air power rather than continuous streams would significantly enhance the combat capabilities of carriers.[32] But it was the solving of the practical problems of operating aircraft at sea that made clear the possibilities of carrier aviation:

> For *Langley's* [the first U.S. carrier] aviators and crews, 1926 was a hectic year. . . . By mid-year [the carrier] had an aircraft barrier which, when lifted amidships, shielded planes parked forward from any landing aircraft whose tailhook might miss the athwartship arresting gear located farther aft. Thus was borne the deck park, a key element in improving the carrying capacity and operating efficiency of aircraft carriers . . . By August 1926, *Langley's* crew could launch aircraft every fifteen seconds and recover them every ninety seconds.[33]

Aviation innovators in the U.S. Navy thus spent much of the 1920s and 1930s developing the ability to launch, recover, and maintain large numbers of aircraft on carrier decks. By the end of the 1930s U.S. carriers could carry and launch far more aircraft than either the British or Japanese navies conceived possible.[34]

The warped visions of the land-based airmen of the RAF and the U.S. Army Air Corps stand in marked contrast to the foresight of the innovators of the *Reichsheer*, the U.S. Navy, or the U.S. Marine Corps – with one highly significant exception. The creation of Fighter Command by Sir Hugh Dowding in the late 1930s stands out precisely because it ran against the grain of RAF practice. It is also a striking example of a revolution in military affairs carried through in a short period of time.[35] Dowding's success was central to the defense of the United Kingdom in 1940. It rested almost entirely on the support he received from outside the air ministry and air staff, and its precariousness underlines the extent to which revolutions in military affairs depend upon circumstances. Dowding himself had been

---

[32] Thomas C. Hone, Norman Friedman, and Mark D. Mandeles, *American and British Aircraft Carrier Development, 1919–1941* (Annapolis, MD, 1999), p. 34.

[33] Ibid., p. 42.

[34] See Watts and Murray, "Military Innovation in Peacetime," pp. 400-04; also David C. Evans and Mark R. Peattie, *Kaigun: Strategy, Tactics, and Technology in the Imperial Japanese Navy 1887–1941* (Annapolis, MD, 1997), p. 323.

[35] See Alan Beyerchen, "From Radio to Radar: Interwar Military Adaptation to Technological Change in Germany, the United Kingdom, and the United States," in Murray and Millett, eds., *Military Innovation in the Interwar Period.*

lucky to survive the First World War both as an individual and as an air officer; Sir Hugh Trenchard had sent him home from the Western Front in summer 1916.[36] His career nevertheless recovered, and by the early 1930s he had become the RAF's chief of research and development. In that position he oversaw the specifications for the fighters that became the Spitfire and Hurricane, and encouraged the research that led to the development of effective radar. He then became chief of Fighter Command in the late 1930s, after losing the competition to become the next chief of air staff to Sir Cyril Newall. At Fighter Command, Dowding drew from 1937 onward on the experience accumulated in creating a British air defense system in 1914–18.[37] The result was a coherent whole: modern fighters, radar, two-way voice radio communications, command structures capable of making and implementing operational and tactical decisions with unprecedented speed and flexibility, and logistical and crew training infrastructures that survived the Luftwaffe's best efforts. Dowding's contribution rested not on technology alone, but on a unified *systemic* concept for its employment.

Of the other factors that contributed to success of the interwar revolutions in military affairs, the foremost were military culture and military education. The Germans took the education of their officer corps very seriously indeed. Seeckt's reforms after 1919 placed the values of the Prussian general staff at the heart of the new German army.[38] The *Reichsheer*'s entire officer corps thus took military education with a seriousness unprecedented in the already comparatively learned pre-1914 German army. Even Erwin Rommel, the archetypal "muddy-boots" soldier of the Imperial German Army, *Reichsheer*, and *Wehrmacht*, wrote books as well as read them.[39]

The other interwar military organizations that innovated successfully took professional military education equally seriously. The Naval War College was examining the possibilities of seaborne air power before the U.S. Navy possessed a single aircraft carrier.[40] Raymond Spruance, the key

---

[36]   Dowding had asked Trenchard to pull his squadron out of the fighting due to its heavy losses. Such a request normally terminated the career of the commander in question; in Dowding's case it did not.

[37]   A major cause of German failure in the Battle of Britain lay in Luftwaffe inability to recognize that the British had integrated radar into an effective air defense *system* that controlled the conduct of the battle; the Germans thus ceased their early attacks on the radar stations because they failed to understand the crucial operational role of radar (which they also possessed).

[38]   On Seeckt's reforms, see particularly James S. Corum, *The Roots of Blitzkrieg: Hans von Seeckt and German Military Reform* (Lawrence, KS, 1992).

[39]   See in this regard the particularly insightful biography by David Fraser, *Knight's Cross: A Life of Field Marshal Erwin Rommel* (London, 1993).

[40]   For the contributions made to naval wargaming by Admiral William Sims see Peter P. Perla, *The Art of Wargaming: A Guide for Professionals and Hobbyists* (Annapolis, MD, 1990).

figure in the two battles that established U.S. naval supremacy for the remainder of the century – Midway and the Philippine Sea – served not one but two tours on the faculty of the Naval War College.[41] The U.S. Army felt seriously enough about the higher military education of its officers to place two of its future senior commanders, Colonel W. H. Simpson and Major J. Lawton Collins, on the teaching faculty of the Army War College for the 1939–40 academic year. The following year Alexander Patch, who also rose to senior command in Europe, was on the faculty.[42]

The claim that military institutions fail in battle because they study the last war too closely is a platitude wholly without foundation. The military institutions that successfully innovated between 1919 and 1940 without exception examined recent military events in a careful, thorough, and realistic fashion. Analysis of the past was the basis of successful innovation. The key technique of innovation was open-ended experiment and exercises that tested systems to breakdown rather than aiming at the validation of hopes or theories. Simple honesty and the free flow of ideas between superiors and subordinates – key components of all successful military cultures – were centrally important to the ability to learn from experience. And the overriding purpose of experiments and exercises was to improve the effectiveness of units and of the service as a whole, rather than singling out commanders who had allegedly failed.[43]

THE U.S. ARMED FORCES AND THE NEXT REVOLUTION IN MILITARY AFFAIRS

In January–February 1991 the United States and its allies devastated the air and ground forces of Saddam Hussein's Iraq. The Iraqis admittedly displayed extraordinary ineptitude at every level. But virtually every other revolution in military affairs has required a victim whose battlefield inadequacies have accentuated the disparity between old and new. Edward III required the poorly organized armies of feudal France to win the great victory of Crécy; Napoleon required the hidebound Austrians and Prussians at Austerlitz and Jena–Auerstädt; Moltke needed the slow-thinking and slow-moving Austrians and French in 1866 and 1870; and the *Wehrmacht* of 1940 required General Maurice Gamelin to show its capabilities to the fullest.

---

[41] These career patterns contrast starkly with those of the current U.S. Navy, in which half the admirals on active duty have not even attended a war college as students.

[42] Leonard J. Holder, Jr. and Williamson Murray, "Prospects for Military Education," *Joint Forces Quarterly*, Spring 1998, p. 83.

[43] For the futility of doctrinal analysis without realistic and demanding experiments, see Robert A. Doughty, *The Seeds of Disaster, The Development of French Army Doctrine, 1919–1939* (Hamden, CT, 1985) and Eugenia C. Kiesling, *Arming Against Hitler, France and the Limits of Military Planning* (Lawrence, KS, 1996).

American victory in the Second Gulf War indeed represented – as advertised – a revolution in military affairs. But it was less a triumph of American technology than a triumph of *concepts and doctrine* that rested firmly on an understanding of the fundamental nature of war. As in all such revolutions, the massive changes in capabilities that showed so clearly on the battlefield were the result of careful doctrinal and conceptual evolution and much investment in training and experiment. The American armed forces had identified and addressed a series of discrete problems that had surfaced during the Vietnam War, from bombing accuracy to the suppression of enemy air defenses, the need for operational concepts in ground combat, and the effective use of helicopters to extend the battlespace.

From 1973 to the mid-1980s, amid debate and experimentation, the four services fundamentally recast their approach to war. "Top Gun" and "Red Flag" enormously improved the training and preparation of U.S. Navy, Marine Corps, and Air Force fighter pilots. The army wrote the operational level of war back into its doctrine.[44] The marines rethought in fundamental ways their doctrine and preparations for war. The publication of the 1986 edition of FM100-5 and of Marine Corps Manual 1-1, *Warfighting*, in 1987 represented a genuine revolution; the concept of air–land battle provided an entirely new doctrinal framework. As with its interwar counterparts, this new concept was tailored above all to a specific enemy and a specific theater of war.

Soviet collapse unleashed the Second Gulf War in two senses. Saddam would never have dared to seek control of the oil of the Middle East in the more disciplined and bracing environment of the Cold War. And Soviet collapse also left the United States with the forces and doctrine developed to fight a sophisticated and capable opponent, and the strategic breathing space in which to redeploy many of them to the Middle East. But in the desert – where the contingent factor of terrain maximized U.S. advantages – the adversary was no Red Army. It was rather a military establishment that superimposed on the inherited cultural defects so amply displayed in the Arab–Israeli wars a character all its own, as a political instrument molded and controlled almost solely by fear. American victory was overdetermined, and only Washington's craven repudiation – "we're not going to Baghdad" – of the principal strategic lesson of the two world wars limited its extent and indefinitely postponed the necessary outcome.[45]

---

[44] For the start of this process see Paul H. Herbert, "Deciding What Has To Be Done: General William E. Dupuy and the 1976 Edition of FM100-5, Operations," *Leavenworth Papers* 16 (1988).

[45] For the nature of the Iraqi dictatorship, see particularly the prescient work of Kanan Makiya (pseud. Samir al-Khalil), *Republic of Fear: The Politics of Modern Iraq* (Berkeley, CA, 1989).

But that "revolution in military affairs" is over. Present and future opponents and allies of the United States know what U.S. forces can do. As the hundred-hours war ended, adaptation, innovation, and strategic and diplomatic realignments aimed at redressing the power imbalance so graphically demonstrated in the Gulf began throughout the world. The art of war is neither static nor unipolar; it is above all a contest of wills: "he dictates to me as much as I dictate to him."[46]

The American response to victory has been far less wise – and less professional – than the steps taken to secure it. Some key figures in the American armed forces clearly concluded that victory had made further effort and thought superfluous: the "American RMA" would permit the United States to rely for the foreseeable future on the forces it already possessed. Others judged that victory in the Gulf was simply a product of a generic U.S. technological superiority – a complete misreading of the previous twenty years, in which conceptual advances derived from defeat and from focusing on a specific opponent had driven innovation.[47] The advocates of that view insisted that continuing technological progress – in which the United States was by definition certain to lead – would confer upon America an effortless superiority over all potential opponents in the coming century. Ironically, given the preeminent role of the analysis of past mistakes in securing victory in 1991, the armed forces made little attempt to learn from the actual events of the Second Gulf War. What little analysis took place largely ignored developments above the tactical level, and for the most part addressed narrow technological issues.[48]

Nor has the scene changed greatly since 1991. The fervent enthusiasm within the Pentagon for the slogan of a revolution in military affairs might seem to offer assurance that the United States will develop revolutionary capabilities and concepts on a continuing basis. But appearances are deceptive. The bureaucratic–technological *Weltanschauung* derived from the seeming perfection of nuclear warfighting, which reduced strategy to mere targeting, once again dominates the civilian

---

46   Clausewitz, *On War*, p. 77.
47   Indeed one of the difficulties that the Director of the Office of Net Assessment, Andrew W. Marshall, has confronted since his office first brought the possibility of a revolution in military affairs to the attention of the services in the aftermath of the Gulf War has been the consistent overemphasis in Pentagon discussions on technology – rather than on *concepts for its use.*
48   No organization made a serious attempt to examine the actual battlefield results on the Iraqi territory the coalition had occupied, and only the efforts of the Secretary of the Air Force ensured the creation of a Gulf War Air Power Survey conducted by an independent group of scholars. But that body's subsequent report was simply filed; few if any officers have read it.

defense community and the military circles charged with administering "the Building."[49]

And the situation that confronts the United States now and for the foreseeable future is different and far less clear than that of the interwar or Cold War periods. No immediate opponent – with the possible exception of the would-be Chinese superpower – bulks large on the horizon. Instead the United States confronts a variety of indeterminate medium- and long-term threats.[50] No direct and unambiguous challengers to the international order demand the development of specific, coherent concepts and doctrine. No effective current regional threat – perhaps not even from China, despite its inability to conceal the far-ranging ambitions and the anti-Western fanaticism that alone legitimate the rule of its Party – provides a semblance of a target against which to develop the specific capabilities characteristic of revolutions in military affairs. The undoubted blessings of peace are in this regard decidedly mixed.[51]

A further obstacle to successful American innovation leading to future revolutions in military affairs derives from the changing institutional cultures of the armed forces themselves. In the post-Vietnam period, U.S. Army, Marine Corps, and Air Force officers who had survived several tours in southeast Asia remained deeply suspicious of the predictive frictionless technological universe inhabited by Robert McNamara and his collaborators, who had led the United States to defeat and humiliation.[52] By the early 1980s this Vietnam generation had risen to positions of leadership, and sought to recast the institutional world-views of the armed forces. They had learned – in the paddies, swamps, jungles, and anti-aircraft mis-

---

49 The congruence in this respect between the civilian and uniformed components of the Pentagon elite is suggested by an article that appeared in the major U.S. foreign policy journal. Its authors, Joseph S. Nye, Jr. and Admiral Owens, proclaimed that "the [U.S.] information advantage can help to deter or defeat traditional military threats at relatively low cost . . . [It] can strengthen the intellectual link between U.S. foreign policy and military power and offer new ways of obtaining leadership in alliances and ad hoc coalitions . . . America's emerging military capabilities . . . offer, for example, far greater pre-crisis transparency. If the United States is willing to share this transparency, it will be better able to build opposing coalitions before aggression has occurred" ("America's Information Edge," *Foreign Affairs*, March/April 1996, pp. 20–36).

50 See The United States Commission on National Security/21st Century, *The New World Coming.*

51 Prolonged periods of peace make it increasingly difficult for military institutions to focus on their business: the waging of war (see especially Andrew Gordon, *The Rules of the Game: Jutland and British Naval Command* [London, 1996]).

52 For a more exhaustive examination of this phenomenon see Williamson Murray, "Clausewitz Out, Computers In: Military Culture and Technological Hubris," *The National Interest*, Summer 1997.

sile barrages into which McNamara and his coterie of economists, political
scientists, and uniformed toadies had sent them – that quantitative indica-
tors of theoretical *efficiency* were not merely irrelevant to battlefield *effectiveness*, but its mortal enemy.[53]

Yet America's Clausewitzian moment did not last. The same inexorable
workings of the promotion pyramid that brought its proponents to prominence led to its passing. With the exception of the Marine Corps and a few
branches of the U.S. Army, the reformers proved unable to recast perma-
nently service cultures that remained profoundly ahistorical and anti-intel-
lectual.[54] Except at the very highest levels, those who had served in combat
in Vietnam retired by the mid-1990s, and a generation of officers with very
different attitudes replaced them. McNamara's mechanistic anti-
Clausewitzian view of future war reemerged seemingly more powerful
than ever from its quarter-century of well-earned disgrace. The watchword
during the post-Cold War drawdown has been that a generic technological
superiority – rather than any searching ongoing reassessment of strategic,
operational, and conceptual possibilities – is the key to the future. And the
services, with the exception of the U.S. Marine Corps, have predictably
once again focused solely upon the procurement of sophisticated high-
cost weapons systems while slighting intellectual and conceptual preparation for war.

CONCLUSION

Revolutions in military affairs – unlike the great military revolutions that
shatter or fundamentally recast institutions and states in their path – offer
broad scope for human creativity and foresight. Past revolutions in military
affairs have given evidence of at least four distinguishing characteristics.

First, technology alone has rarely driven them; it has functioned above all
as a catalyst. The armored divisions that broke the back of the French army
in May 1940 did not wield a superior technology – German tanks were if
anything distinctly inferior to those deployed by the French.

Second, revolutions in military affairs have emerged from evolutionary
problem-solving directed at specific operational and tactical issues in a
specific theater of war against a specific enemy. Successful innovators
have always thought in terms of fighting wars against *actual* rather than
hypothetical opponents, with *actual* capabilities, in pursuit of *actual* strategic and political objectives.

---

[53] This point is dedicated to all who have ever endured the absurdities of the U.S. Army's
    Command Maintenance Management Inspection (CMMI).
[54] See Williamson Murray, "Does Military Culture Matter?," *Orbis*, Winter 1999 and
    "Military Culture Does Matter," *Strategic Review*, Spring 1999.

Third, such revolutions require coherent frameworks of doctrine and concepts built on service cultures that are deeply *realistic*. Innovation, to be successful, must rest upon thorough understanding of the fundamentally chaotic nature of war. It must derive from experience acquired both in war and in exercises and experiments. Organizations that attempt it must reward native honesty and privilege open discussion of the lessons of combat and of exercise and experiment. For the value of exercises, particularly when resources are short, lies not merely in their conduct, but in their planning and in their after-action analysis, which must aim at understanding rather than at the validation of doctrine, concepts, or weapons systems. And armed forces engaged in such revolutions must provide mechanisms for effectively disseminating and implementing concepts and lessons; the world's military archives are littered with far-seeing reports that no one reads.[55]

Fourth, revolutions in military affairs remain rooted in and limited by strategic givens and by the nature of war. *They are not a substitute for strategy* – as so often assumed by the utopians – but merely an operational or tactical means. National Socialist Germany's catastrophic failure against Soviet Russia serves as warning against the delusion that leading an RMA confers strategic freedom. Nor can technology abolish war's central essence as the realm of uncertainty and of the clash of wills. Processing power can no more replace discernment and sheer guts at the strategic level than on the battlefield itself: "machines do not win battles, even if battles are won with machines – a very great difference." And in war, "the result is never final."[56] Every RMA summons up, whether soon or late, a panoply of direct countermeasures and "asymmetrical responses."

The armed forces of the United States, as the twenty-first century opens, face a perplexing world. They must address on a limited budget the imponderables unleashed by the end of the Cold War. They lack a major competitor or specific immediate large-scale threat against which to prepare. And they have involuntarily acquired for the foreseeable future a variety of perplexing and often militarily dysfunctional subsidiary missions seemingly calculated to plunge those required to perform them into deepest cynicism – from peacekeeping among populations thirsting for blood, to small wars under absurd inhibitions – no killing on TV – that seemingly preclude decisive strategic results, to open-ended police actions, futile efforts at drug interdiction, thankless humanitarian missions, and the occa-

---

55 For the German army's deplorable effectiveness in disseminating and implementing tactical principles derived from combat lessons, see particularly Timothy T. Lupfer, "The Dynamics of Doctrine: The Changes in German Tactical Doctrine during the First World War," *Leavenworth Papers* 4 (1981), pp. 21–9, 46–9, 55–8.
56 Ernst Jünger, *Das Wäldchen 125. Eine Chronik aus den Grabenkämpfen 1918* (Berlin, 1926), p. 59; Clausewitz, *On War*, p. 80.

sional hostage rescue effort. Yet they must also face and prepare for a future in which major challenges to the interests and perhaps the survival of the United States will inevitably arise.

The present strategic pause – like the blessed European armed peace from 1871 to 1914 – is unlikely to last. While it endures, the U.S. armed forces have an opportunity to address fundamental weaknesses. They must beware above all of substituting technology for strategy and of fielding superior weapons *platforms* rather than effective military *forces*. They must always bear in mind the danger that one of America's many proclaimed or covert enemies – rather than America itself – may launch the next revolution in military affairs. And they must understand that if the past is any guide at all, the cost of failure to change now will be a far higher price in lives and treasure to be paid later. For battlefield adaptation – OJT or on-the-job training in the jargon of America's combat units in Vietnam – has always proven exceedingly bloody, costly, and painful.[57]

Relentless concentration on intelligently reshaping doctrinal concepts, on the analysis of experimentation aimed at solving specific identifiable problems, and on durably recasting service cultures could indeed pay the massive dividend of a further American revolution or revolutions in military affairs. But the present trend is far from promising, as the American government and armed forces procure enormous arsenals related only distantly to specific strategic needs and operational and tactical employment concepts, while "continu[ing], in the immortal words of Kiffin Rockwell, a pilot in the legendary First World War Lafayette Escadrille, to 'fly along, blissfully ignorant, hoping for the best.'"[58]

---

57 For the American experience in this regard, Charles E. Heller and William A. Stofft, eds., *America's First Battles, 1776–1965* (Lawrence, KS, 1986); for the dysfunctional military culture of the early twentieth-century British Army and its battlefield consequences, see particularly Timothy Travers, *The Killing Ground: The British Army, the Western Front, and the Emergence of Modern Warfare, 1900–1918* (London, 1987) and Martin Samuels, *Command or Control? Command, Training and Tactics in the British and German Armies, 1888–1918* (London, 1995).

58 Quoted in Robert Gaskin, "The Great 1996 Non-Debate on National Security," in Williamson Murray and Allan R. Millett, eds, *Brassey's Mershon American Defense Annual, 1996–1997* (Washington, DC, 1996), p. 27.

Index

Agincourt, battle of (1415), 28, 29
air force
    British (RAF), 163
        Bomber Command, doctrine of,
            meets combat reality, 169,
            183–84
        culture of, largely impervious to
            experience, 183–84
        Fighter Command, success of,
            186–87
    German (*Luftwaffe*), 170, 171
        close-air support doctrine of,
            184–85
    United States
        Air Corps Tactical School of,
            182–83
        doctrine of, meets combat reality,
            163, 182–84
        post-Vietnam rethinking by, 189
        use of PGMs by, 3, 188–89
air power
    interwar British and American
        development of, 182–83, 184
    in 1914–18, 148, 150, 183
aircraft carriers
    development of, by U.S. Navy,
        186–87
    first air strike by (1918), 129
    as RMA, 10, 13, 129, 181, 186–87
American Revolution, War of the
    (1775–83), 63
Amiens, battle of (1918), 152
Ardennes

German attack through (1940), 165,
    167–69
German attack in (1944), 168–69
armor, armored formations
    German development of, 12, 154ff.
    limited effectiveness of in 1914–18,
        143, 146
    as revolution in military affairs, 12,
        13 (Table 1.1), 154–55 and note
        1, 172–74, 192
armor, medieval, 22, 46
    improvements in, 20–21
army, *see also* military culture, by
        country
    British, 132ff.
        and lessons of 1914–18, 157
    Confederate States of America,
        recruitment of, 78–79, 81
    English (medieval)
        mobility of, 25
        recruitment and payment of,
            23–26
    French, 93–94
        and "battle culture of
            forbearance," 45–47, 50, 54, 61
        creation of modern military
            culture in, 50–53
        importance of drill in, 47–50
        interwar doctrinal shortcomings
            of, 164–65
        and the legacy of the First World
            War, 157
        recruitment of, 60